THE SPEED OF HEAT

THE SPEED OF HEAT

An Airlift Wing at War in Iraq and Afghanistan

Thomas W. Young

McFarland & Company, Inc., Publishers
Jefferson, North Carolina, and London

LIBRARY OF CONGRESS CATALOGUING-IN-PUBLICATION DATA

Young, Thomas W., 1962–
    The speed of heat : an airlift wing at war in Iraq
and Afghanistan / Thomas W. Young.
        p.   cm.
    Includes bibliographical references and index.

    ISBN-13: 978-0-7864-3798-6
    softcover : 50# alkaline paper ∞

    1. Iraq War, 2003– —Personal narratives, American.
    2. United States—Air National Guard.   I. Title.
    DS79.76.Y68   2008
    956.704'4348   dc22   2008008048

British Library cataloguing data are available

Cover photograph: C-130 Hercules aircraft from the West Virginia
Air National Guard return to Martinsburg on August 1, 2003
(courtesy the 167th Airlift Wing). *Front cover by TG Design*

Manufactured in the United States of America

McFarland & Company, Inc., Publishers
  Box 611, Jefferson, North Carolina 28640
  www.mcfarlandpub.com

For my squadron mates, past and present.

And to the memory of Major Brian Downs,
a former member of the 167th Airlift Wing,
killed in Iraq on Memorial Day, 2005.

ACKNOWLEDGMENTS

First and most important thanks must go to my wife, Kristen, who provided so much invaluable assistance suggesting improvements, editing, and selecting photos that she's practically a co-author.

I also extend warmest gratitude to neighbor and fellow UNC alum Elizabeth Lee for her rigorous proofreading, and also to former squadron mate Joe Myers for his attention to detail in reading the manuscript.

Thanks also to others who made suggestions for fine-tuning the book. They include Dick Elam, Laurel Files, Steve and Jodie Forrest, Janet Murray, Jim Marrs, and Jim Vergilio.

For help with photos, many thanks to Emily Beightol-Deyerle, Andy Schmidt, Bud Martz, John Alderton, and Tony Henry.

Additionally, thanks to Andrew Carroll, editor of bestsellers *War Letters* and *Behind the Lines*, for his encouragement and kind words—and for his tireless work to honor American veterans and to preserve their war letters.

There aren't a lot of movies made about airlifters. There's no Twelve o'Clock High *or* Top Gun *about those heavy aircraft, but despite their lack of glamour, they are arguably the most potent tool this nation has for shaping the international arena.*
     —Air Force Secretary Sheila E. Widnall, in a December 3, 1996, address at American University in Washington, D.C.

Airlift is the cornerstone of our nation's ability to project military power worldwide. Airlifters transport troops and equipment from our nation to foreign shores, evacuate wounded soldiers, sailors, airmen, or Marines and resupply forward-deployed ground forces. The capability to conduct global, sustained airlift operations, in hostile or permissive environments, is unique to the United States and is critical to achieving our national objectives.
     —Air Force Manual 3-3.35B, Combat Aircraft Fundamentals

TABLE OF CONTENTS

PREFACE

Many things make the United States a military superpower, and not all of them involve directly engaging the enemy in combat. Airlift, the movement of troops and cargo, ranks high in the equation. With its fleet of large transport aircraft, the United States can put personnel and equipment anywhere on the globe within a matter of hours. That's the mission of the service members whose first-person accounts make up this oral history.

Books and media coverage on the wars in Iraq and Afghanistan have focused mainly on the ground forces, and rightly so. The people carrying the rifles also carry the greatest burden of risk and hardship. When reporters and academics do turn their attention to air operations, they usually focus on fighter planes and bombers. Bookshelves and journal articles reveal little about airlift forces, although no other part of the military machine can operate without them.

Practically every soldier, every bullet, every pint of blood, every bite of food arrives in the war zone by airlift. Transport aircrews accompany the troops from the beginning, flying them in, supplying them, bringing them out for medical treatment or rotations home, and in the most heartbreaking missions, carrying them on their final journey back to grieving relatives.

This book is the story of one airlift wing, as told by its members. The 167th Airlift Wing of the West Virginia Air National Guard consisted of a squadron of twelve C-130 cargo planes and their crews, plus all the supporting sections, such as maintenance, motor pool, aeromedical, and civil engineering—in all, more than twelve hundred people. A former Associated Press reporter turned aviator, I flew as an active member of that unit.

For this book, I interviewed nearly seventy servicemen and women. Most of them deployed to the Middle East at various stages of the Iraq and Afghanistan wars, and many volunteered for multiple deployments. Some went directly into harm's way, coming under fire in various circumstances. Others performed critical functions outside combat areas, in locations such as Uzbekistan, Kuwait, and Pakistan. In these interviews, fliers tell of dodging missiles fired at their C-130s, mechanics talk about making combat repairs, nurses discuss saving lives, and two motor pool truck drivers describe the explosion of

1

a roadside bomb. Other interviewees illustrate the variety of specialties connected with the airlift mission, such as civil engineers who design airfields, security policemen who guard planes, instructors who teach troops how to watch for roadside bombs, and commanders who run forward air bases.

This oral history serves three important goals. The first is to provide historians and laymen a portrait of airlift operations, a military mission that's crucial but not well known outside the Air Force. These eyewitness accounts are a resource for researchers who want more than facts and dates, for people who want to understand the role of airlift and how this critical function works. By focusing on the experiences of one airlift wing, the book illustrates airlift in general, capturing a snapshot of this seldom-publicized mission.

The second goal is to show an airlift wing's uniquely broad perspective on war. Because of the nature of this unit's work, its personnel were not only participants in the conflicts, but witnesses on a grand scale. Crews from the 167th flew into every part of Iraq and Afghanistan. They carried virtually every kind of cargo and weapon. While treating and transporting the wounded, the wing's aeromedical personnel saw every kind of trauma the horrors of modern war can inflict.

The third goal is to provide insight into the motivation of an all-volunteer, wartime military and to communicate the emotions experienced by these service people as they carry out their mission day by day. The stories show what it feels like to live in a desert camp, to watch tracer fire arcing toward you, to bandage wounds of a soldier much younger than you are, to fly with near silence in the cockpit because of the flag-draped boxes in back. They show the pain and the rewards of putting years of training to work. As one sergeant states with simple eloquence, "We were doing our job."

The timeline for the oral history begins on September 11, 2001, with unit members describing the realization that the nation was under attack and discussing the preparations for war that began even before the first tower fell. In the case of this Air Guard wing, 9/11 came at a time when flight crews and support personnel had polished skills to new levels, not realizing how soon they would be taking those sharpened skills to war.

The history continues with accounts from the early part of the Afghanistan war, then moves on to the start of the Iraq conflict and its transition from a classic victory of one army over another to a bloody and thus far inconclusive battle with an insurgency.

As this book goes to press, the fighting and dying continue in Iraq and Afghanistan. The book cannot end with observations on the outcomes of these wars. Instead, it concludes with unit members reflecting on their experiences and on their reasons for doing the things they do.

Fliers often speak in jargon impenetrable to everyone else. I have tried to provide translation where necessary. In addition, the interviews were edited for brevity and clarity.

I extend deepest gratitude to my comrades-in-arms, the men and women of the 167th Airlift Wing. I owe my life to their professionalism, and this book to their willingness to share their stories.

Thomas W. Young • Alexandria, Virginia • Spring 2008

INTRODUCTION

On the morning of September 11, 2001, I arrived at the gate of my West Virginia Air National Guard base and saw a warning I'd learned in training but never expected to see outside a classroom: "Threatcon Delta." That's the highest level of alert.

I had a day off from my civilian job as an airline pilot, and I expected to spend it flying in the flight engineer's seat of a C-130 Hercules. My unit, the 167th Airlift Wing at Martinsburg, West Virginia, had scheduled a number of routine missions that day.

Instead, we huddled around television sets, horrified by the images of the burning Twin Towers, the black smoke of ignited jet fuel boiling into the violated morning sky. My training flight, like all other flights that day, was canceled because of something else I'd never expected to see. The government had implemented a modified form of SCATANA, or Security Control of Air Traffic and Air Navigation Aids.

SCATANA was a holdover from a bygone era, a measure to take if the Soviets ever decided to make the Cold War hot and nuclear. Now this quaint relic of the twentieth century became suddenly relevant with the arrival of terrorists who chose to make their holy war a campaign of mass murder.

We felt a nearly impotent rage, but we did what we could. Maintenance crews fueled airplanes. Flight engineers and loadmasters conducted preflight inspections. Administrative personnel started checking fliers' records for currency. People in the Life Support section inspected parachutes, oxygen masks, survival vests, and other gear. Combat arms specialists reviewed inventories of rifles and handguns. The wing also includes doctors, nurses, military lawyers, truck drivers, and cargo handlers, all of whom began making preparations— some even before the first tower fell.

We didn't know what taskings would come down for our unit, but we knew we'd be going somewhere, sooner or later. Each person seemed eager for a job, for a chance to do something other than just stand in front of the television and take it.

Normally, one flight engineer needs a little less than an hour to preflight a C-130. That day, four or five of us jumped on each airplane as maintenance turned it over to us, finishing the preflight inspections in fifteen or twenty minutes apiece. Between inspections we headed back into Operations to hear the latest developments, our flight suits bearing more stains from grease and sweat with each trip.

Some dates in our history become permanent signposts, markers for an age. Those living on those dates can never go back to the world they knew just the day before, and they know it immediately. The Declaration of Independence, the surrender at Appomattox, the attack on Pearl Harbor—all were portals to a new era, for better or for worse, and forever. So was this day.

We airlifters aren't trigger-pullers; we're logisticians. We put the trigger-pullers and their supplies on the battlefield. We knew the perpetrators of the 9/11 attacks had brought upon themselves a terrible, swift sword, and we would help wield it.

Our base at Martinsburg lies in the Shenandoah Valley, an area thoroughly devastated during the Civil War. Union General Ulysses S. Grant famously ordered the valley laid waste so that "crows flying over it...will have to carry their own provender." Our instrument landing system approach to Runway 26 takes us over the Antietam battlefield, where twenty-three thousand Americans were killed or wounded in one horrific day. One of our low-level training routes passes by the town of Winchester, Virginia, which changed hands about seventy times during the Civil War.

Now a bizarre twenty-first-century war had begun on American soil, and supersonic fighters General Grant could not have imagined flew combat patrols over home cities.

When I returned home late that afternoon, my neighbors were outside, sitting on stoops, standing on porches, discussing the awful news. I felt their eyes on my dirty uniform and me as I emerged from my car. I guessed they wondered what more I knew, what inside information I possessed that they lacked. The answer to that was pretty much nothing.

But there was something more in their silent, stricken stares. They saw that flag on my sleeve, and they expected my squadron mates and me to do something.

I

TRAIN LIKE YOU FIGHT

We got a lot of good training done during that period of time. It definitely prepared us for what we didn't know was coming up.
—Master Sergeant Dave Twigg, 167th AW

Even prior to 9/11, there was no such thing as one weekend a month for an Air Guard flier. During the previous decade, the 167th and other units stayed busy with various deployments all over the globe. These included the first Gulf War—Operation Desert Storm—and the numerous related missions that followed. Operations Northern Watch and Southern Watch maintained no-fly zones over Iraq. Operations Provide Comfort I and Provide Comfort II sent relief and protection to Kurds in northern Iraq. All these efforts needed airlift support from C-130s.

At about the same time, Yugoslavia began its bloody self-dissolution. In the early 1990s, Bosnian Serbs opened a campaign of ethnic cleansing against their Muslim neighbors. Air Guard C-130s flew into action, dropping relief packages and supplying peacekeepers. Ironically, some of us got our first exposure to combat in missions to defend Muslims.

In 1999, NATO forces began bombing Serb positions to stop ethnic violence in Kosovo. Again, airlifters carried troops, ammunition, and cargo to make the operation possible.

We didn't realize it at the time, but we were honing skills we were about to need even more. At Martinsburg, our commander had simple expectations: You will become fully qualified, current, and proficient, and you will stay that way. Any questions? See previous statement.

Colonel Jesse Thomas (ret.), pilot, former wing commander

Let me just say this about training: people said I was a stickler for training, and they were right. You go through your lifetime and there are certain

Two views of a 167th Airlift Wing C-130 Hercules on a low-level training mission. Flying through the mountains of West Virginia provided good training for negotiating the mountains of Afghanistan. The aircraft can land on short, rough airstrips to offload cargo on the ground, or it can drop supplies by parachute (courtesy the 167th Airlift Wing).

things that occur that direct you in a certain way of thinking. I came right out of college into the military, and I went into the Air Training Command, so training was embedded into me for safety purposes.

Also, as I grew up and got married and had my own family, two men had a big impact on my thinking. One was my father and the other was my father-in-law. Both of those individuals served in World War II. My father was in Patton's infantry, Third Army, and my father-in-law was in Patton's armored division. Both of them said the same thing.

They said their experience during boot camps and training camps was that the individuals who paid attention in training and practiced it lived longer and survived the war. They said people who didn't do what they were trained to do, many times they got killed on the battlefield.

That always stuck with me. Training was essential. It wasn't essential only for yourself but for the protection of your buddies-in-arms around you. If you aren't trained, you're the weak link, and you could cause the death of someone else.

I held people's feet to the fire on training. I wouldn't compromise on that. It also was driven home to me when I attended the Army War College. Training, readiness—you had to pay attention to that if you wanted the unit to succeed.

Over the years I would go out to various conferences, depending on the position I held, and we were always on the leading edge of training. It began back in the Gulf War. It became obvious that the Air National Guard had to do SKE training. [SKE, or Station-Keeping Equipment, allows aircraft to fly in formation even in bad weather when the aircrews can't see each other.] Some people kept saying we couldn't do SKE training; it was too hard to do.

Well, we came out of the Gulf War, and it became obvious to me that we had to do SKE, and we started it in '91 or '92. A lot of units weren't doing it; they were saying it was just too hard. We didn't have a requirement to do it, but we set up training programs. As a result, after we trained the people in SKE, it wasn't long before we got involved in Bosnia. There, SKE was used to do airdrops at high altitude at night. We went over there and we were very comfortable with SKE because we had been doing it.

We then began working with NVGs [Night Vision Goggles]. We actually started doing NVG training in 1996. No requirement to do it, but it was obvious if you looked at the conflicts we were in, the U.S. military owned the night. If you were going to be part of it, you were going to learn to operate at night. So we started NVG training back then, at first just formation flying and then airdrop training.

But after 9/11 it became real obvious we needed to start NVG air-land training. [Air-land refers to doing all flight operations on NVGs, to include takeoff and landing.] It was a problem getting the syllabus from command; it eventually came out. We pushed to do that air-land training, and as it turned out it was needed over in Afghanistan. A lot of units weren't prepared for it, and all of a sudden they were forced into it.

I always defined combat readiness in simple terms: that people are combat ready if they feel comfortable in their mission environment. In other words, you're going to have enough stress going into combat. You don't have to be stressed by not knowing how to use the goggles and everything else. If you're comfortable using your equipment and your radios, you're more combat ready.

For example, we made people, every day we flew, load up the secure voice radios. If they were comfortable using that on a day-to-day basis, when they got into a combat environment they wouldn't have to worry about it. They could go ahead and just do their mission and feel comfortable with the equipment.

I made people do it on a day-to-day basis to where it became so mundane and second nature that they had no problem with it. I saw other units struggle with that. They'd get over there and they couldn't do the secure voice; they were just struggling trying to learn how to do it. I didn't want to put people in that position.

After the wing commander set the standard for training, it was up to the operations officer and others to make sure we all reached that standard. Operations officer Steve Truax describes seeing the payoff with his own two eyes.

Lieutenant Colonel Steve Truax, navigator, operations officer

People had kicked against getting these advanced qualifications, but when it came time to go to war, so many of the things we did in combat were guided by airborne radar, NVG aided, and so forth. It was painful getting the qualifications at the time, but it followed the dictum that the more you sweat in peace, the less you bleed in war.

Once we got there we had a much easier go of it than other units who were not so well versed. Some of our guys had some resentment because other units couldn't do some of those missions, so we got stuck doing them—particularly going into Afghanistan when everything was bombed out. You went in at night, you went into blacked-out places, you went into damaged places, and that was a real eye-opener.

I remember doing an approach by airborne radar, landing in Kandahar, and thinking, "Boy, this works well." We had a very smooth landing on a runway that had all kinds of restrictions, and then as we were rolling out, I flipped up my goggles and realized it was pitch black. Without NVGs, you couldn't have even seen the airport, let alone land there. And I dropped the goggles down again and said, "Oh my God; we're the real deal now."

We really can do these things that would have seemed special ops and spooky just a couple years ago. I remember being impressed with our ability to do missions we would not have been able to do earlier in my military career.

Air Guard members bring a variety of skills with them from civilian jobs and prior military experience. Our chief flight engineer began his military service as a helicopter crew chief in the Army, where night vision goggles are second nature.

Chief Master Sergeant Billy Gillenwater, flight engineer

I came to the unit qualified. We got qualified on NVGs in the Army back in 1980 on helicopters. It was new to the C-130 world. The NVGs were always kept to the active duty as a special type thing. Some people said about the Guard and Reserve, "That's too much of a mission; you guys wouldn't be able to handle it."

It was fortunate for the unit that the base commander required everyone to become NVG qualified. People didn't like it. They thought we were doing too much training. They thought we were doing too many low-levels and air-drops. But being in the military, I can't see how you would not want to be ready to go do what it is you're supposed to do.

When it came time to go to war, I was glad we were in the position we were in. We were ready. We didn't have to worry about getting ready. We did what we had to do. Our in-commission rate, our launch times, our recovery times, were second to none. I wouldn't have traded that experience for anything in the world.

Night vision goggles can do more harm than good if you haven't trained hard. Pilot Brandon Taksa offers an explanation.

Captain Brandon Taksa, pilot

It reminds me of looking through a fog. Not a thick fog, not a pea-soup fog, but a fog where your depth perception is a little distorted. Things may or may not be what they seem. You think about a fog, usually you don't have real discernible color variations, and the same is true with NVGs. Everything's green. You don't have a lot of depth perception. Same with fog.

So you're handicapped, but in another way you're enabled in a way you would never have been before. I think everybody who wears NVGs lifts them up and looks out with their naked eye, and it's amazing how dark it is outside. So in that respect you're highly enabled, which is a confidence booster.

It makes you feel better realizing that you can see them, and they may not be able to see you, which is a good survival tactic.

Walking around on NVGs is sometimes difficult, let alone flying an airplane. Depth perception is distorted, and you particularly notice that in the dark room where you're just testing your NVGs. It's completely dark, you lift your NVGs, and you can't see your hand. But with your NVGs, you see your hand reaching for something, and it's not exactly where you think it is. You have to reach farther and farther and farther. It's a good reminder for me that the depth perception is off.

So if something as simple as reaching for an object on a desk is hard, imagine trying to walk, let alone maneuver, and now you compound that by moving at the speed the C-130 flies—the speed of heat. Then throw in maneuvers and unfamiliar terrain. It can be disorienting, but on the flip side, if it's used properly it's very enabling.

A lot of NVG training took place both before and after 9/11. Sometimes it was hard to do a night flight after working during the day, but that's the essence of the Guard—citizen-soldiers maintaining readiness for war.

Technical Sergeant Kenny LaFollette, flight engineer

I remember our flying schedule moved to mostly night flights to try to get everyone current on night vision goggles. Of course, that came down from the base commander, Colonel Thomas. He could read the future. At the time it seemed hard because it was long days. It definitely paid off because we had way more experience working with them by the time we actually deployed, versus the units who pretty much showed up and were told, "Here's your NVGs. Start flying."

Master Sergeant Dave Twigg, loadmaster

There was a lot of training that took place during those times. We did a lot of night vision combat offloads, engines-running onload-offloads. Backings for us were very important. [The C-130 can use reverse propeller pitch to back up on the ground. During this procedure, loadmasters ensure clearance from any obstacles. This is often done in complete darkness with the aid of night vision goggles.]

Checklist flow was very important. To this day I could probably run the checklist without the checklist in front of me. Repetition is key. After completing that checklist a hundred or so times, it sticks.

I told other loadmasters I instructed that when you get in this environment,

Airmen push cargo rigged for airdrop aboard a C-130. Loadmasters rig and secure the cargo. During airdrops, they make sure the load exits the airplane safely. They also calculate weight and balance to ensure nothing makes the aircraft too over-loaded or too nose- or tail-heavy to fly (courtesy the 167th Airlift Wing).

you don't want to be digging around for your checklist. You want to know where you are, what's going on, and what your next steps are. I tried to push that to a lot of the younger guys. It paid off. A lot of them came back and said, "You were absolutely right."

We got a lot of good training done during that period of time. It taxed everybody, believe me. It definitely prepared us for what we didn't know was coming up.

Brigadier General Wayne "Speedy" Lloyd (ret.), former commander of the West Virginia Air National Guard

In the time that I've been in the Air Guard from 1967 until the present, I've seen it evolve from a force that really did not have much capability. We had old, outdated aircraft that really couldn't do very much. Then in 1972, near

A 167th crew at work in the cockpit of a C-130. The pilot and copilot sit up front with the flight controls. The flight engineer sits between and slightly aft of the pilots, and most of his instruments are on an overhead panel. The crew also includes a navigator and at least one loadmaster (not shown) (courtesy the 167th Airlift Wing).

the end of the Vietnam War, we started to transition. The 167th moved out of the Lockheed Constellation, which was a logistics nightmare to support.

We moved into the C-130s, and we evolved from a force that was not very relevant to one that can perform as well if not better than our active-duty counterparts.

In the years before the Twin Towers fell, we weren't the only ones honing skills. One of our loadmasters, Master Sergeant John Ratcliffe, witnessed the other side at work during a deployment with an active-duty unit to Saudi Arabia. In June of 1996, John was billeted at a place called Khobar Towers.

Master Sergeant John "Ratman" Ratcliffe, loadmaster

It was my last deployment with active duty. I went over there for one last fun time. I think we went over there three times, in '93, '94, and then '96. In Saudi Arabia we always stayed in the Khobar Towers.

There's like a perimeter road that runs around the whole complex of big, tall apartment buildings. We used to go out and jog on that perimeter road. We decided not to run that night, for whatever reason. I was taking a shower and that's when it happened.

Apparently they tried to get in the front gate, the terrorists. They had a truck. The guys at the gate turned them around; they didn't have proper paperwork or something. They were trying to go to the chow hall with the truck.

They turned them around and there was an SP [Security Policeman] up on top of a building, I guess doing a lookout or something. And he's what really saved a lot of lives. He saw this truck, and as soon as it parked, there was a Caprice, and the guys jumped out, got in the Caprice, and sped off.

That's when the SP started running down through there, banging on doors: "Get out, get out, get out!" And so a lot of people got out of there. It was in the evening. I guess nineteen ended up dying because of the blast.

I was in the shower, and that was probably best because there were no windows in there. All the windows that were facing west, all the glass blew in, of course. The guys all the way to the Navy base in Bahrain said they felt the rumble of the blast. We had a lot of guys who got Purple Hearts because they were cut open and stuff.

It was like, BOOM, and then "What the heck?" We're running around and people are screaming, "SCUD! They attacked us!" People were putting gas masks on. It was very confusing. When it all got settled down, the commander started telling us what had happened. Some of the guys ended up doing detail carrying bodies to the chow hall.

That was 25 June '96. About two days later we flew our next mission. We went into our intel brief, and they told us about Osama bin Laden. That was the first time I'd ever heard of him.

2

CONDITION DELTA

Threat Condition Delta: Attack Imminent or In Progress

Every airman in Basic Training learns about Threat Conditions. From least serious to worst, they are Alpha, Bravo, Charlie, and Delta. The Greek letter Delta looks like a triangle, and it's the mathematical symbol for a difference or a change. For us, Threat Condition Delta on that morning in September meant a permanent change in our lives as citizen airmen. Many members of the 167th found themselves at our home base in Martinsburg that day, and they took part in immediate preparations for missions or deployments. However, because of the civilian work some of us do, along with a few twists of fate, there were Martinsburg guardsmen involved at all three major sites of the 9/11 attacks—New York, the Pentagon, and rural Pennsylvania.

For Major Pete Gross, the events of 9/11 would eventually lead to a position as an active-duty adviser to the 167th Airlift Wing. Furloughed from his airline job just weeks after the attack, he returned to full-time military service. Like hundreds of other airline pilots, his company laid him off because of the economic impact of 9/11. But on that black Tuesday, he was beginning what he hoped would be a long career at American Airlines. He describes watching from the cockpit as the horror unfolded.

Major Pete Gross, pilot

I had gotten hired by American Airlines in the summer of 2001, so I started working for them in June. September 10th was my first day of IOE [Initial Operating Experience, flying with an instructor pilot until fully qualified]. That first day, we took off from our Dallas base, and we flew to Oklahoma City, back to Dallas, and then to Newark. I was a flight engineer, or a second officer, on the 727.

We got into Newark and spent the night in Manhattan. There were crazy

16

thunderstorms that night. Got up the next day, and it was a beautiful fall day. We had a scheduled 8:45 departure from Newark, and we were just going to fly straight back to Dallas, a pretty easy day for us.

When we came out of the gate, we were facing east. We basically released our brakes to push back right at the time the first tower was hit by the first aircraft. [According to the 9/11 Commission Report, American Flight 11 struck the North Tower at 8:46:40.]

A minute or two later, we had our engines running. We saw a little wisp of smoke off the towers. I thought it was kind of a beautiful view because we had the sun off the east, and it was perfectly clear from the rain last night that had moved on. You could see forever. I saw that little wisp of smoke, and I thought, "That's odd; I wonder if that's steam venting off." We didn't think much of it, and we went ahead and taxied out.

We were probably number five or six for takeoff. They told the airplanes in front of us to hang on, that their clearance was canceled. They were going to keep them on the ground; there was a temporary ground hold. This isn't unusual, especially at a busy place like New York. We were more thinking about our fuel because that day we were very tight on fuel. We had just enough to get to Dallas. If we burned two or three hundred pounds more on taxi, we'd have to go back to the gate; we wouldn't have enough gas to depart. We were working pretty quickly to shut all our engines down and switch over to APU [Auxiliary Power Unit] power to save fuel.

So we sat there. We were asking why we were on hold. They said they couldn't tell us. At that point we had no idea. So we waited and waited and waited. Everybody's talking on the radio and looking outside. It was a good twenty minutes into it, and guys were curious about whether they'd have to go back to the gate, because they needed to tell the passengers and make some decisions on fuel.

When the second plane hit, I was in a checklist; I was looking down. The captain happened to be looking in that direction and saw the explosion. [According to the 9/11 Commission Report, United Flight 175 struck the South Tower at 9:03:11.] By now there's about thirty planes all stacked up waiting for departure. We're all just three miles from lower Manhattan. Instantly the radios just erupted and you knew something had happened, but you didn't know exactly what. People were talking in short phrases like:

"Did you see that?"

"What was it?"

"Was it an airplane?"

"No."

"I think it was an airplane."

At that point the captain pulled up the ADF [Automatic Direction Finder], which is a navigational instrument, but it also allows us to listen to AM radio frequencies. He found a news station up there in New York. The initial report was that it was two small airplanes. My thought was, "Why would anybody fly into the World Trade Center today?"

Right about then we got a printout on our ACARS [Aircraft Communication Addressing and Reporting System], which is a digital link with the company. It said: "There is a ground hold. All aircraft are to check in. Airborne aircraft are to check in and land immediately at the closest suitable airport." I had to respond to let them know where we were. Shortly after that, Newark Tower directed all planes back to the gate. Took us a good forty-five minutes to get all the planes back to the gate.

Our initial concerns were for our families, the initial reports being that American Airlines planes had crashed. We knew our families would be seeing that, and nobody would know where the planes were or even what type of planes they were, so we wanted to get information to our families. Because everybody in New York had seen this, the cell phones were completely locked up, and there wasn't a payphone open in the entire airport by the time we got back to the gate. Once we got the airplane parked, we were furiously dialing our cell phones nonstop for about a half-hour. Finally the first officer got ahold of his wife, and we passed all our phone numbers to his wife so she could call our wives to let them know we were safe on the ground.

We kept the passengers on, not having any idea what was going to happen. Eventually we took them off after about a half-hour. We told them, "You know something's obviously going on. We don't want to tell you details, because we're getting several different versions. But we'll let you get inside and get more information from the TVs, and you can call your families to let them know you're safe."

The captain went out to call the company, and the first officer went up the jet bridge [the moveable walkway from the terminal to the plane] to look at the computer [to check for schedule changes or messages from the company]. So I sat there with the ADF on, monitoring the APU. I was looking out my window, and by now there's a lot of smoke, and it really was changing the skyline. Then we heard the Pentagon got hit, and we were in that surreal twilight where something you thought was never going to happen, or was unthinkable, was happening. We were also hearing reports of people falling off the towers, and they were pretty spectacular stories. You kind of wonder what's true, and unfortunately, we found out in the end that ALL of it was true, and a lot of it was worse than the radio reports.

Then I can remember listening to the reports from New York, where they're talking about how the tower looks like it's falling. I'm sitting on the flight deck in the 727, three miles away, listening to this in total disbelief, and it didn't even occur to me just to look out the window. Then I did look out, and all I could see was a tremendous plume of smoke that now covered the entire skyline. I couldn't see that it fell, and I couldn't even imagine what it would have done—something that big, falling. After about ten minutes, you could see only one tower. That was a pretty amazing thing.

Right about then things started happening pretty fast. I heard the shaking of the jet bridge as the captain was running down. He said, "Grab all your stuff and shut down the airplane. The company says there's about fifteen planes unaccounted for around the United States—not just American Airlines planes. They believe it's a coordinated attack. They think they're going to hit every city in the country. The FBI is now running through the airport, and they're shutting off all the airplanes, and they're raising all the stairs and pulling away all the jet bridges."

So I started turning everything off, going through a shutdown checklist. The captain, fortunately, was smart enough to pull all our bags out of the airplane and onto the jet bridge, which later would prove to be a big deal. When we ended up at the airport hotel for the next few days, we saw about half the crews wore their uniforms for three or four days.

I was in the middle of shutting everything down when the FBI came running onto the plane with automatic weapons in their hands. They started screaming at me to get everything shut down. I just took my hand across all the panels and pulled everything down. The agent started literally pulling me out of the cockpit. He said, "I need you out, and I need the jet bridge away."

He started yelling at the gate agent to start backing the jet bridge away. She started backing it away. I jumped over onto the jet bridge, and the gate agent ran over and closed the door. Now the FBI agent is chasing us up the jet bridge, and we're running, and he's running behind us, pushing with one hand, and with the automatic weapon in the other. I got up to the terminal, and you could see a mob migrating toward the exits. They cleared out a pretty big airport pretty quick. The people literally couldn't fit through doorways as fast as they were running.

Because I'm in uniform, passengers are yelling at me, asking where they're going to get their bags or when they're going to get their next flight. Of course, we didn't know any of that.

Those of us in airplanes—where everything started—ironically were often the last to find out what was happening. As Gross and his crewmates taxied their civilian airliner at Newark, the crew of a C-130 was preparing to take off from Martinsburg on a routine training mission, equally unaware of unfolding events.

Captain Curtis Garrett, navigator

We were going to do an airdrop mission down at Pope Air Force Base, and we had gotten on the airplane and started engines here at Martinsburg. We were going to take off on Runway 17, and we had clearance to take off.

By the time we taxied down and turned around, we were told by tower, "Your clearance is canceled."

We were sitting there at the end of the runway, and we asked, "Can we at least fly in the traffic pattern?" We thought we'd do some pattern work. The tower goes, "You don't understand. We are closing the airspace." We said, "Is there an emergency? Why are you closing it?" The controller said, "You don't know what's going on, do you?"

Master Sergeant Tim Nicholson knew all too well what was going on. A firefighter and paramedic for Fairfax County, Virginia, he and his ambulance partner were among the first responders when American Flight 77 slammed into the Pentagon at 9:37:46 in the morning.

Master Sergeant Tim Nicholson, loadmaster

Things were getting a little crazy on the radio. They said all emergency vehicles that were out on the road, not responding to calls or in transit with a patient, needed to return to their stations. We were en route back to our station, back to Vienna station.

On the way back to Vienna station they dispatched several units, us being one—Medic 402—to the Pentagon for a plane crash. Holy shit, you know. Wow. When we were a few miles out you could see the black column of smoke. You're trying to paint a picture of what to expect when you get there. I'd been on the job four years at that point, and that was probably going to be the biggest incident I'd ever been on. So we were talking about it, wondering about other firemen, wondering about the fatalities we were going to find, injuries, etc.

We showed up, and they were shutting down the roads. The closer we got, the more men in black suits and machine guns we saw. I don't know where they came from, but we were only twenty minutes after the crash, if that.

We pulled up and I noticed there was one fire truck there, and it was burning up. I said to my partner, "How in the hell did they burn up a fire truck already?" It was a large fire and it was very hot, obviously. The first thing we were thinking was we hope the firemen are OK, and how did they catch a fire truck on fire?

About that time a second fire truck showed up, and they started to use a master stream, which is a humongous column of water shot out of what's like a deck gun. We had to drive around some light poles that were knocked down, and I mean HUGE light poles, like three feet in diameter at the base. Maybe eighty feet in the air when they're standing. So that wasn't making sense, you know, a lot of things were just weird. People were coming out like you poured gasoline on an anthill. Evacuating, obviously.

We got all our bags out; we were talking about how we're gonna manage this incident. We gotta find out what other units are here; we're going to have to triage people, etc. And these firemen came walking to us, and they had this look in their eye, a far-off stare. They were cut up, banged up, scratched up, small injuries.

We said, "Hey guys. What's going on?"

The officer said, "We were on that engine there that's on fire."

"Shit—what happened?"

He said, "We were sitting there at the helo pad."

The Pentagon has its own helo pad. They were manning the helo pad; I guess they always keep a fire truck there in case they have an incident. They were sitting there seeing the airplane coming towards them, and that's when it clipped the light poles. They had nowhere to go, so they jumped out of their rig, jumped under the rig. Of course, the plane impacted the building, blew debris, fire, and that's how they got banged up.

I said, "You guys OK?"

They said, "Yeah, we're OK."

I said, "Well, we got a boatload more people coming if you guys need help."

More and more units were showing up, so we were starting to get some help. Also, military people from the Pentagon, full bird colonels, were coming out, saying, "What can we help you with?"

Me being an enlisted military man, I'm like, "Sir?! Well, sir, you can carry this bag for me; you can help me set this tarp up."

By that time you had engine companies, trucks, other med units, ambulances. Everybody was very coordinated. It was actually amazing for a chaotic situation like that, how well disciplined and organized the people there were—the fire-and-rescue people as well as the military people.

We were starting to set up triage to treat people, putting them on the red tarp, yellow tarp, green tarp, black tarp. Black tarp was the dead people. Green was minor injuries, yellow not so bad, red serious. Just spent hours doing that. That's the hard thing. You gotta make decisions. Is that somebody you're going to be able to save? Can you tie up your time and resources to save one person, or do you need to write that person off and go help maybe save more people? That's how triage works. It's to help the most and do the most good. You can't save everybody in a big scenario like that. You have too many other people who need immediate attention who WILL make it. The other guy, even if you can help him he may not make it. You have to make those decisions.

We emptied our med unit, [used up] all our supplies, all our controlled medications, morphine being one of the big ones—gone. Just wiped out. We had no supplies left. A plane explodes—you can imagine the massive amount of heat, so you're going to have blast injuries from flying debris, glass, bricks. You have injuries anywhere from smoke inhalation to cuts to burns. You have those who were dead on impact, then any degree of injuries. Severe burns will shut your body down right now. People will quickly go into shock.

Every time we would start to do something, they would evacuate us. They wanted us to evacuate, like three hundred yards. How are you going to walk that far in any amount of time and still take care of people? Your first priority is to take care of people, but at the same time your safety is very important. The first time they did it, I asked, "Why in the hell are they having us evacuate?"

Of course, by that point they were grounding all aircraft. The problem was not all aircraft were on the ground. They had planes that were still in the air, heading towards National. They didn't know whether there was going to be another attack. That just added to the stress and chaotic mess.

An engine company showed up from our station. Not only am I utilized as a paramedic, but I do the firefighting. So I got our firefighting gear off our unit and assisted them in fighting the fire. It looked like spaghetti with the lines everywhere, firehoses everywhere. I had no idea there were so many corridors in the Pentagon. We had to go so deep into the Pentagon because the plane's impact went all the way to that third corridor [the C ring]. Black smoke, heat. You'd step across people, dead people, and you'd think it was just a piece of office furniture; you didn't know. They were charred, and you couldn't see very well because it was so smoky. Somebody's burned and you step on them....

I did try to break some windows to help clear out smoke. You ventilate by breaking windows, cutting holes in roofs, whatever. That way you get the fresh air in there. It helps you see better and it cools it, releases the heat. Well, the windows on the Pentagon are some kind of material so that you can't hear through it, and supposedly it's blast resistant. Firemen, you know, love breaking windows when they have to. Man, you'd hit one of them things and it was like hitting a drum—DONG. It would just bounce off. You had to get saws. I don't know if you've ever used a circular saw to cut something like Plexiglas, but it gums it up. Doesn't cut it nice like a piece of wood. Ventilating was very hard. I got through the windows with a saw, but the saw blade would gum up. And those are big windows, man.

Another thing that was amazing—and I have no idea how long into the incident—no concept of time—there was so much going on, you'd just lose track of time. But people were showing up, just regular Joe Schmo civilians. I remember this one contractor—he had a big F-250 truck. He took it upon himself to go to Costco, loaded a whole pallet of bottled water, came down to where we were, dropped the pallet of water on the ground and just left. Later on, people were coming with great big orders of pizza and stuff, just dropping them there. Nobody asked them to do it, and they were just regular citizens.

Most regular citizens, of course, watched the events on television, and the same held true for those of us back at base.

Lieutenant Colonel Steve Truax, navigator, operations officer

I was galloping around here doing the things I normally do, you know, clerical things, scheduling things, and I noticed a bunch of guys out here in the pilots' section looking at the TV. I walked up and said, "What's going on?"

They said a plane hit the World Trade Center. People started to speculate about what had happened and what it meant, and we're sitting watching that tower with a huge plume of smoke coming out of the side, and I started to refer to historical things.

I said, "This is probably an accident. You know, a B-25, I believe, flew into the Empire State Building years ago in bad weather."

Somebody said, "Look, you dumbass. There's not a cloud in the sky, and look at the size of that hole. That's not a friggin' Cessna."

We were sitting there scratching our heads trying to figure out what had happened, and BLOOEY, as we were watching we caught that blue blur as the second one hit the second tower.

I can't remember who said it, but someone said, "Oh my God, we are under attack."

Then the phone nets got all tied up because everybody was trying to call home. And then the cell phone nets got tied up because everybody had tried the hard line, and they were trying to call home wireless now.

Pretty soon everything was very busy. We started to hear all these things about another plane hitting the Pentagon.

At first it wasn't evident to me how bad it was, and then you heard about a plane crashing in Pennsylvania. When things started to really become clear about what was actually happening, I came back and looked at the news again, and the towers collapsed. That's when I said, "Oh, my God." That's when it first became evident to me how catastrophic this was. It was bigger than Pearl Harbor.

We began to try to prepare for the future. We knew something very, very big had happened. We weren't initially sure what.

Colonel Jesse Thomas (ret.), pilot, former wing commander

In the morning, we were in our staff meeting up in the conference room. We had just finished the meeting and someone from the office came back in and said, "I think you better turn on the news. There's something happening up in New York."

At that time, when the first plane flew into the World Trade Center, people might have thought it was an accident. But when the second one went in, it was obvious that something was going on. And then of course, another plane hit the Pentagon, and then you had the aircraft crash up in Pennsylvania.

Surprisingly, we had a member in the unit who lived where the aircraft went down in Somerset County, Pennsylvania. That aircraft went down about a half a mile to a mile from his home. On September 11, he happened to be down at the unit; he was over at our audiovisual department. I got a call saying that he was concerned. His wife was at home, and so we made arrangements for somebody to go with him up to his home and make sure he got there safely. As it turned out, the aircraft had crashed within a mile of his home.

In a very short time we started getting messages to ramp up our force protection, and also the DefCon [Defense Condition] went up. Never in my career in the continental U.S. had the DefCon gone up. The last one I can remember—and I wasn't in the military then—was the Cuban Missile Crisis in 1962.

Technical Sergeant Bob Leverknight is the guardsman Colonel Thomas mentioned who lives near the Flight 93 crash site. Bob works for the Somerset Daily American *newspaper, and he has served in the Army as well as the Air National Guard. His military background and his knowledge of his home area made him a valuable resource for the authorities investigating the crash.*

Technical Sergeant Robert Leverknight, combat camera photographer

I was coming into the base at Martinsburg. I was on orders. As I came down River Road, I heard on CNN Radio that a plane had hit the World Trade Center. My initial thought was a Cessna or a small private aircraft. Didn't think a whole lot of it. The next news item was that Saddam Hussein was bragging about shooting down a Predator drone.

I came on into the base and told [Master Sergeant] Bill Wolfinger what was happening. We switched on the Today Show. Just about the time the TV warmed up—it was an old TV—Matt Lauer was sitting there reporting it was an airliner, and then the second plane hit.

When the second plane hit, we began to realize it was a terrorist attack in New York. I called a friend of mine down at Andrews Air Force Base, Maryland. As I was on the phone with him, the plane hit the Pentagon. I decided at this point I better call my wife and say, "I'm OK; they're not hitting here."

I called her and I got her calmed down. She was a little upset and a little panicky. Just as we hung up the phone, she walked out the door, and Flight 93 went ripping over the house and crashed.

By this time NBC had brought Tom Brokaw in, and he said a plane had crashed eight miles east of Jennerstown, Pennsylvania. That Saturday night I had covered the races in Jennerstown. That's when a little bit of panic set in. I tried calling my wife back and got no answer. Got a busy signal. The next time I tried dialing, I got an "all lines are busy" message, and it was because of the volume of traffic calling 911.

By this time the base had locked down. We were at Condition Delta, which was the first time I had ever heard that outside of training and this was real world. I was trying to figure out what was going on. Unlike DC and New York, there weren't a lot of TV cameras out in rural Pennsylvania.

I asked Colonel Thomas if he had heard anything from his channels, and he said no. Eventually—it seemed like ten hours, but I'm guessing it was at the most, forty-five minutes after the news came across about Flight 93—Colonel Pat Burkhart had Bill Wolfinger drive me home because I was in a fairly upset and agitated state, to put it mildly. I was almost hysterical.

As we're driving, I'm trying to use his cell phone to contact home. I finally got through about noon. I talked to my son Matthew, and he said everybody was OK. So we turned around and came back to the base. I switched to my Jeep to drive home, so I was on the road about four hours, five hours from the time we had left the base.

When I got home, I didn't even change clothes; I was still in my uniform. I was watching the local news coverage, and I saw the one neighbor I wanted to talk to was down at his grandfather's. So I walked down there, and I was talking to him. About that time this big black Suburban with dark tinted windows, West Virginia tags, pulls up. Power window comes down. This younger gentleman looks out at me and says, "You're West Virginia Air Guard?"

"Yes sir."

"Martinsburg, right?"

"Yes sir."

"You from here?"

"Yes sir."

"Get in."

"Yes sir."

It was the FBI evidence collection team out of Charleston, West Virginia. It was Agent John Fields.* I kept calling him "Sir," and he'd say, "No, it's just John." For the rest of the day and from then on, it's been just John.

I showed them around the debris field area, the road into the debris field. We went door to door letting folks know not to take their pets out because some of the debris was toxic and could make their pets sick. We also didn't want somebody's dog eating evidence. We finished that up about ten-thirty or eleven o'clock at night.

---

*Not the agent's real name.

We went over to the command post at the crash site to sign in. Everything was lit up, and they were already starting to do the investigation. The FBI, the FAA—it was just an alphabet soup of everybody there.

I was maybe five feet from the impact crater and didn't even realize it. Pieces of wire in the debris field—the biggest piece of aircraft I saw was a piece of landing gear. Most pieces were the size of a dime or smaller.

They were already starting to collect evidence. They were basically setting down the procedure of what would happen when they found the flight data and voice recorders. They were eventually found. One was buried at fifty feet under the ground; the other was seventy-five feet under the ground.

You gotta understand that it didn't hit, as the media said, in a field. That's not a field; that's a reclaimed strip mine. It's broken soil down to about three hundred feet. The ground basically swallowed the airplane, like it hit water.

Agent Fields said they might need me again throughout that week or so. As it turned out, I think they were out there almost six weeks collecting evidence and recovering parts of bodies.

Within two or three days, the visitors to the crash site—not just the families, but the public—started showing up, and it hasn't stopped since. It's still going on. The day the Afghan war started was the day of the first organized motorcycle run out there, and they've been going on ever since. I think it's an unwritten rule that if you have a Harley-Davidson, you have to take the mufflers off and you have to go out to the crash site.

It has changed the community, in some ways good and in some ways not good. We have a lot more traffic than we ever had before. There's the real possibility of having a government entity telling us what we can and cannot do with our properties. But on the positive side, it's brought a close community closer. We watch out for each other a little bit more now.

As Bob Leverknight headed home to the smoking wreckage of United 93, back in Martinsburg our maintenance crews began preparing aircraft for launch.

Technical Sergeant Tim Shipway, crew chief

I had some drills to make up, so I was in here helping out with the aircraft. We had to take a break at nine o'clock. We normally have CNN on just to catch up with the news and everything, and we saw that the first tower was struck. Then we saw the dark image of the second plane.

We knew we might be called. So we completed all the inspections and got all our aircraft ready to go. If the commander had gotten a phone call that we needed five planes to go right now, maintenance had the aircraft ready that very day.

One of the hijacked planes, American Flight 77, took off from Dulles International Airport, which lies only a couple of ridges east of Martinsburg. A number of us have civilian jobs based at Dulles. In fact, on duty with the Guard or with our companies, we often recognize each other's voices on the congested Dulles radio frequencies. At the base, we sometimes see a crew member enter the locker room wearing the dress shirt and epaulets of an airline pilot and come out wearing a green flight suit.

Major Carla Riner worked as a flight attendant and later as a pilot for American Airlines. She describes the realization that some of her civilian colleagues had died.

Major Carla Riner, pilot

I had been at the Guard the weekend before because it was drill weekend, and I stayed with a good friend of mine in Winchester, Virginia. I was living in Miami at the time because I was flying as a pilot with American down in Florida. But I stayed that Monday, just kind of hung out, because I was going to fly a training mission that night.

So I woke up that morning, a relatively leisurely morning, turned on the Today Show, and I was talking to my dad, who was then a ramp guy with Delta Air Lines.

We happened to be on the phone when the Today Show cut to a reporter who said, "Evidently a small airplane has flown into the World Trade Center." And my dad was looking at the same thing, and I go, "Dad, that just doesn't make any sense." It was clear and a million out there [pilot slang for unlimited visibility]. If some little private airplane guy had a problem, there's no way he'd fly it into the towers; it just doesn't make sense.

So we're just talking about the events on the television, and that's when the second airplane went in. And my dad went, "Oh, no." Nothing had sunk in yet; I couldn't conceptualize what was happening. I just remember Dad saying, "Hey, I need to go, and they're talking about stopping the takeoffs here, so let me go see what's going on."

I hung up the phone, and I just remember when they started saying what was happening, all the phone lines were packed. I couldn't get anything on the home phone. I couldn't get anything on the cell phone.

I just remember sitting there looking at the TV, and then I thought to myself, "Oh my God, I need to get to the Guard because we don't know what's going to need to be flown." I was thinking, you know, medevac out of there; I had all kinds of ideas. So I jumped in a flight suit and came up to the Guard, and I sat with everybody else listening to the stories as they came in throughout that day.

When I learned that American 77 went into the Pentagon, I just remember thinking, "Oh, God," because I flew that exact flight as a flight attendant for about three years straight. I have a lot of friends who are 767 pilots at American, based in DC, as well as flight attendants. I remember being particularly shaken about the fact that the airplane had taken off from Dulles.

That evening, I went back to Winchester to a different friend's home. She's a flight attendant with American. She was home with her husband and two children, and I remember walking in the door with a bottle of Jack Daniels. She doesn't drink, but you know, in a couple hours that whole bottle was gone because we were just in such shock about it.

Though the shock of 9/11 affected military people like everyone else, those in uniform could at least take satisfaction knowing they were in a position to do something about it. Crews immediately went on standby to wait for whatever mission might come along.

Master Sergeant John "Ratman" Ratcliffe, loadmaster

I called here to the unit and talked to Bill Scott [the loadmaster supervisor at the time]. I said, "Hey, what's going on?"

He said, "Get dressed and get in here if you can."

I live only two miles from the base, so I was like, "Sure!" So I threw my flight suit on, and I ran in there and sat with everybody else. We sat there for a while, watching the news in the loadmaster section. Troy Smith and I were sitting there, and Scott said, "You guys are both in Bravo Alert. Go home." They put us right into crew rest for Bravo Alert. [A Bravo Alert crew stands by in a rest status and is available for launch within three hours.]

As soon as I went home I called Lowe's and said, "I'm not coming in." They said, "We've been waiting for your call. We expected not to see you."

Lieutenant Colonel Mike McMillie, navigator

As soon as we found out the second building had been hit, I immediately called the unit and said, "Hey, I know there's something bad going on. Whatever you need me for, just give me a call." I know that I was probably about third or fourth in line as far as the nav section was concerned. By the end of the day, I think just about everybody had called up and said, "Sign me up. I volunteer."

Later in the day they actually gave us a couple of Bravo Alerts. People were put on orders later that day. For me, it was like two days later I was sitting on Bravo Alert, just to make sure we had people available to go fly.

Major Mike Langley, pilot

I was at my civilian job with American Airlines. I had landed at National Airport the night before, on the tenth, in an MD-80. There was a cloud deck at about 3,000 feet, and I remember popping out of the clouds and thinking how beautiful all the lights of Washington were.

It was around ten o'clock at night. I could see the Washington Monument. I could see the Capitol and the whole Mall area, and of course, Washington National Airport sits right there on the Potomac. I remember doing the approach and landing and thinking: how neat.

I got in my car and drove right by the Pentagon and came home. The next morning I had to go to the doctor's office with my son for some routine shots. He was two at the time, Joshua. I was coming in later to fly at the unit. I picked up the phone and called in to ask something about the flying, and Bill Farrell [another pilot] said, "You need to turn the TV on."

I got the TV on just as the second aircraft hit the second tower. The whole day I relived that. My wife and I talked about taking our kids out of school. We did not do that. Then that evening we sat and we talked about what had happened.

We explained to them, but we didn't go any deeper than they wanted to know. We didn't try to explain more than what they actually asked. Then it was to the unit: What do you need? When do you need me to come in? What are we going to do? They had some of us on alert for a few days, and I was doing that. I think it was Operation Noble Eagle, they called it.

I flew with American Airlines the Friday they opened the airspace back up to normal flying. Thursday they allowed airplanes to reposition back to their original locations for the companies, but I flew on that Friday. And it was one of the eeriest days. It was a beautiful clear day, and all the way from Baltimore to Chicago it was so eerie because it was quiet. I would check in with air traffic control, and I'd say, "American twenty-thirty-nine, checking in at one-nine-oh, glad to be back." And the response I would get sometimes over the radio was controllers answering back in a choked-up, teary voice because of the emotions they had gone through.

Master Sergeant Les Morris, loadmaster

My wife and I saw our first-born child on the ultrasound that day. After we looked at the ultrasound that night, I told my wife not to count on me being home when the baby came. I thought for sure we'd be gone. Shortly after that, in October, I was gone.

3

AFGHANISTAN

Combat airlift is a mentally and physically demanding mission. It requires the highest standards of flying skills and professional conduct.
—Air Force Manual 3-3.35B, Combat Aircraft Fundamentals

As the United States geared up for what would become Operation Enduring Freedom, I sometimes chatted about the situation with one of our pilots, Lieutenant Colonel Joe Myers. Joe used to teach English. I remember him quoting ominous words from Rudyard Kipling's poem, "The Young British Soldier:"

When you're wounded and left on Afghanistan's plains,
And the women come out to cut up what remains,
Jest roll to your rifle and blow out your brains
An' go to your Gawd like a soldier.

Fortunately, Americans didn't get stomped in Afghanistan the way the British had in the nineteenth century and the Soviets in the twentieth, but we didn't know what to expect at the time.

On September 20, 2001, President Bush spoke to the nation and the world before a joint session of Congress. Of Afghanistan's Taliban government, he demanded, "They will hand over the terrorists, or they will share in their fate."

Perhaps the mullahs didn't believe him, or perhaps they thought Allah approved of mass murder and would intercede on their behalf. The air strikes began on October 7.

As the Afghanistan war went on, C-130 aircrews from the 167th Airlift Squadron deployed to Masirah Island, Oman, to haul troops and cargo in and out of the war zone. Masirah Island Air Base was a busy place in the early days of Operation Enduring Freedom. It hosted both airlift crews and special operations forces. Transport planes and AC-130 Spectre gunships took off nightly from the dusty desert island and crossed the Gulf of Oman to reach airfields or targets in Afghanistan.

Our fliers and support personnel arrived in time for one of the Afghanistan war's major battles, Operation Anaconda, in March of 2002. By this time, C-130 crews had become the logistical lifeline for Coalition troops in Afghanistan. You never knew what cargo or personnel would show up in the back of your airplane. Ammunition, Meals Ready to Eat, oil and hydraulic fluid, Humvees, bomb-sniffing dogs, or helicopter parts might wind up on the manifest.

Passengers might include soldiers from any U.S. Army division, or perhaps British Special Air Service troops, Spanish pilots, or French mechanics. You might see bearded special operations guys carrying weapons in long cases, wearing little if any insignia and saying nothing. They could have been Delta Force, Green Berets, or OGA—which stands for Other Government Agency and is widely understood to be CIA. A few of our crews carried Afghan soldiers of the Northern Alliance. Still others flew detainees, hooded and shackled.

Night missions brought blacked-out landings on night vision goggles. Nothing marked the runways except infrared lights invisible to the naked eye. All this took place in some of the most forbidding and remote terrain in the world. During the day, we saw the devastation of decades of war, Soviet occupation, and Taliban rule. Pitiful abandoned villages marked homes and lives destroyed, leaving only what appeared from the air as tic-tac-toe patterns of roofless mud walls.

Arriving at air bases recently taken in war, we found scenes of post-apocalyptic destruction. At Kandahar and Bagram, bomb craters made much of the runways unusable, and we had to land on one side of the pavement, using the longest undamaged sections the civil engineers could mark off.

A C-130 lands at an Afghan airfield. Air bases in Afghanistan bristled with hazards such as construction equipment, bomb craters, and land mines (courtesy the 167th Airlift Wing).

Bullet gouges and fire stains scarred airport buildings, glass broken and crunching underfoot. Soldiers or Marines bristling with body armor and automatic weapons guarded the perimeters, and specially trained Air Force Security Police called Raven teams sometimes flew with us to protect crews and planes. They reminded us not to stop off the concrete because we could get blown up by land mines. At night, they made us keep our penlights off and wouldn't let us smoke cigarettes because we could get drilled by snipers.

Mission after mission, fliers strapped into the airplanes, tamped down their emotions and their fatigue, and flew their C-130s in ways they never had before. The extraordinary became routine.

Captain Curtis Garrett, navigator

The fight was going on. It was busy. During Anaconda it was mainly Special Forces. They had all the good toys. We talked on secure radio all the time. A lot of flying on your own—there'd be sections with no air traffic control, no nothing except AWACS [Airborne Warning and Control Station, an aircraft that provides control of air traffic and air strikes].

They had to use AWACS just for traffic deconfliction because there were still fighters and gunships; there was still shooting going on. [Deconfliction refers to the intricate business of keeping airplanes out of each other's way.] You had to know what was a live area and what was not. You didn't traverse those areas without good reason.

The only NVG training we'd had by then was airdrop and taxi, but things had gotten to the point where we were using night vision goggles in just about every phase of flight. It was pitch black. The runway lighting was near non-existent. Just about all the flying we did that month was at night.

Imagine yourself on the ground, having just landed in Afghanistan. You're in a strange land in total darkness—darkness that's hiding enemies, real or imagined. Man's primeval fear of the night stems from situations like this. Is there a sabre-toothed tiger beyond the light of the cave's fire? Is there a Taliban fighter low-crawling toward the airplane? The NVGs help, but their field of view is narrow. Still, as Captain Garrett explains, technology makes the night your friend. The darkness may hide enemies, but it also hides you, and you want that darkness complete.

We were down at Bagram one night; we were sitting on the ground, and Special Forces guys came up and said, "We can see your lip lights." [Lip lights are tiny green lights attached to the microphone on a flier's headset.] We remembered you don't even leave your lip lights on. That's because you want complete blacked out operations on the ground. Light as minimal as you can get because you still had problems with snipers.

If you're worried about snipers or sabre-toothed tigers or any other kind of enemy, there's nothing like a gunship to make the problem go away. Flight engineer Mike Bayne and our wing commander, Colonel Eric Vollmecke, recall seeing AC-130 Spectre gunships—the killer version of our own familiar C-130 Hercules—bristling with gun barrels on the left side of the plane. Over a target, the Spectre makes left turns in a circle of fire and destruction.

Senior Master Sergeant Mike Bayne, flight engineer

I remember the AC-130 gunships were with us there at Masirah, going in and out of Afghanistan, and they were doing live stuff every night. They had what they called the "kill boxes," where they were doing their operations. [A kill box is a zone to be attacked, and to be avoided if your aircraft is not part of the attack.] You could hear them on the radios; their call sign was "Safari," and they were out hunting.

Colonel Eric Vollmecke, pilot, wing commander

My first mission in January of 2002 was into Kandahar. It was all at night, on the night vision goggles. At that time we still had a lot of offensive operations going on, so there was a lot of deconfliction with close air support missions, AC-130 gunships. I once got blinded by an AC-130 gunship firing down on a target, with all the tracer fire. I thought, "This is the real deal, and hopefully none of that stuff will be coming my way."

Then as we got close to Kandahar, we realized the weather was going to be more of a challenge than the enemy because I couldn't see anything due to the dust.

Captain Curtis Garrett, navigator

I remember seeing a dust storm starting. This was during the day. We were flying along and it was real clear, and you could just see this wall of dust, almost up at your altitude, marching its way across the terrain. You see these dust storms in the movies, and here I got to witness one for real. That would have been in southern Afghanistan, near Kandahar.

In addition to dust storms, Southwest Asia also offers an oppressive, humid heat not relieved by the hot winds. To approximate it, you'd have to sit fully dressed, loaded down with gear, in a sauna—with a hair dryer blowing in your face. Flight engineer

Mike Bayne describes conditions at a Pakistani airfield often used during Operation Enduring Freedom.

Senior Master Sergeant Mike Bayne, flight engineer

We had a prop valve housing go bad on us leaving Bagram, so we ended up spending the night in Jacobabad, Pakistan. We didn't get there until the wee hours of the morning, and they put us up in the transient tents. We all slept in, since we were going to leave later that night after they fixed the airplane. At about ten o'clock, we all headed down to the cafeteria tent, and it was unbearably hot. We were talking to the guys outside the chow tent and we said, "Hey, how hot is it?"

They said, "We don't know. The thermometer stops at 140." So it was pretty hot. They also told us not to swat any bugs on you because the bugs have an acid content; they will actually leave burns on your skin. That really made it a garden spot.

As our Afghan allies, the Northern Alliance, rolled across what had been territory held by the Taliban, they began taking prisoners. The Coalition built a holding facility at the Kandahar airport for captured Taliban and al Qaeda fighters. Major James Powell recalls being rattled at the sight of a group of detainees.

Major James Powell, pilot

We went to Kandahar and we met a guard from North Carolina, a reservist. He gave us a little tour of the holding facility they had for some of the al Qaeda people. It was kind of eye-opening to see the way they brought them in, the way they processed them.

They were waiting to be transported. I think some of them ended up in Guantanamo, or they were just interrogated there and then released. As we were walking through, they were kind of watching us. Some of them would definitely give you a stare, and you'd feel the hackles on the back of your neck stand up. It was a little unnerving walking through there, thinking what if they had some uprising or something at that moment.

Most of them looked like they were fine, physically. They had clothes that looked like hospital scrubs; some were light blue and some were orange. I don't know if there was any significance to that. They fed them three times a day; they had pre-packaged meals. One guy said they had put ID bracelets on them, and they had to change a lot of the bracelets after a month or two because the prisoners were gaining weight.

For most of us, this strange environment of hazards both natural and man-made seemed otherworldly. But a certain type of soldier feels right at home here— the special operator. Which brings up a strange question: If you run across a saw-scaled viper, one of the deadliest snakes in the world, which of the following do you do?

A) Kill it
B) Get the heck away from it.
C) Catch it and keep it for a pet.

If you're a special operations commando, apparently the answer is C. While at Masirah Island, some of them captured a saw-scaled viper, put it in a terrarium, and fed it mice. They don't call those guys "snake-eaters" for nothing.

The war in Afghanistan gave the snake-eaters an unprecedented opportunity to showcase their talents. The job of hunting down jihadists in remote, rugged mountains called for a heavy emphasis on special operations. American Special Forces, Delta Force troops, and Navy SEALs joined with NATO colleagues such as the British Special Air Service and the German Kommando Spezialkraefte. The missions against al Qaeda and the Taliban involved elite commandos from several nations to such an extent that some observers called the Afghanistan war "the Olympics of special operations."

Many of our unit's airlift missions into Afghanistan carried special ops personnel or supplies to support them.

Major Chris "Mookie" Walker, navigator

At that time in Masirah we had a lot of special ops people there. People wearing beards and such, snake-eaters, special ops people from Germany, as well. They'd come to Masirah for quick R-and-R. That goes to show you how rough they had it, if Masirah was an R-and-R for them. They'd go back over there trudging through the rocks and the sand and hunt down people, and we'd fly them in and out.

The mission of airlifting special operations forces into a hot area brought together two groups of people with vastly different skills and concerns. We fliers worried about approach tactics, runway lengths, and making contact with all the right air traffic controllers. The snake-eaters worried about ambush tactics, rifle barrel lengths, and making contact with all the right tribal leaders. But the mission required all of us.

Captain Curtis Garrett, navigator

It felt good to support Special Forces there. They liked us because we were mission hackers. [Military slang for people who get the mission done instead of finding excuses not to fly.] They loved us to death, and when we were there at Masirah they'd say, "Come on over. We're having a barbecue."

Of course, they've got their neat toys and they've got their money. They have their own rules. The military needs them, has to have them. But sometimes higher ups don't like the loose ends they bring. These guys had beards, long hair. We had water battles with these guys; they played hard. They liked us because we were getting them to places they needed to be, into dirt strips. If there was a mission that needed to be done, we were there with them.

They have that can-do attitude, in fact, maybe too much so: "Boy, high-risk mission and everyone's going to die? All right, let's go!" That's the kind of attitude they have. Maybe we weren't quite as bad, but we'd say, "Sure, we can do that." It felt good to be appreciated by those people.

Loadmaster Lee Deyerle volunteered for some of the unit's first Afghanistan missions. Ex-Army, part Native American, no nonsense, he has a way of saying out loud what everyone else is thinking to themselves. A former ground soldier himself, Lee had more of a connection with the special operators than most of us.

Technical Sergeant Lee Deyerle, loadmaster

I remember getting on the airplane one night, and this guy looked like he was straight-out Taliban, dressed up. Talked perfect English, and the only reason I knew he was American was his weapon. It was a standard-issue M-4 with the SP-2 or SP-4 laser sights on it. And he had a set of Seven-Bravos, which are the NVGs.

It was Wild West. There was not one mission that we flew in Afghanistan after 9/11 that was bullshit. We didn't haul air around. We did the job. Always busy. It wasn't any rear-echelon guys running the show. It was operators running operators, and you were allowed to do what you had to do.

We would haul a lot of troops. These guys had been out in the weeds for a long time. Dirty, filthy. We'd haul them either to other locations in Afghanistan or we'd haul them back to Masirah for a little R-and-R.

Had a friend come up to me at Masirah. Didn't even recognize him, he'd lost so much weight. He was a combat controller buddy of mine. [Air Force combat controllers travel with ground units and direct air strikes.] He came up and I said, "Hey, Jake. Dude, you don't even look like yourself."

He goes, "Yeah, I been up in the weeds for four months."

I said, "Well, you're drinking with me tonight. Come on."

We carried a lot of special weapons. I remember seeing a John Deere Gator with some kind of missile launcher. A lot of desert patrol vehicles. We'd be hauling Humvees back that had not even twelve hundred hours on them that were just bent and beat to hell.

All the aircrew and operators were getting along wonderful. It was just like a brotherhood. You'd sit there and you wouldn't even talk about flying or fighting and what they were doing up there. You'd talk about where you came from, good places to party when you got home. And we'd talk about the weather a lot.

You didn't want your airplane to break down in Afghanistan. But inevitably, it happened. That's when a Maintenance Recovery Team would come in, and with safety wire and creativity, fix the plane at least well enough to get it out of harm's way. Technical Sergeant Jay Barrow recalls working on an aircraft in the dark with other planes landing nearby—with all their lights off.

Technical Sergeant Jay Barrow, engine specialist

We went to Kandahar to recover an airplane from Dyess Air Force Base. We spent the whole night there. All we had for light was flashlights. It wasn't necessarily a by-the-book fix, but we were able to use what we had to make it work so they could get out of there. They were there for two or three days.

We worked on this thing through the night, watching C-130s come in with lights out. It seemed like they were landing maybe twenty feet away. I'm telling you, it was close. You'd hear a plane rush in and all you'd see was a little bit of light in the flight deck. That made my hair stand up. Everything was dark. I'd look around, like, "Holy crap!"

We were getting kind of hungry, and we started looking around the airplane and found a bag of sodas and Nutter Butters. We cleaned 'em out, brother. I was getting nervous because I thought the crew would show up and see we'd eaten all their food.

Actually, the only thing that made me nervous was everybody else was carrying an M-16 and we weren't. And you had to stay on the pavement to avoid land mines.

While mechanics did their normal jobs in abnormal conditions, so did everyone else, including loadmasters. On one particular mission, the loadmasters kept Major Chris Sigler posted on something going on inside the cargo compartment that unnerved them. Sigler and crew had a sad mission that night; they were transporting the body of a foreign soldier who had given his life in the fight against the Taliban. Some of the Muslim soldier's surviving comrades were riding with him.

Major Chris Sigler, pilot

We were carrying some of the foreign soldiers that were overseeing the body. We were flying out at night. But when the sun started to come up, the loadmasters got a little excited because the foreign troops stood up and started moving around. They started kneeling down in the back of the airplane.

The loadmasters weren't sure why four or five of these guys were getting up at the same time. They called up and said they were getting a little nervous. Then the loadmasters realized what the troops were doing. They were praying when the sun came up.

The pace of operations in Afghanistan left little time for reflection. But on occasion, crew members had a chance to marvel at the rugged land passing under their wings.

Lieutenant Colonel Steve Truax, navigator, operations officer

I remember flying over the Hindu Kush for the first time. I thought, "My God, this is the terrain that stopped Alexander the Great and the British Army."

I also remember dropping the NVGs and seeing a meteor shower. It was either the Perseids or the Leonids. There was no moon, very dark over there. And we were watching the little meteors, a couple, two, three a minute. And that was an awesome sight.

Major James Powell, pilot

In the day, if you happen to fly over western and central Afghanistan, you look down and there's nothing, miles and miles of nothing. But at night on NVGs you would see some tribesmen or whoever with campfires or using some sort of lanterns. You'd see these light sources dotted all over the country. It's kind of unbelievable.

As you fly over this forbidding terrain, you try not to think about crash-landing into it and having to fend for yourself, wounded and left on Afghanistan's plains. But in case that happens, you have stuff in your pockets you really don't want to need. There's a blood chit—a piece of cloth with a message in several languages that says, essentially: "I'm an American flier, and I just had an airplane blown out from under me. If you help me, my government will try to repay you. And I really hope I didn't just show this blood chit to the wrong person."

The vest also contains camo face paint, in case you know the blood chit won't help.

On your side or your thigh you have a Beretta nine-millimeter. A fine, reliable handgun, but no match for an AK-47.

Your survival vest bulges with pouches, and one of them contains a lensatic compass. *Fliers are used to navigation at the push of a button, guided by GPS signals from space. But this damn thing just points north. And then you start walking. Sometimes you do have a handheld GPS, but when the batteries run down, you go back to the old school.*

A little pillbox contains water purification tablets for drinking undrinkable water. You have flares and signal mirrors for bringing in a rescue chopper—and you hope that happens before you need the water tablets.

You have a first-aid kit in case a bad day gets worse. There's even a fishing kit for those with more hope than sense.

Loadmaster Doug Ferrell describes how some USO performers became worried at the sight of an aircrew donning survival vests and other gear.

Master Sergeant Doug Ferrell, loadmaster

We landed at Seeb International Airport in Oman to pick up a load, and the PR man came out and told us, "You're taking Joan Jett and the Blackhearts to Kandahar."

We're like, "Yeah, get out of here."

Sure enough, here they came, and we took her to Kandahar. She slept most of the way. Her drummer was doing a film documentary during the whole concert tour there, and he came back and interviewed me.

His eyes kind of grew larger as we started down and did our combat entry checks and put on our armor and survival vests and helmets. He's like, "What are you doing?"

I said, "We're getting shot at."

He goes, "What do you mean, 'We're getting shot at?'"

They had no idea what they were going into.

We had to fly in and out of hell, but other people got stuck there. For troops stationed in remote areas, small treats like soft drinks or fresh fruit became luxuries. In addition to our official cargo, we tried to bring a few morale boosters to people whose assignments were tougher than our own. Navigator Mike Foley says his crew did a favor for the air traffic controllers in Kandahar.

Major Mike Foley, navigator

I remember going into Kandahar, we went up in the control tower one time. I was with [pilot] Mike Langley. He wanted to go up in the tower and thank the guys for the job they were doing. Mike asked them if there was anything they couldn't get in Afghanistan that they would like. One guy said he'd been there about six months and he hadn't had a good cigar. Mike told him he'd see what he could do.

Somehow—I don't know where he got it. Maybe he went to downtown Doha. He must have bought a couple of them there. Next time we went up to Kandahar, we called the tower and told them we had some cigars to deliver. We shut down and delivered them. The guy really appreciated it.

Another memorable thing we did was September 11, 2002. We were there in Kandahar, and I had taken some flags with me. We told the guys in the tower we wanted to run a few flags up the flagpole on the anniversary. They said, "Come on up." We ended up having about thirty flags. They had a couple flagpoles, and we stood up there and ran the flags up the flagpoles. I have a couple of flags that I've given to my kids and family members and some special people. [The certificate says], "This flag was raised over Kandahar tower on September 11, 2002."

4

WHERE'S THE RUNWAY?

They told us, "We think it's important enough to send you right now. Make it happen."

—Captain Curtis Garrett, 167th AW

On a typical flight to Afghanistan, we would take off from a forward base in Qatar or Oman. When on night missions, we sometimes saw gas flares of oil rigs in the Persian Gulf flickering like candles on black velvet. Climbing for altitude and coordinating with controllers on AWACS planes or Navy ships, we carefully avoided Iranian airspace.

Crew members might take advantage of the relative calm to slice open Meals Ready to Eat and have a cold dinner before entering hostile air. To avoid collisions with all the American metal in the sky, we climbed to assigned altitudes in corridors known as "driveways."

Over Pakistan, we began running the Combat Entry checklist to configure the aircraft for war:

"Lights."
"Off."
"Defensive systems."
"On."
"Night vision goggles."
"On."
"Survival equipment."
"Donned."

Soon came the eerie glow of a runway lit only by infrared lights. Flaps down. Gear down. Cleared to land.

The missions demanded all the skills we'd practiced so thoroughly at home.

Major Chris Sigler, pilot

It's one thing to learn how to do a tactical arrival and land an airplane. Normally when you do that, you can see the airfield plenty far out. But the whole new challenge is acquiring the airfield on NVGs. You have to learn some little tricks, like maybe look under the NVGs and see if you can find some other lighting near the airfield. You look through the NVGs, under the NVGs, whatever you can to find the airfield. From that point on, you have to trust the aircrew. The navigator's giving you input on the altitude. The copilot's backing you up on the airspeed because you're looking outside the airplane. You expect the rest of the crew to keep you posted on the inside of the airplane, with what's going on with the instruments.

Then add heavy military air traffic to all the challenges described above. Lieutenant Colonel Steve Truax says he had a close call that didn't involve the enemy at all.

Lieutenant Colonel Steve Truax, navigator, operations officer

One of the biggest incidents I had was an Army helicopter. When we were taking off from a blacked-out runway in Afghanistan, the chopper called clear of the runway, and just about the time we were hitting 100 knots he said, "Actually, I don't think I'm all the way clear. Can you stop?"

Of course, by then we couldn't. We said, "No we can't." Wisely, the pilot put the power to it and got us off the deck, and we went over the guy's tail rotor. If we had tried to stop like he had asked, we might have nosed into him.

Lieutenant Colonel Shaun Perkowski, pilot

Most of our excitement happened because of other airplanes doing exciting things. Anytime you got around the airfields, I thought that was the biggest threat—getting in and out of the airfields safely with all the traffic.

There was one specific situation when we were going into Bagram. It frustrated the you-know-what out of me. We were taking particle-board furniture there in the middle of the night. As we're descending into Bagram, they clear two A-10s out of Bagram, climbing up into us. I'm blacked out in a random steep descent, and they're coming up into us. I can see their lights.

I'm like, "Well, turn on all of our lights." So I've got to deconflict myself with those guys while doing a descent on NVGs. You were always cautious about what other planes were doing.

During the deployment, unofficial patches started to show up on flight suits. A popular C-130 emblem said, "Combat Airlift After Dark." One crew's patch was solid black except for four sets of eyes. Across the bottom it read, "Where Is The Runway?"

Navigator Curtis Garrett flew some of the early missions in Afghanistan, when fliers had to think on their feet and improvise.

Captain Curtis Garrett, navigator

We're stepping out to the airplane. We have our standard mission—fly up to Bagram, down to Kandahar and back to base at Masirah Island, Oman. The tactics guy comes up and says, "You've been refragged, but you gotta leave now. First stop is the same." [A "frag" is a fragmentary order. To be "refragged" is to be assigned a different mission.] He hands us the new frag, and he goes, "What do you need?"

I'm like, "I need runway coordinates to this place." We were going to Kabul. Kabul at that point was run by the British.

They give me the coordinates over the radio there at Masirah and we take off, and I have to plan this mission on the way to Bagram. From Bagram we

167th Airlift Wing navigator Kelly Washington with the tools of his trade. His laptop computer shows an aeronautical chart display, just underneath the radar screen. On the table he has paper charts and photographs of the landing zone or drop zone. The panel in front of him contains navigational instruments and controls for the aircraft's defensive systems. The navigator's station is on the right side of the flight deck, aft of the pilots and flight engineer (author's collection).

went to Mazar-e-Sharif to pick up Afghan nationals who were going to join the army. Mazar-e-Sharif is a day/VFR only field. [Certain airfields in mountainous terrain are used only during the day, under Visual Flight Rules. No approaches are allowed at night or in the weather under Instrument Flight Rules.] We get in there right at sunset; it's getting dark. The discussion on final approach is, "Where's the runway threshold?"

We're getting closer and we're looking down and wonder—what is that gray spot in the middle of the runway? It's a crater. It still hadn't been worked on since we'd bombed it. So we had to land beyond the crater.

We touch down and they've got all these cardboard boxes beside the runway, marked M-I-N-E. We're making jokes like, "Yeah, that's not your box, it's mine."

We taxi in and we wait for these guys. We finally get them on board, and they come in with their AK-47s, and they just throw them all in this big wooden crate that's strapped onto the ramp. Our soldiers make them disarm and put all their weapons in there. They just toss their weapons in—CLANG! Their weapons are all beat up; they're nasty-looking things. They'd walked around with weapons their whole life, it seems.

Of course, we fly them to Kabul. We had a low-level briefed. [A route flown at high speed and very low altitude to avoid surface-to-air missiles.] We were going to do an NVG landing. Our intelligence was poor because the mission was kind of handed to us. I have a PowerPoint intel brief they'd just handed to me. I flip through and I draw all my intel off this—where we can fly and where we can't and what frequencies we can use. I'm trying to glean all this information because it's not on any of the American instructions. This was a field the Brits controlled; in fact, it was closed airspace to us. It was the first time we'd been in there. So we're trying to cipher through all this stuff, and we think we have it pretty much made. Our approach took us on a forty-five-degree dog-leg to final. At about two and a half miles to final, I'm doing an ARA [Airborne Radar Approach, an instrument approach during which the navigator provides guidance to the runway based on his radar picture without use of any ground-based navigational aids].

The pilots ask, "You got the field yet?"

"No."

I'm starting to get nervous now—and then I'm painting the runway on radar at about two miles. I'm feeling pretty good. I'm painting the runway now.

We're on glide path and we see these runway lights. The Brits had lined only one side of the runway, and it was like, is it the right side or the left side? Maybe the other side's broken. We're on final and I go, "Here it is: left side. Land to the right."

The copilot goes, "Are you sure?"

This is our discussion on final, on NVGs, while I'm trying to read out of this airport data. We get it worked out; we can see the runway at a safe distance and we land. We turn off the runway; we're taxiing back in and the tower goes, "Have you landed yet?"

We say, "Yeah, we're on the apron; we're about to pull into parking." He didn't know where we were [due to the extreme darkness and the aircraft landing without lights] and we'd been talking to him a few miles out. So we knew if he didn't see us land, maybe the bad guys didn't either.

It was a pitch-black night. It was probably one of the worst NVG nights I've ever had. I remember looking out, and you couldn't see anything. In fact, I gave up looking outside and just terrain-cleared by the radar.

We got the Afghan troops on the ground, and the Brits wouldn't let them off the airplane because the people who were supposed to pick them up weren't there. So now we've got all these guys stuck on the airplane.

At the time we didn't have an iridium satphone. I remember wishing we had a satellite telephone. This would have come in handy. To show you how sometimes things work out, we're on the high-frequency radio, trying to call people. I finally get Yakota Air Base, Japan.

Here I am in Afghanistan and I get Yakota on the HF. I have a phone patch back to Prince Sultan Air Base in Saudi Arabia, which patches me into this guy's cell phone who's probably only thirty miles away, to say, "We're here. We need you to come now because these people won't let them off the airplane, and we're running out of crew duty day."

It was just one of those last-minute missions. They said it needed to be done. The mission hacked. ["Hacking" a mission is military slang for getting a mission done despite obstacles and perhaps despite regulations.]

They told us, "We think it's important enough to send you right now. Make it happen."

A native son of Alabama, Major Mike Langley keeps his crews at ease with homespun humor. The redneck jokes mask a technical expertise that served him well during a stint as our unit's chief of tactics. He describes needing every bit of that expertise while negotiating the Hindu Kush mountain range and landing at fields in Afghanistan.

Major Mike Langley, pilot

The Hindu Kush is just an area of the world—I don't think I could explain it to someone if they had not ever been there. You just can't really explain how dark and how rugged and how bleak everything is there.

I remember being somewhat apprehensive but also excited because it was going to be the first time in my career that I actually got to do what I had been trained to do. I had to evaluate not only my own ability, but my crew's ability. If at any point I lose the confidence of one of my crew members, the whole system does not work inside of our airplane. So I have to be able to maintain a complete closed loop, if you will, so that everyone stays inside of it. And if I lose anyone, then the loop is no longer there.

Whenever we would do things as a crew that were nonstandard, we tried to go over it; we tried to brief it. I tried to verbalize what we were doing, also adding that if they had a problem with it, they needed to speak up. We're all big boys and girls here, we need to speak up.

The fight against the Taliban involved some of America's highest technology, such as air strikes called in by coordinates from satellites and bombs guided by lasers. But it also involved troops on horses, and it included Afghan allies who had never flown before. Flight engineer Mike Bayne recalls some Afghans who got their first airplane ride.

Senior Master Sergeant Mike Bayne, flight engineer

We went into Mazar-e-Sharif, and we picked up sixty of these really young Afghani guys. We took them into Kabul. There were some Delta Force guys with us, and it turns out that the Afghans were part of the first groups that were going to be trained by the Coalition. They were coming to Kabul to be trained by the Belgians and somebody else. We were the first C-130 to fly into Kabul.

I got to see these young Afghan guys who were going to be the new Afghan army. We didn't get to talk to them because they didn't speak English. But it turns out none of these people had ever been on an airplane. On the approach into Kabul, we had to come in away from the city. They didn't want us flying over the city. So we come in over these mountains, do a right turn, and slip the airplane down into the valley, pull some negative Gs. The loadmasters said these guys, their eyes got as big as saucers.

Major James Powell, pilot

We flew into Bagram and picked up some security forces guys, and we went up to Mazar-e-Sharif and took the first batch of Afghan National Guard or police force. Picked those guys up and brought them to Kabul. Most of them had never been on an airplane before. You could just see the big, wide eyes: "Are we going to make it?"

Had the whole crew all in the back, telling them, "Here's some earplugs; here's how you put the seatbelt on." They were giving us the thumbs up. The loadmaster said as we came down into Kabul you could see them white-knuckled in the back of the airplane, and then a big sigh of relief as we touched down and started taxiing off the runway.

Although some of our Afghan friends had never experienced flying before, they probably had more familiarity with something that was new to many of us: getting shot at.

Senior Master Sergeant Mike Bayne, flight engineer

We left Kandahar one night, and when we got back for our debriefs, intel had us retrace our departure flight path because there were tracers following the airplane. We hadn't seen them, but the people on the ground reported it, so they wanted to know our path so they could try to pinpoint where the bad guys were hiding. In retrospect I'm glad we didn't know they were shooting at us at the time.

Major Chris "Mookie" Walker, navigator

Most of the time, we were going into Afghanistan dead dark, and we'd be using our NVGs to try to locate the field and land there. Really just trying to keep a low profile, all lights off, in and out. We'd talk every once in a while to the Task Force Eleven guys we'd transport, and they'd say, "Sometimes when you guys are taking off, we see tracers coming after your plane. But the bad guys are missing you, so we figured why radio to you to maneuver, because the guys are missing you anyway."
We said, "Oh, really? Thanks for the info."

Major James Powell, pilot

I was talking to one of the guys on the ground and I asked him, "Has there been much action around here?"
He goes, "Oh, not too much. But every time you guys depart out of here we see tracer rounds going off behind your airplane."
We're like, "REALLY? We haven't seen them."
He goes, "Because you guys are so dark without lights, they can't see you." We think they were aiming at the sound of the airplane.

Lieutenant Colonel Mike McMillie, navigator

We had one sortie that we were flying out of Kandahar. They were talking about gunfire that was taking place south of Kandahar, and we had to take off in that general direction. We took off, and because there was supposed to be some gunfire, we said we're not going to give them a real good chance to shoot at us. We kept it real low until we got over the desert, and this was right after sunset.

We started climbing out, and we had the night vision goggles on. We saw what looked like a mountain out in the distance, and there seemed to be gunfire because you could see lots of flashes. We kept flying and we kept seeing this gunfire, or at least what we thought was gunfire.

It turned out this was actually a thunderstorm we were seeing that was about 150 miles into Pakistan. It kind of looked like a mountain, and we were so spring-loaded after someone said there was gunfire out there.

Major Mike Foley flew as a navigator on the B-52 Stratofortress during Gulf War One. He says in the C-130, like in the B-52, navigators have to keep their priorities straight while picking their way through hostile, rugged terrain.

Major Mike Foley, navigator

We had corridors to fly, certain places we could and couldn't fly, altitudes we could or couldn't do. Had to keep track of that.

The biggest thing was the landings and takeoffs. That's when you're near the ground—too many threats. We were very vigilant on our approaches and departures.

I let the pilot do what he needs to do, and I try to help him if there's something that he needs to know about avoiding a threat; that's the number one important thing right there. Number two was a very close second: don't hit the ground. Those were my two priorities.

We were supposed to be landing at a certain time. We had a certain window, a time frame we could land or take off. But you know what? If you crash the plane, you're not going to be on time. So number one is you have to keep the plane flying. We decided we would worry about avoiding any threat we knew about, and then all the terrain, of course. Time control was third or fourth down the list.

Of course, we wanted to make our times as best we could because they did have a flow they had to do. Only a certain number of planes could be on the ground at a certain place because it gets busy, and it gets too crowded sometimes.

We did mostly nighttime stuff in the Afghanistan theater when we started. We were flying with our night vision goggles. I remember one night, we were flying in Afghanistan and I looked up. I like astronomy, so I like to look at the stars every now and then. You could tell where the Milky Way was. It was a streak with a lot more stars in a certain area of the sky that you can't see with the naked eye. We would see lots of meteors. In Afghanistan, it's very dry. Low humidity means better visibility, and at the altitude we were flying we were above the dust, so it was very clear where we were.

A lot of times if we were in a terrain area, I'd sit down and watch the radar for the terrain instead of looking visually. Kind of like the old B-52 days. Couple of eyeballs looking out the window and somebody looking on radar, it's safer than everybody looking out the window.

Major Chris "Mookie" Walker, navigator

Thank God we had the H-3 model of the C-130 because with its radar we could at least see what was happening in total darkness. You could say, "OK, we're in a valley now, you can descend." Or, "There's a mountain ridge about three miles to the right, just don't turn that way." Eventually we started using a GPS moving map display, and that really helped because we could say, "I'm right HERE on this chart, and if we're at this altitude we're not going to have to worry about smacking into a mountain."

When you're flying down with no lights into a totally pitch-dark valley, knowing there are mountains all around, that can be really, really nerve-racking.

For American fliers in Operation Enduring Freedom, the environment probably posed a greater danger than the enemy. Although the 167th never lost an aircraft, other units—including C-130 units—were not so lucky.

On January 9, 2002, seven Marines died when their KC-130 tanker went down near Shamsi Air Base in western Pakistan. On February 12, 2002, eight aviators were hurt when an Air Force MC-130 Special Ops bird crash-landed in Afghanistan. On June 12, 2002, another MC-130 crashed on takeoff from a base near Gardez, Afghanistan. Three of the ten people on board were killed.

5

VALLEY OF DEATH

That was the closest to death I ever fell.
—Technical Sergeant Kenny LaFollette, 167th AW

Bagram Air Base lies at the foot of the Panjshir River valley, north of the Afghan capital city of Kabul, where the valley opens into the wider Shomali Plain. Jagged peaks surround the base, making for tricky approaches. Each time we flew into Bagram, we could imagine a Taliban fighter with a shoulder-fired missile waiting for us on one of those peaks. The Panjshir valley hosted some of the fiercest fighting during the Soviet war in Afghanistan, and parts of it remain heavily mined. American forces have taken their own share of casualties there, including at least two helicopter crashes that killed nine service members in 2003. Literally translated, the name means "Valley of the Five Lions." We called it the Valley of Death.

Senior Master Sergeant Mike Bayne, flight engineer

I remember the first time we flew into Bagram—at night. When we first got there, everything was at night; they weren't doing any day stuff. The Bagram airstrip was 5,050 feet by 75 feet wide useable at that time. And the first time we went in there in the daytime, we saw why. Just to the left of where they had the [useable] area marked off was a bomb crater big enough to hide a C-130.

When we went back during the last deployment, part of it had been repaired, but they were still working on it. I believe the whole thing's 10,000 feet now.

Major Mike Langley, pilot

First time into Bagram, we were flying a downwind leg, then a right break into two helicopters that were on approach. Tower told us to do it, and my copilot couldn't see them. I blindly turned into where I knew the field was, and I knew it was a valley, but I had never been there before. It was all strictly based on my having map-read and terrain-read all the information prior to getting there, so I had a visual picture of where I was.

It worked out; we were able to land and taxi in and have no real problems, but I do remember that flight very well. And then coming out of there, in the pitch dark of night, there's nothing but ten-thousand-foot mountains everywhere, and coming out the valley, we'd go up, take a left, and go up through the valley. You're climbing constantly and the terrain's still rising above you.

Major Carla Riner describes flying as a copilot on an early mission into Bagram Air Base, facing the dangers of the mountains, the unfamiliar fields, and the darkness. She says if not for quick and well-coordinated teamwork, the flight might have ended in disaster.

Major Carla Riner, pilot

Oh, yeah. The most challenging flight of my life, by far. My crew—an extremely experienced crew—was going into Bagram one night. This was the very next mission after our initial theater check. And back then we had not had much formal training on night vision goggles. I mean, we had sort of done a little low-level, you know, 500 feet at night, but nothing like this.

Bagram was particularly challenging because it's in a bowl, and you never went there during the day. Never, ever. The weather wasn't that bad, but it was pretty windy. It was an assault landing. [An assault landing is a procedure involving aggressive use of brakes and reverse thrust to get the airplane stopped on a short runway.] Half the runway was closed due to bomb damage.

It was enough to make us think about it before we even started the approach. Back then, the navigators were building airborne radar approaches, and our navigator had made a mistake in something that he put into our SCNS [Self-Contained Navigation System], so our data wasn't accurate. We were flying over the runway edge lights at like, 400 feet. And the navigator kept saying, "No, we're not there yet—no, we're not there yet." I was like, "There's the runway, RIGHT THERE. GO AROUND!"

The flight engineer came up out of her seat, pushing all four throttles as much as she could. The pilot pulled back on the yoke, but pulled back too much [causing the airspeed to drop]. So the flight engineer's got the throttles; I've got the yoke, pushing forward, going "Airspeed, airspeed!" Meanwhile, it was pitch dark. So it took literally every person on the airplane to keep the airplane flying.

Finally the airspeed indicator came back into the pilot's crosscheck. He got a good pitch set, therefore I let go of the yoke. The flight engineer pulled back on the throttles like normal.

It didn't hit me until we landed back at Masirah at sunrise. I just remember shaking when my feet hit the ground. From walking there to the bus, riding back to Ops, I was just shaking the whole time.

You're cleared for a night descent into Bagram. That means spiraling into a black hole surrounded by menacing ridges.

The radar altimeter picks this time to give you a strange anomaly: When you put the landing gear down at higher altitudes, the instrument occasionally cycles itself and gives a momentary reading of about one foot. That, in turn, confuses the Ground Proximity Warning System, which screeches in an artificial voice: PULL UP, PULL UP! For a millisecond you wonder whether the radar altimeter will be the last thing you ever see. At least one crew shoved the throttles and roared away from a mountain that wasn't there.

But then the warning stops and your heart restarts. The infrared runway lights appear in front of you, and the combat controller clears you to land.

On touchdown, iridescent moths, sparkling in the night vision goggles, swarm around the airplane like snow. Some corner of your mind wonders, "What the hell ARE those things?" But you have higher priorities right now.

Flight engineer Kenny LaFollette describes how the combination of darkness, unfamiliar terrain, and instrument failure caused his crew to think they were dangerously close to hitting a mountain.

Technical Sergeant Kenny LaFollette, flight engineer

We had never been into Bagram Air Base before, so I had no idea exactly what this place looked like. However, we had been well briefed that it sat down in a bowl with a lot of tall mountains around it.

On the approach in there, you stayed high, then came down rapidly. As we were turning onto final approach, I was running the Before Landing checklist, and the radar altimeter failed. At the time we had rolled out to a heading that the navigator was questioning. We knew there was a ridge off to our left. With the NVGs you could see an outline, but it was so dark you really couldn't tell if it was the first ridge or the second ridge behind it.

As we were descending, the radar altimeter was just counting down, and you could hear everyone's voice start to get rather tense. And the copilot and I both at the same time said, "Airspeed!" because we had gotten slow. I would have to say that was the closest to death I ever felt. That's because according to the radar altimeter, which was counting down, we thought we were going to be running into that ridge.

It was actually just a malfunction of the radar altimeter, and we were actually right where we were supposed to be on course. Everybody was rather shaken up after that experience.

Captain Curtis Garrett, navigator

We were hauling Special Forces guys and bullets and water into Bagram. Just bare essentials for the base. We landed on the field, and we'd just about finished unloading, and I think I was talking to AWACS at the time, saying we're about to leave. The copilot was talking to tower, which was just a guy in a tent with a hand-held radio, helping deconflict with the helicopters that were there.

All of a sudden, tower frequency called up and said, "We've got enemy force movement and ground fire in such-and-such a sector. Small arms."

The aircraft commander, James Powell, looked around and he went, "Curtis, where is that?"

I pulled the sector chart down and I'm looking at it and I can't find this sector; I'm missing something here. I'm looking all around the field, trying to find where this firefight's going on, then I look right where the field is.

I said, "That's a sector on this field. That's right where we're at."

Old James about broke his neck, saying, "WHAT? We're getting out of here."

Tower got on the radio, yelling, "GET OUT OF HERE! Cleared to take off."

We're taxiing out and stuff's going on. You're on NVGs, and of course, the taxi's a little bit faster than normal, and we turned around and took off. There's helicopters flying overhead and we're going down the runway. Kind of like controlled chaos—the helicopters were trying to put something down in there. The helicopters were going to blow something up as we were getting airborne.

Master Sergeant Doug Ferrell, loadmaster

I think the only time I actually had triple-A [antiaircraft artillery] close to me was the very first missions we flew into Afghanistan. They had the gun mounts in the mountains, and as you would fly by, you would see it come across at you instead of up at you, which was weird. It was lucky that we were flying low. That's because you could look out, and when you saw it, it was actually coming behind the airplane. They couldn't judge it at night. They would just fire, and most of it was behind the airplane. About every third or fourth flight, you'd see tracer fire. Kandahar wasn't that bad. It was usually going into Bagram.

In January of 2003, four Americans died when a UH-60 Black Hawk helicopter went down near Bagram. In November of that year, five more U.S. service members were killed in the Bagram-area crash of an MH-53 Pave Low special operations helicopter.

6

KYRGYZSTAN

I wanted to make the people who did that realise they made such bull of a
mistake.
—General Wayne "Speedy" Lloyd, on those behind the 9/11 attacks

During the war in Afghanistan, the top West Virginia Air National Guard com-
mander left his civilian job with Atlantic Coast Airlines to run an air base in Kyr-
gyzstan. The Kyrgyz government allowed Coalition forces to use Manas International
Airport in Bishkek as a base for fighters, tankers, and transports. The facility, unofficially
named Ganci Air Base, was crucial to air operations into Afghanistan after 9/11.

Brigadier General Wayne "Speedy" Lloyd (ret.), former commander of the West Virginia Air National Guard

Kyrgyzstan, it's a great country; it's a beautiful country. High mountains just to the south of the airport go up fifteen or sixteen thousand feet. We would launch fighters out of there, F/A-18s and Mirages; we would launch fighters down over Tajikistan, and as they entered the airspace there in Afghanistan, they would refuel. We had tankers there, also.

We'd refuel the fighters and then they would be on alert, and they'd be called in for strikes. From the time they'd take off in Kyrgyzstan until the time they'd return, the average mission would last about six hours. In many cases, if they had a number of targets and had to refuel a number of times and the weather was bad, missions would last upwards of nine hours.

The French in the Mirage, they had a masseuse there who would work their guys over when they got back. You can imagine sitting in a small fighter for that number of hours, how painful that would be. I never could get the Marines to make use of the masseuse. It was very interesting times. The Mirage brought one capability to the fight; the Marine F/A-18s brought something else, and it was really very interesting.

54

The French had two tankers there, KC-135 R-models with the CFM-56 engine on them. The Australians brought in two of their Boeing 707s that they had converted to tankers, which had drogue refueling capabilities. They had only four of those aircraft in their fleet, and at one time I had three of them when they were rotating one in and out.

Because of the language difficulties, I had daily staff meetings with people, and I really spent a lot of time making sure that my direction had been understood. We conducted training exercises, which is something you normally don't do in a wartime environment when you're forward deployed. But because of the language difficulties, I had to make sure we could work together if we were attacked.

In pep talks to troops, General Lloyd would look back on a personal loss from 9/11.

I would go in and talk to the people as the wing commander. At one point I would tell them I didn't know why they were there, but there were four reasons why I was there.

The first two reasons were my two grandsons; I call them the dynamic duo. I wanted to make their future more secure and more like what I'd known as a kid. I don't think we'll ever get back to those kind of days, but whatever I could do to help rid the world of terrorism, I wanted to play a part.

The third reason was a young lady by the name of Michelle Heidenberger. Michelle used to work for me at an air charter service. Her husband, Tommy, worked for me. She was a ticket agent and he was a pilot.

I always would ask whether anyone had heard of Michelle, and nobody ever had. The bottom line was Michelle had become a flight attendant for American Airlines, and she died at the side of the Pentagon when American Airlines Flight 77 crashed.

The fourth reason was Chief Peter Ganci. We named the base in Kyrgyzstan after him. He was the fire chief in New York City who died when the towers collapsed.

I wanted to make the people who did that realize they made one hell of a mistake.

When General Lloyd arrived in Kyrgyzstan in March of 2002, he found himself coordinating forces from several nations in a host country plagued by civil strife.

We were standing up a coalition there of eight nations at the time. It was Spain, France, the Netherlands, Norway, Denmark, Australia, Korea, and we were bringing in a contingent of the United States Marines. We had the Army there doing electric power production. And then we had about nine hundred Air Force personnel who were erecting the tent city and supply and all the other support services to the other nations.

It was an interesting assignment. Kyrgyzstan is a very small, impoverished

Agricultural land in an Afghan valley. Fliers departing Kyrgyzstan for Afghanistan soon found themselves over hostile territory. In some situations, fliers dropped down to a low level, using the terrain to hide from enemies carrying shoulder-launched missiles (courtesy the 167th Airlift Wing).

country in Central Asia. It was part of the former Soviet Union. It was the location where they trained their helicopter pilots.

Very poor country. Average person makes less than twenty dollars a month. They almost had a civil war while I was there, and they had a shooting down in a place called Osh, close to the Fergana Valley. They shot into a crowd, kind of like our Kent State shooting, and killed five people and almost brought down the government. The prime minister and his entire staff did in fact resign.

I'd negotiated an agreement to put in a munitions storage area, which we needed at the time to store the bombs for the French Mirage fighters and the Marine F/A-18s. All of a sudden, the prime minister who had agreed that I could go ahead with this project resigned, and the liaison with the ministry of defense was fired and brought up on corruption charges.

So I found myself in the unenviable position of having dug big holes and put in security fences and all these kinds of things, and yet didn't have a written agreement. It was later signed by one of the commanders who replaced me. It's now all legal, but at the time it made me feel kind of nervous.

I was there during the period when it looked like India and Pakistan were going to go to nuclear war with each other. We had evacuation plans to bring the U.S. dependents out of India and Pakistan up to Kyrgyzstan to house them if such an event took place, which required a lot of preparation. It was a very interesting time.

At nearly every air base in the world, and certainly those in Central Asia, the commander has to deal with the terrorist threat.

We knew we were under threat by the Islamic Movement of Uzbekistan, the IMU. We were being observed. A lot of people didn't like the fact that we were there.

I conducted training for emergency response to bomb threats. There were roads near the base that went right beside the barriers we had constructed with concertina wire on top of them. We had the microwave detection system outside, but still we were very vulnerable to attack.

My biggest fear was that we would come under attack and not be prepared in some way to respond and protect our people. My mission was to put bombs on target; my goal was to not allow anyone to be hurt while I was there.

That's harder to do than you might think, with people going downtown. You can't keep them in that compound indefinitely. So I made people travel in groups of four, with a cell phone. I had a security detachment downtown, integrated with the local law enforcement. If people started getting in trouble, they just punched the SEND button on the phone, and immediately it went back to a security detachment we had there in the Hyatt hotel.

We had a very well-defined area that people could go to. So, anyway, in the course of my command over there, nobody was ever kidnapped or killed because of stupidity.

We had some folks that got beat up, just typical city crime. A couple of the Frenchmen got stabbed one night being downtown when they shouldn't have been. They were outside the designated area. But no one was killed when I was there.

Lieutenant Colonel Mike McMillie worked as General Lloyd's executive officer in Kyrgyzstan. McMillie describes some of the unique challenges of coordinating forces from allied nations.

Lieutenant Colonel Mike McMillie, navigator, executive officer at Ganci Air Base

The neat thing about it was getting to work with all the different allies and trying to remember all the different rules that all the different allies have. We think of all the rules that we've got in the U.S. Air Force, but we had to worry about Australians and their tankers. We had the French and their tankers and their fighters. We had Marine Corps Hornets; we had Spanish C-130s, Dutch C-130s, Norwegian C-130s, Danish C-130s. We had Spanish helicopters.

We had to figure out how to support them, how the different nationalities were able to meld together. It was a unique experience because I think this was the largest Coalition organization in one wing, ever, as far as the Air Force is concerned.

It was a tremendous experience watching this thing go from a base of six hundred people to just over two thousand. When all these Coalition forces are assigned to the wing, because there's no military law across the different services, the toughest thing is getting them to buy into the U.S. standard.

I'm not demeaning the French in any way, but the French have different laws in how their people are treated. One case is that when they're not on duty, they're not on base, and they're not in uniform, their commander really doesn't have the same authority that we have over troops in the United States. So we had some French guys that went off, doing what their standards were, got a little drunk, got in a little trouble. We had to ask to have them sent home.

We had a Spanish C-130 pilot who wanted to be very brave, so he flew low-level over Afghanistan when he shouldn't have been flying low-level. Unfortunately, he had a USO show called "Cheerleaders of America" in the back, and he made some of the gals really, really sick. We were able to find out about it and he would not admit he was making an error. That's because in Spain that was one of the things you could do as an aircraft commander.

He was flying low-level all the way across Afghanistan, through the mountains, and making a pretty rough ride. There was no way he could deny it; I got to see some videotape that one of the gals shot out the window. He was probably flying 150, 200 feet, and he didn't need to do that. He was putting himself and his passengers in danger.

We eventually had to ask the Spanish to take him back, and we said, "This is not the United States standard." And they did. It hurt his career probably for a couple months, but he was on the fast track anyway.

As of this writing, Ganci Air Base continues to serve as one of the Coalition's most important airfields in the Afghanistan theater. The Air Force's 376th Air Expeditionary Wing has replaced nearly all the tents with more comfortable permanent structures. The facilities include a cantina called "Pete's Place," also named for Fire Chief Peter Ganci. Inside Pete's Place, there's a wooden sign that reads: "THIS BAR DEDICATED TO COALITION MEMBERS WHO GAVE THEIR LIVES IN THE WAR ON TERROR."

7

SALERNO LZ

WARNING—Use of the following procedures ... should be performed only when authorized by the major air command concerned. Engine failure after refusal speed ... makes it unlikely that a successful takeoff can be made.
—From the C-130 flight manual, section
on maximum performance takeoffs

In civilian life, you fly an airliner as gently as possible. Somewhere in those rows of seats behind you sit nervous passengers frightened by the slightest bump. The company wants their repeat business, so you try not to scare them. The folks spooked by the mildest turbulence don't realize the airplane can handle far more than anything it's likely to face flying Grandma to Topeka.

In the military it's a different story. You fly the airplane to the extent of its capability, and of yours. You memorize limits of weights, speeds, G-forces, and temperatures because you will go right up to those limits. Fliers sometimes joke, "That number's not a limit; it's a goal."

In Afghanistan we encountered a landing zone that demanded maximum performance flying. Flight publications described Salerno LZ as 4,000 feet of packed clay, with a runway condition reading of sixteen, which meant a runway slightly less slippery than wet pavement.

Bull.

Salerno LZ was 4,000 feet of soft dirt and big rocks, with a runway condition reading of God knows what. On the side of a mountain of loose shale, limestone, and scraggly evergreens. In Khowst Province, smack in the middle of that wild border region between Afghanistan and Pakistan that no one has ever really governed. A forward operating base for Army troops at the tip of the spear.

To shoehorn the aircraft into places like this we use something called an assault landing. For such a landing, speed control becomes critical. Pilots usually ask copilots and flight engineers to back them up: "Call me five knots high or three knots low."

It involves a high rate of descent, slamming the airplane onto the dirt, then standing on the brakes and using full reverse pitch on the props. The propellers growl

59

and strain as dust billows over and around the aircraft, which bounces and groans as it slows to a stop on the rough surface.

To get the plane out of there, the pilot pushes the throttles up to max torque, and despite miserable heat, the flight engineer turns off the air conditioning. That's so every ounce of power goes to producing thrust. Sweating in the vibrating, roaring machine, the pilot releases the brakes while the navigator times the acceleration with a stopwatch. You have so many seconds to reach a speed of so many knots. If the speed checks good, the pilot lifts her off at minimum flying speed, clawing for altitude on the cusp of a stall.

Before you do all this, you run the performance charts to make sure the plane can make it off that length of runway with that weight of cargo and fuel. The calculator gives you your final answers, and you pray you got the numbers right.

Major Mike Langley, pilot

It was a hot zone; we were supposed to have A-10 fighters for an escort, but we never actually saw them. They had to break off early because of bingo

Pilot Scott Hostler of the 167th Airlift Wing studies aircraft performance data before takeoff from a desert airfield. C-130 crews carried out "maximum performance" takeoffs when they needed to get a heavily loaded airplane off a short airstrip (courtesy the 167th Airlift Wing).

fuel. [Bingo fuel is a low fuel state, the point where you must either return to base or conduct an aerial refueling.]

So we were on the ground there, and they loaded us up and I got out of the seat and went to the back and helped push cargo on. We had backed all the way up to the very edge of the fence, and then we pulled forward slightly so they could get the trucks behind to load us. Hindsight being 20/20, I would have liked to have backed up and had that extra twenty feet. Later it became evident we could have used every inch.

I remember sitting there and looking at the fence that was no more than twenty or thirty yards off my left wing. Afghanis were walking along there, and I was thinking they could launch a mortar and it would go over the airplane and over the entire field. It was such a small field and runway.

Also, there was some chatter on the radio. We didn't find out until later that there had been an ambush. Afghanis, about twenty of them, had jumped out of a truck and fired on some Americans. It happened to be some of our Special Forces. The Special Forces mowed down about ten or twelve of them and captured eight of them. That was all going on with helicopter support taking off from this field while we were waiting to take off. And on the radio they were telling us not to go to that area because there was a firefight going on.

They got us loaded, and we had already figured out all the data for getting out of there with the requirements to make sure we were legal. The winds were kind of squirrelly: it was a headwind, a crosswind, and occasionally a tailwind. We checked all our data; we ran the power up. Everything looked good across the board and we released the brakes [and began timing our acceleration].

[For an acceleration time check, the aircraft must reach a certain decision speed within a calculated time limit. If the actual acceleration does not meet these numbers, the pilot aborts the takeoff.]

We had our decision speed calculated to seventy knots and there's a three-knot tolerance for error in the gauge. The navigator started timing and I believe the time limit was twenty-two seconds.

The navigator said, "Time," and the copilot said, "Go," because we had met the sixty-seven knots. He did exactly what I asked him to do.

We got to the end of the runway, last dirt clod, with a ravine probably thirty yards ahead of us, and we were maybe eight to ten knots below takeoff speed. I pulled it off into the air.

It flew and I leveled right on top of the treetops, and we managed to get about 125 knots as we crossed the very first ridge extremely low—at about 100 feet. We slowly started gaining airspeed and a little bit of altitude.

I remember we probably second- and third- and tenth-guessed that whole scenario, wondering what we did wrong. And I think the consensus was that we didn't do anything wrong; it was just that close. It was that much of an assault procedure that we actually hit all the numbers as advertised except the takeoff speed. But by then it was take it flying or go off the end of the runway.

I remember thinking later that if we'd taken fire at any moment within that first minute or two after takeoff, there would have been nothing we could have done other than put it back on the ground somewhere. There was no leeway.

Our load may have been heavier than reported. I'm not blaming anyone, but it may have been heavier than advertised. When you're at an austere field like that, you have to trust the people who are loading that the load is exactly what they say it is. We may have gotten a little bit of a tailwind at the time of our takeoff. Several factors didn't work in our favor, making it that close. It was a real, no joke assault procedure.

Lieutenant Colonel Steve Truax flew as Langley's navigator on that mission. From his seat toward the back of the cockpit, Truax couldn't see much out the windows, and he didn't like what he saw on his radar.

Lieutenant Colonel Steve Truax, navigator

We weren't quite climbing as well as we expected. We thought either the winds had shifted or the cargo scales were wrong, and we probably weren't doing quite what we had calculated. And what we had calculated was tight for getting out of that dirt strip and getting above the mountains and getting out of there.

I'm in the back and I can't see. I can see my radar and my radar is showing black, which means you've got mountains in front of you, and you're not seeing the stuff behind it. And I thought, "This is dicey." I remember trying to communicate my concerns with the pilot, not sure if he could see his way to pick through visually and at the same time not wanting to distract him.

I was looking out the windows and seeing mountains in most of them and thinking, "I'm not sure how serious this is, but I'm alarmed." I also thought, "We'll be OK as long as we don't lose an engine. Then it'll be dicey." And there was no place to put it down. It was very rugged terrain and the terrain kept rising.

I accompanied Langley and Truax on that mission. While Truax looked at terrain on his radar, I had full view through the windscreen, and it didn't look good from that angle either.

From the author's journal, 21 July 2003

A wild ride through Afghan mountains yesterday.
The day began with a flight from Masirah to Bagram Air Base, Afghanistan.

We carried two Land Rovers to Bagram. After offloading the vehicles, we picked up a prefab building on a pallet, along with about thirty troops from the Tenth Mountain Division.

Departing Bagram, we headed south toward Salerno LZ near the town of Khowst. Our planned escorts, two A-10s, did not make the rendezvous; they had to break off to refuel. So we flew low-level through the mountains alone, following the terrain.

We landed in a cloud of dust at Salerno, a dirt strip littered with rocks that have been tearing up tires and antennas. The landing came without incident, though, and we offloaded our cargo. Then we picked up a pallet and thirty-seven troops.

For takeoff, we ran her up to full power and still used all the runway to get airborne. We barely made our acceleration check time. Unsure whether the problem was heavier-than-reported cargo, deteriorating runway conditions, shifting winds, or some combination of all the above.

Another scorching low-level route, blasting through the peaks of loose shale. Several troops got airsick and vomited into their helmets. We hated to do that to them, but it's better than getting shot down.

Senior Master Sergeant Steve McDonald is a former Navy flight engineer, and he had years of experience flying P-3 Orions before joining the Air Guard. He often reminds us that the submarine-hunting Orion is a "real man's airplane."

He has a hard-drive memory for aircraft systems and performance. When you ask him a technical question, he usually knows the answer off the top of his head.

Mac may have flown a real man's airplane, but he didn't like Salerno any more than the rest of us.

Senior Master Sergeant Steve "Mac" McDonald, flight engineer

You did max performance in and out of there. The dirt runway was just terrible. Big rocks and stuff. Every time you went in there you damaged something.

My most memorable thing was when we were going into Salerno, somehow the wheels kicked up a big rock and it knocked off a brake line. We went to the end of the runway and started the offload. The loadmaster started calling up saying, "Hey engineer, we're leaking hydraulic fluid."

Meanwhile, we're doing everything with engines running. So I went back there and looked, and sure enough, the left main gear is pissing hydraulic fluid. So we shut down the hydraulics and it's still pissing hydraulic fluid. Made a huge puddle. I was worried about emptying the system. Brake fuses are supposed to stop all that, but it wasn't happening. So we hurried and closed up, and we went up the runway a little ways and shut down to get out and look at it.

Sure enough, a rock had gone up right where the line went into the brake and knocked the fitting off. So we were shut down, and we were worried about snipers there. We were all wearing our flak jackets and all that stuff. We really didn't want to be sitting there on the ground.

I got into the hostile environment kit [a toolbox designed for quick and dirty fixes in a combat situation]. I capped off the brake and some lines, did the best I could. We really didn't have enough caps; I used tape to tape some things up just to keep the dirt out. We started up and took off with one less brake.

The rocks at Salerno LZ seemed to know exactly how to damage our brakes. Flight engineer Kenny LaFollette had a similar experience on a different mission.

Technical Sergeant Kenny LaFollette, flight engineer

We went into Salerno LZ. We did an engines-running offload of troops, rotating guys in and out. We had just loaded up and the ramp and door were still down. Someone tapped me on the shoulder; it was one of the troops. He said, "You're leaking something in the back of the airplane. It looks like it's coming from underneath the landing gear."

I went back, and I was leaking hydraulic fluid out of the brakes. I got up underneath the brakes there. I had the pilot cycle the brakes through to see if it was doing it in emergency mode or normal mode, and it was doing it in both. What actually happened was the pucks on the brake assembly were leaking.

I capped those lines on those brakes, so we had three brakes. We went to Kandahar after we left there. We talked it over as a crew and decided it would be fine to fly back to Masirah. That runway was rather rough. I guess what happened was we kicked a rock up on landing and maybe hit that puck. I'm just thankful that the guys getting on the back of the airplane saw it. That was a good thing.

8

DEFENSOR FORTIS

Defensor Fortis [Defender of the Force]
—Air Force Security Police motto

On missions into Afghanistan and elsewhere, many transport aircraft carried with them specially trained Air Force Security Police called Phoenix Raven teams. It's their job to protect the aircraft and crew in nonsecure areas. Originally, the Raven concept involved inconspicuous troops bearing concealed weapons, mainly for antiterrorism and antihijacking. But in the post-9/11 world, they began flying very different kinds of missions for which there was no guidebook.

Master Sergeant John Cordova, 167th Airlift Wing Raven team member

Phoenix Raven teams comprise two to four security force members who went to the Air Mobility Warfare College at Fort Dix, New Jersey, to become certified Ravens. They fly with the aircrews to airports that do not have security or have inadequate security.

After the event at Khobar Towers, they stood up the Raven program as the first line of defense for antiterrorism. Right now there are nineteen hundred Ravens Air Force-wide. We have the oldest flying Raven team in existence right now. Our average age is forty years old, where in active duty it's twenty-two.

We fliers like Ravens because they keep bad guys away from our airplane and us. As John explains, they get training in several skills—all to ensure that attacking a U.S. Air Force aircraft will become a very bad career move for a terrorist.

They bring the best of the best instructors to the schoolhouse. You get training in ground combat fighting, which is weapons retention, grappling, and ground wrestling. You go to a close quarters house and you do shoot/no shoot situations with simunitions and paintball. They bring in federal air marshals and you train on aircraft to defend the cockpit. They also bring in the Army and you do some of their convoy training. How to safeguard VIPs. They teach you Combat Lifesaver skills. You're certified as a pressure point control tactics instructor, a defensive tactics instructor, and an expandable baton instructor while you're there.

Second Lieutenant Mike Lemon, now a security forces officer, worked his way up to the rank of Master Sergeant before receiving his commission. As a senior NCO, he served as a Raven team manager on missions immediately following 9/11.

Second Lieutenant Mike Lemon, 167th Airlift Wing Raven team member

The Raven program is kind of a bastard child because Ravens are a different type of security force person. I have a hard time saying they're elite; they're just a different tool in the tool belt. You don't send a thirteen-man squad to do what we do. They can't do what we do and we can't do what they do. So we're kind of shunned by the security force guys, but then again, we're not fully accepted by the operations guys. We're cops to them.

Ground personnel loading cargo at Kandahar. During operations like this, Raven teams stood guard to protect the aircraft and crew (courtesy the 167th Airlift Wing).

We deployed very quickly after 9/11. We left September 28, 2001, and we initially deployed to Travis Air Force Base in California. It was such a surprise and shock to everybody. They got us activated and out into hubs so they could utilize us, and Travis was our hub. They really didn't know what to do with us. There was a lot of confusion, but eventually we deployed to Malaysia. That was our first deployment.

Lemon explains that he thought he was missing the action by going to Malaysia at that time, but the assignment to guard airplanes turned out to involve more than he expected. As he tells his story, he refers to his partner on that mission, fellow Raven Vince Shambaugh. Shambaugh is a burly former Marine who served in Gulf War One and now works as a deputy sheriff and part-time Air Guardsman.

In transit to that mission in Malaysia, we were in Hawaii when the initial bombing in Afghanistan started. This was a real kick in the balls to us because Afghanistan was going on, September 11 had just happened, and we were away from our families. We got sent to Malaysia because Boeing was trying to sell the new F/A-18 Super Hornets to the Malaysian government. We went over in a KC-135 tanker and took three F/A-18s. We landed there in Malaysia and we did an air show. I'm like, "We're at war, and we're in a Muslim country, and we're at an air show."

The first two days, the company reps and the dignitaries, the generals and the purchasing people were going to look at the airplanes. The next two days were open to the general public. We had four Ravens, a KC-135, and three F/A-18s in a country that didn't particularly care for us at the time. They were expecting fifty thousand people on this tarmac. We had no rope, no stanchions, no nothing. It's so hot there, people were trying to get under the KC-135's wingtips to get in the shade.

I was at the tail and he [Shambaugh] was at the nose. People were climbing up the ladders, trying to get in the airplanes. People were everywhere and the threat was real. They would confront us: "How come you're not killing children in Afghanistan? How come you're here?" The tone was very tense.

We had literally a thousand people within a hundred feet of this KC-135 fully loaded with fuel, sitting on this ramp, and we had almost nothing. You can't display weapons there. We had concealed weapons and batons and we had our little radios.

It's a hundred degrees, right? Humidity is a hundred percent. And there's two guys underneath the airplane, under the wing. There's people lighting up cigarettes, everything. But there's these two guys with real long trench coats, leather. You had MiGs up there, flying crazy acrobatics. And they're not looking up at the airplanes flying at all. They're looking up underneath the wheel wells of our airplane. They're looking up the cowlings. They're looking at the landing gear, and they're very interested in it.

I said, "Vince, you see those guys?"

He's like, "Yeah, I see 'em."

I said, "Man, they're making me nervous."

He goes, "Yeah, me too."

So we sat there and watched them, and this went on for probably twenty minutes. I was like, "Fuck this. This is enough, man." They got these big, long coats on. Something's not right. They're not paying attention to anything except our bird.

I went over and got the Malaysian military police. They didn't speak any English. I pointed to the guys and I said, "Those guys right there are making me nervous. They're not watching anything; they're looking at our airplane." He didn't understand. I said, "I want them out of here. Get them away." [motions with his arm] He understood that. He snapped to, man. He went over there and grabbed those guys by the back of the neck, drug them out from under the airplane and led them off at gunpoint. That was it. Never saw them after that.

Not long after the Malaysia mission, Ravens from the 167th deployed to the Middle East. There they protected airlift and tanker aircraft going into Afghanistan. Martinsburg's Raven team does not necessarily deploy with the unit's own aircraft. For their first Afghanistan missions, they flew on active-duty C-17s, which are the newest transport jets in the Air Force. During the early days of Operation Enduring Freedom, the Ravens flew in and out of Landing Zone Rhino, a forward base in the southern desert of Afghanistan.

Staff Sergeant Eddie Rollyson, 167th Airlift Wing Raven team member

When you first went in, you didn't know what to expect, what kind of forces were there. You didn't see a whole lot of what was going on, but I guess they had the perimeters pretty secure. We were told to stay on the runway because they weren't sure what was out there. People were still getting blown up by unexploded ordnance. Once you landed you were looking for devices like that and also keeping an eye out for people approaching the plane. We were watching the plane to make sure no one was coming around it.

Master Sergeant John Cordova, 167th Airlift Wing Raven team member

It was a new experience for us going in at night. Once you get there, it's totally different from anything you've ever seen. You get off the plane, it's pitch black, and you make contact with somebody. It's pretty exciting because you have a whole planeload of people and gear going into a place where heavy aircraft haven't been. They had just cleared the runways of mines and old ordnance left over from the Russian invasion. It was pretty scary. I'm not ashamed to say it.

Second Lieutenant Mike Lemon, 167th Airlift Wing Raven team member

That was the insertion of the 15th and the 24th Marine Expeditionary Units into Afghanistan. It was the farthest inland insertion of Marine Corps forces in their history. Afghanistan is landlocked.

As American forces pushed farther into Afghanistan, they set up operations at Bagram Air Base near Kabul. As Lemon explains, the missions got more hairy because Bagram is nearer populated areas and therefore more vulnerable to attack.

When we started flying into Bagram, that was a totally different thing because that was about thirty-five miles from Kabul. We would fly in on a spiral descent and we'd be up on missile watch, looking for SAMs and RPGs [Surface-to-Air Missiles and Rocket-Propelled Grenades].

Myself and Eddie flew with the first C-17 into Bagram. That was December of 2001. At that time there had been some Marine Corps C-130s in there, and they were getting RPGs shot at them a lot. That's when we started taking Special Forces guys in there. It was kind of a pucker factor because I remember walking into mission planning, and the nav and pilots were saying, "I need to know who has control of this intersection right here because I'm going to be flying right over top of it."

I also remember walking back to the loadmaster and the loadmaster goes, "This is going to be a little sporty." Usually those guys were pretty calm and cool because they were special operations. I talked to the pilots later and they said it looked like that Mel Gibson movie, *Road Warrior*. Stuff burning, cars on fire, tracers flying everywhere.

At that point there were some CIA guys on the ground in Bagram, along with Northern Alliance fighters. The main fear at Bagram was sabotage. They were afraid we were going to land that big C-17 there, and there was going to be a Northern Alliance turncoat. He'd wait until the airplane got right there and he'd throw a satchel charge and blow up the airplane. That was our main threat.

It was night when we went in. You were wearing night vision goggles. There were people moving all around and you didn't know who they were. The Northern Alliance dressed just like the Taliban at the time. We put one guy at each wingtip, one guy at the tail, and one guy at the nose of the air-plane. Engines were running the entire time. You couldn't hear anything; you were just doing sight checks with each other. We were looking for somebody who would break away and try to make a run for the airplane and throw an explosive charge.

The Ravens had never been used in combat before. Ever. We weren't designed for combat. We were designed for antiterrorism. We were designed to blend in with the aircrew and be benign security. We were designed so that if you'd look out and see an aircrew, you wouldn't be able to say, "That's a Raven, and that's a Raven." We'd wear flight suits and blend in with the flight crew. This was a totally different function for us. We'd come off the airplane in full body armor, weapons displayed. Normally we'd carry concealed weapons and you wouldn't be able to pick us out. This was a totally different mission for the Ravens.

We were basically writing the book. There was no field manual; there was no operating instruction for how we were supposed to do it, so we basically made it up. We decided that our threat was close in, so I'd have guys go on missions with shotguns instead of rifles because it was a close-in threat. Nobody told us to do that; we just did it. It was basically, "Go there, do the job, and get it done. We don't care how."

Our leadership at the higher headquarters level really just wanted the mission done. They didn't care how it got done; they wanted it done. They wanted the airplanes back, and they didn't want to see a burning shell of an airplane with people getting dragged through the streets. They didn't want that to happen.

Master Sergeant John Cordova, 167th Airlift Wing Raven team member

At the warfare center, they teach you that the aircraft is sovereign U.S. territory. Nobody, without the pilot's permission, gets on board that aircraft. That's what we're there for.

We got to see a lot of things you normally don't see, and it's a totally different role from what we were taught at the schoolhouse. We tried a lot of new equipment, a lot of new gear, and a lot different tactics. We'd fly in blacked out on night vision goggles. We'd go outside and set up a perimeter around the aircraft. The lead Raven would make contact with the troops getting on the aircraft, or if troops were getting off the aircraft, we'd make sure they met up with a safe contact.

All the Ravens recall the Bagram missions as their scariest assignments, espe-cially during the approaches into the airfield. That's because military people like operating in their own element: fliers feel comfortable in the air, but trigger-pullers want to be on the ground.

Second Lieutenant Mike Lemon,
167th Airlift Wing Raven team member

For example, we'd do our intel briefings beforehand. Exclusively, the intel was all about the approach and stuff like that. We don't care about that as Ravens. We want to know what's happening on the ground. The intel was all tailored towards the pilots, their spiral descent, and so on. And us in the back— when we were going into Bagram, I was like, "Please get on the ground, get on the ground, get on the ground." And it's so rough and it's dark and it's blacked out and there's turbulence.

Finally, when I got on the ground, I felt more secure. Once you got on the ground, you had stuff going on at a very fast rate. Everything's blacked out, and people are running and hollering and engines are screaming. Machines, Humvees, everything flying around you. You don't really feel secure, but you feel calmer, I guess. It's our thing; we're on the ground now. We're ground fighters. At least on the ground, I can shoot; I can run away; I can do something. In the air, there's nothing I can do.

Technical Sergeant Vince Shambaugh,
167th Airlift Wing Raven team member

There's nothing more helpless. All the training you have and all the guns you have ain't doing a bit of good when you're in the air getting shot at.

We knew somebody was going to die. We submitted to the idea that we're going to lose some people. That Marine Herky crew ate in the chow hall with us that same morning they took off and hit the mountain. [On January 9, 2002, seven Marines died when their KC-130 Hercules tanker crashed near Shamsi Air Base in western Pakistan.]

Second Lieutenant Mike Lemon,
167th Airlift Wing Raven team member

There were letters written to family members that would be left behind. People wrote letters to their families. We all expected that something bad was going to happen.

Perhaps the closest call for the Ravens came in November of 2001 in Kandahar, when the airfield came under attack.

Master Sergeant John Cordova, 167th Airlift Wing Raven team member

[Another crew was] taking prisoners out of Kandahar to Guantanamo Bay, Cuba. We were there just to offload equipment from a C-17. The plane beside us was actually loading prisoners. We were closer to the perimeter fence. We had just finished pushing the last pallet off, and we saw people running by us, taking up positions. Next thing, the Marines were telling us to go.

We're standing there looking, like, "What's going on?" All of a sudden you see tracer fire coming in through the perimeter fence. Al Qaeda had seen where they were loading detainees and they'd decided to mount an assault from a nearby village. That was, the least to say, exciting. We got on the aircraft and took off. With no lights, just took off and it was like an amusement park ride going practically straight up. You're just wondering what in the world's going on. The whole time you're just hanging on to your strap, waiting for this plane to level out. We didn't find out the details of the attack until we got back to Oman and watched it on CNN.

Staff Sergeant Eddie Rollyson, 167th Airlift Wing Raven team member

The bird that was taking out the first detainees was in front of us. Right when it was getting ready to leave, there were flashes over from the perimeter. Everybody started saying, "There's an attack!" We started throwing off our cargo, which was mattresses. Mattresses were going everywhere, and they were trying to get all the planes out of there. We didn't know how bad the attack was. As Ravens, we were trying to stay on the ground to make sure nothing was coming for the bird. The plane was actually going while we were trying to run and get on it. As far as I know, nothing happened to an airplane. We got out of there safe, but it was a little weird seeing an attack come over the perimeter.

In addition to flying on airlift missions, the Ravens often protect aircraft and crews on tours by dignitaries. After 9/11, the Raven team from Martinsburg took part in a number of high-level trips, including presidential visits. Assignments to support presidential trips are called Phoenix Banner missions.

Master Sergeant John Cordova, 167th Airlift Wing Raven team member

We did a thirteen-country Middle Eastern tour with Condoleezza Rice, Donald Rumsfeld, and Tommy Franks. Thirteen countries in twelve days, stop and go, stop and go. That was at the end of 2001, going into 2002.

In the spring of 2003, President Bush held talks with Vladimir Putin, and we flew with the president to St. Petersburg. From there we went to Moscow. To be part of the team with the Secret Service and the Hostage Rescue Team, being snagged from a little Guard base in West Virginia, it's pretty exciting.

When we have missions like that, we're authorized a civilian clothing allowance. The Secret Service tells us what to buy and how to wear it, so we all look the same. The job of the Secret Service, of course, is to protect the president and the presidential aircraft. But in addition to Air Force One, there are other aircraft from the military that fly backup and support. They'll have the press corps on one; they'll have the luggage on one; they'll have the Secret Service and Hostage Rescue Team on one. We protect those other aircraft and crews.

Second Lieutenant Mike Lemon, 167th Airlift Wing Raven team member

We did Banner missions to China, Russia, Rome, Israel. We did a lot of Banner missions. We also flew CODEL [congressional delegation] missions. Peter King—he's the chairman of the House Homeland Security Committee—we flew him and the secretary of energy into Libya. It was the first mission to Libya for years and years and years.

When Libya got out of the WMD game [Weapons of Mass Destruction], we went over there to verify that they were actually doing it.

Those missions are unique because we fly in a Boeing Business Jet, a C-40A, and it has no military markings at all. We fly in civilian clothes, usually a blazer, carry a concealed weapon, and it's usually either a U.S. senator or a U.S. congressman we're escorting. But it doesn't take a rocket scientist to figure out what it is. You got this big airplane; you got American-looking guys with short hair standing around in civilian clothes. They know who it is.

During the Libya trip in February of 2005, Lemon and Shambaugh had a close call with what appeared to be either terrorists or criminals in Amman, Jordan.

Second Lieutenant Mike Lemon, 167th Airlift Wing Raven team member

We got to Jordan. We were on the way to Libya. It was the first blizzard in Amman in like, ten years. Snow was flying sideways and it was cold. The U.S. embassy was supposed to come out and provide us transportation from the airport to our billeting location, which was like, an hour away. That's all we knew; it was an hour away. We didn't know north, south, what route to take, anything like that.

Since there was a snowstorm, the embassy said, "We ain't coming to get you. You're on your own."

It was up to us, me and Vince, to get through customs and everything at Amman. That took hours, getting in and out. I'm on the phone with the embassy guys, and I'm like, "Man, we need a ride out here. We don't know where we're at or anything."

The embassy guy goes, "There'll be a van there waiting for you."

So me and Vince come out of the airport. We're standing there and everybody's staring at us. We got our gear and everything. It's obvious that we're U.S. military. This van pulls up and this guy goes, "We're your ride." I didn't know. He said, "Go ahead and get in the van." He was a Jordanian.

I hop in the van, and as soon as I hop in the van, I notice there's somebody behind me. There's four or five Jordanian guys sitting behind us. I looked at Vince, and we're unarmed. I looked at him and he looked at me, and I was like, "This ain't right."

We were in the van and it was full of Jordanians. We had no idea where we were going.

Technical Sergeant Vince Shambaugh, 167th Airlift Wing Raven team member

They were talking in hushed tones. They were about to jump our ass.

Second Lieutenant Mike Lemon, 167th Airlift Wing Raven team member

We thought they were going to take us out in the desert and kill us. I was like, "Come on, Vince. Get out."

The guys go, "No, no, get back in."

I said, "No. Get. We ain't taking you."

I got back on the phone to the embassy and I said, "This is bullshit. You need to get somebody out here right fucking now."

I don't know if was an abduction attempt or not, but I tell you what—it looked like one; it smelled like one. I swear to God, if we would have left in that van, I don't know what would have happened. They weren't the welcoming committee; I guarantee you that.

Lemon says in the post-9/11 world, Air Guard Ravens have proven themselves to the aircrews.

Initially we were perceived as being lesser because we were Guard, but we totally changed their attitudes about it. After that, they exclusively wanted to fly with Guard guys. They were used to flying with active-duty guys. Their active-duty guys were first-term airmen, maybe a staff sergeant, and they really didn't have any life experience. Their experience was going to basic training.

We started showing up with guys who had so much more experience. We had guys who'd flown seventy or eighty missions at that time. I'm a state trooper. I got deputy sheriffs. We have a lot of life experience and we brought a lot to the table. They started wanting to fly with us exclusively because we were more mature; we had more life experience. We were better suited for the missions because we'd had experience in pucker factor situations.

9

SEE YOU IN BAGHDAD

I called people and said, "Well, we're getting activated. We don't know anything else."

—Major Mike Foley, 167th AW

While we helped take care of business in Afghanistan, other wheels were turning far above our pay grades. As far back as 1998, America's official policy had called for regime change in Iraq. In President Bush's State of the Union address on January 29, 2002, he listed Iraq as a member of the "axis of evil."

While Saddam Hussein resisted pressure to cooperate with United Nations arms inspectors, another war looked more and more likely. I can recall watching the news one afternoon at our Martinsburg base and remarking to a squadron mate, "See you in Baghdad."

Sure enough....

Major Jeff Lane, pilot, squadron commander

Starting in January 2003, I had numerous discussions with squadron leadership as to what would be the best method for selecting people. Thinking about it ahead of time in December and January was very helpful in that we didn't have to think about it right before we left. We were over ninety percent prepared already. We had already made up a list of lead crews. By the time we got our mobilization notice, all that was left to do was the tasking.

Major Mike Foley, navigator

I was one of the guys who called the navs when we got activated. Attitudes really impressed me as I called people—this was in March of '03. I called people and said, "Well, we're getting activated. We don't know anything else."

Their response was, "What day, and where are we going?" Nobody said, "I can't go. I don't want to do it. It doesn't make sense. We shouldn't do this." The answer was, "What day, and where are we going?"

Master Sergeant John "Ratman" Ratcliffe, loadmaster

I went to the manager at Lowe's and I said, "Well, if Iraq doesn't happen, then I'll be back in March." You know, everybody watching the news just knew it was leaning that way. You felt it.

Lo and behold that Thursday, Roger Nye [the unit's director of operations] called and said, "Hey, I want a meeting with everybody in the building."

I walked in and Roger said, "We've got a Three-Nancy package."

Everybody said, "What's that?"

He said, "Everybody's activated."

I was on the last airplane, March 5 or March 6. Took the long tour. Volcanic ash was in the Mediterranean, so we had to go up to Aviano Air Base, Italy, and spend the night there when everybody else was already in Masirah.

Lieutenant Colonel Steve Truax, navigator, operations officer

I asked my girlfriend to marry me because we'd been planning for marriage. I could see how if you're deployed and there's nobody at home with your power of attorney to take care of you, it's tough. I did not know what was next, so we ran to the courthouse, got married, and sure enough they deployed us again right after that. I just gave her a blanket power of attorney for everything, forwarded all my mail to her house, and she took care of everything for the five months we were deployed.

We at the squadron level wanted to lead from the front, to lead the troops into the tents, into the desert, and I felt very much that that was my place. And then as I was preparing to go, I was told I was staying back with another package.

So I went home and called the wife up and went to Baltimore where she was still living. It was my birthday, as a matter of fact. We went out to my birthday dinner, came back, and my cell phone was sitting in her living room with a message on it. I dialed it up and it was somebody saying, "I've tried to reach you all weekend. It's Sunday right now; you need to be here eight o'clock Monday to leave."

I looked at my watch and said, "Great. I've got eleven hours to go home, take care of all my business, pack up all my stuff, and get ready to leave." So that was the notice I had. Leaving my wife on those terms was terribly depressing, and I went home and packed all night. I probably got an hour or two of sleep. I wasn't crew for the flight going over, so I could sleep on the plane. My apartment complex had a night drop, and I ended up dropping off several months' worth of rent and a note saying, "I don't know how long I'm going to be gone. Please look after my apartment."

Lieutenant Colonel Bill Clark, pilot

When I walked off the ramp here, I turned around and looked back, and I'd never seen my kids cry so hard. That was the worst part.

Guard members have their own rituals for deployment day. Some bring their families to the base for tearful goodbyes. Others say their goodbyes at home, drive themselves to the airfield, and leave their cars in the parking lot for the duration.

Upon arrival at the base, a flurry of predeparture chores comes before takeoff. We go through intelligence briefings, public health briefings, and legal briefings. We stand in lines for immunizations and finance. The chaplain gives out encouragement and Bibles, paperback editions small enough for a flight suit pocket. They come with a bookmark featuring the Twenty-Third Psalm, including the famous verse: "Yea, though I walk through the valley of the shadow of death...." Forklifts rumble around belching smoke and carrying pallets of baggage. As we leave the Operations building to step to the flight line, we pass a sign that reads: "You Are Our Greatest Asset. FLY SAFE And Have A Great Day."

Finally, sitting in the cockpit, we regain at least some measure of control. Checklists done and engines on speed, we lift off the runway and point the nose toward the Atlantic. Usually three or four planes deploy at once, and we might see our squadron mates a few miles ahead, a speck in the windscreen and a voice on the radio.

Over the ocean, static on the hissing high-frequency radios pops like distant rifle fire. Droning across the sea, we have hours to think about what we're getting into.

From the author's journal, 5 March 2003

Twenty-one thousand feet over the Atlantic, a relatively low altitude because we're heavy with fuel and cargo. En route to Lajes Field in the Azores, the first step on a journey of unpredictable duration.

I'm guessing this day of departure will be the hardest of the whole deployment. A sip of coffee from my Thermos, rich French roast with a touch of cinnamon from my own kitchen, emphasizes the separation from all things familiar. Homesickness in a foam cup. I could open my checklist binder and steal a glance at the photo of my wife, but at this moment it would just make things worse.

Though you think you're prepared for this, it hits harder than expected. One loadmaster told me, "I'm having a hard time putting on my game face." Another said he broke into tears when he dropped off his daughter at school this morning.

Meanwhile, one troop's wife has supplied us with a huge pot of chili and some cornbread. We dine on the home cooking as we drone over a dark ocean.

Technical Sergeant Kenny LaFollette, flight engineer

Waiting to actually get to the destination is a little unnerving if you've never been there before. You're reviewing your desert procedures and things you haven't ever used. You want to get yourself ready.

From the author's journal, 6 March 2003

Touched down in the Azores last night amid howling wind and lashing rain. C-130s and KC-135 tankers line the ramp, more than I've ever seen there.

Lajes Field is usually a good overnight stay, but by the time we got there, all the aircrew rooms were taken. We slept on cots in an old dorm building, three and four men to a room. I think we tossed and turned all night. One man said he hasn't slept well since he got the mobilization call from the unit.

This morning dawned clear, with a heaving blue sea down the hill from the base. Aviators are still in the process of tearing themselves away from home. One guy says his toughest moment came when his eight-year-old told him to have a good trip.

"But we gotta do this thing," he added, "or else my little boy will have to deal with it."

Aloft and en route again, we hear almost nothing on the radio except Air Mobility Command call signs. The United States has launched an aluminum overcast; transports and tankers fill the jet routes over the Atlantic.

As scores of American planes head east over the ocean, the high-frequency Military Affiliate Radio System, or MARS, hums with conversations between fliers and their families. Good Samaritan ham radio operators make phone patches for us: "I love you—over."

You can't be too intimate; the whole crew and half the damn Air Force are listening. Occasionally some wife or girlfriend doesn't realize that, and she tells us all what some embarrassed pilot can look forward to when he gets home.

The Air Force's credo is "Global Reach, Global Power." Airlifters contribute much of the reach—to the extent that the word "Reach" becomes our call sign.

From the author's journal, 8 March 2003

Long after midnight my time, still Friday evening at home. The MARS operator patches me through to my wife, Kristen.

"It's so good to hear your voice," she says, wisely keeping the conversation boring. "What are you doing?"

"Flying over North Africa." Egypt, actually. But I keep things vague in what's probably an overly conservative effort at not telling the enemy anything useful.

"I love you—over."

"Reach Three Six One Yankee terminating phone patch," I said, oddly mixing official procedure with a chat with my wife. The ham operator wishes us Godspeed.

We touched down at a place that had become familiar to many of us early in the Afghanistan war—Masirah Island, Oman. When the U.S. drove the Taliban from power in Afghanistan, operations at Masirah scaled back. Now fresh rows of tents had been set up, our new homes waiting for us. From Masirah, C-130s could reach not only Iraq, but also Afghanistan and the Horn of Africa, where antiterrorist operations were going on.

Masirah's location in the Arabian Sea has given it strategic military value since the days of Alexander the Great, who called the island "Serepsis" and made it a staging base. Approximately forty miles long and ten miles wide, the island hosts an air base at its northern end built by the British Royal Air Force.

If you had to deploy to the desert for Operation Iraqi Freedom, Masirah was the place to be. To begin with, it was in Oman, perhaps America's strongest Arab ally in the war on terror. Oman has demonstrated that a country can be staunchly Muslim without teaching its citizens hatred of non–Muslims. You seldom hear of an Omani terrorist. Oman's brand of Islam, Ibadhism, may help account for that; Oman is the only Muslim country with a majority Ibadhi population. Ibadhism is a moderately conservative form of Islam that stands apart from the Shiite and other Sunni sects of the religion.

In addition, the island was safer from terrorist attack than mainland bases, and it was out of Scud range from Iraq, so we didn't have to worry about diving for bunkers and pulling on gas masks.

Our Camp Justice at Masirah was a smaller camp than some of the bases in Qatar and Kuwait, so you never had long lines for showers or meals. And although it was hot, the ocean breezes seemed to give us a bit of a break.

Compared to other people involved in the war, we had little reason to complain.

However, as Major Jeff Lane explains, we did have to do some work to make the place ready for military operations.

Major Jeff Lane, pilot, squadron commander

We deployed to a facility that had a certain amount of infrastructure already there, but it was not set up for flying when we got there. Our facilities were largely bare, with wires sticking out of the walls. Our communications were really like World War II at first; we didn't have cell phones. Telephones weren't hooked up yet to our tents. Most of our communications was driving around in vehicles and talking to each other.

Although our crews were ready to start flying, the infrastructure in mission planning and command and control were not set up. The obstacles to flying were administrative, from a crew member's standpoint. You go somewhere and you assume your communications are going to be there. Before we can fly combat missions, we need classified computer access to receive our mission taskings, or an encrypted telephone capability to pass those verbally. We need a capability to write orders, to fabricate the mission planning kits, to operate the whole maintenance scheduling process. The Air Force left all the details up to us, as far as getting up and running. We're used to going to places where there's a little slot we fit into and we start flying. When you go somewhere and you have to kind of make that slot, it's a different experience.

From the author's journal, 9 March 2003

Home sweet tent, Camp Justice, Masirah Island, Oman. It's four in the morning here, but my body thinks it's seven in the evening. Actually, my prop-lagged body doesn't know what to think, but I'm wide awake.

There's a pleasant, constant rustling sound as the air conditioner blows cooling air through the cloth plenum that runs overhead through the length of the tent. We have hung bedsheets and shower curtains from parachute cord to mark off each man's space and provide a small degree of privacy for each of the five members of our crew.

I write with a camouflage-colored handkerchief draped over my reading lamp to keep from disturbing my neighbors. A journal will help pass the time, but I hope I'm not here long enough for a book-length project. A short story would be good. Better yet, one brief haiku poem.

There's a memorial outside, just a few steps from my tent. It honors the eight men killed in the accident at Desert One. That took place in 1980, during the failed attempt to rescue hostages at the American embassy in Tehran. The C-130s in that mission, Operation Eagle Claw, took off from Masirah.

I've seen photos of the crews before launch—confident, jovial men in flight suits and survival vests, ready to pull off a stunning rescue. They'd have done it, too, if not for horribly bad luck.

I once read an op-ed piece that described the Iranian hostage situation as the first battle in a war on the West by militant Islam. Maybe the author was right.

Meanwhile, there's interesting wildlife here on the island: scorpions, camel spiders, and sand vipers. I'm told sand vipers are among the deadliest snakes in the world. Nice.

Thousands of miles from home, some of the stateside spit and polish goes away. In fact, you don't polish brown suede desert boots at all. At least they don't show the dust that permeates everything.

Neither do our uniforms. Ground personnel wear the familiar DCUs, which stands for Desert Camouflage, Utility. Fliers walk around in light tan desert flight suits, sometimes a little baggy. In the rush to deploy, you take what you can get from supply.

A 167th aircrew at Masirah Island Air Base, Oman, in 2003. From left to right: loadmaster Roland Shambaugh, flight engineer (and author) Thomas W. Young, navigator Kelly Washington, pilot and aircraft commander Mike Langley, copilot Jon McCullough. Note the nose art to the left of the crew door, the "Let's Roll" slogan inspired by the actions of passengers aboard United Flight 93 on September 11, 2001 (author's collection).

Nearly every aviator wears a tiny utility light hanging from his flight suit's zipper tab. The light emits a green beam compatible with night vision goggles. You aren't supposed to hang sunglasses, utility lights, or any other ornaments on your uniform, but out here no one cares. Besides, when the lights go out in the desert, it gets very, very dark.

On our left sleeves, above the pen pockets, we wear the usual flag patch. But even the star-spangled banner makes concessions for desert camo. Instead of red, white, and blue, it's brown and darker brown, like everything else in this sandy expanse.

From the author's journal, 10 March 2003

Hotter today. Still waiting on word of when and where we'll fly. Crews are still settling in, setting up their living arrangements, e-mail accounts, etc.

When not flying, there's not much to do on this desert rock of an island. There's a beach open to us, guarded by Air Force Security Police. Occasionally a boat will begin criss-crossing a little too close for comfort, and the SPs will blow a whistle and get everyone off the beach. Whether the boats contain terrorists or just curiosity-seekers is anyone's guess. One of the troops here had enough foresight to bring a surf rod with him. Wish I'd thought of that.

Meanwhile, we can work out in the exercise facility, watch DVDs, or e-mail home if the servers are up. This is also a good time to study flight manuals.

The island itself is a pretty barren place. A few scrubby trees insist on eking out an existence. Other than that, it's just rock and sand, fit mainly for the scorpions. Mice like the tents, though, and cats like the mice, so half-wild felines roam the base to keep the rats and mice under control.

Colonel Eric Vollmecke, pilot, wing commander

My wife and I watched a movie recently, *Jarhead*, and she asked me about how that related to some of my war experiences. The one thing I really liked about the movie was that it captured well what it's like to wait and not know exactly when the operation's going to kick off. That actually can be very stressful. You're in that holding pattern; you have to keep your skills sharpened and be ready to go at a moment's notice—but that moment's notice might be a month away.

From the author's journal, 11 March 2003

Still waiting for our Air Operations Center to get set up, and we're waiting for orders to fly. We'd like to be busier, but this could become a good case of how you should be careful what you wish for.

10

ALARM RED

                                        —From AFMAN 10-100, The Airman's Manual

In March of 2003, the 167th Airlift Wing had four airplanes and eight crews based at Masirah Island, Oman. Crews from Georgia and Texas units also joined us. We sat through briefings and reviewed tactics. We checked and rechecked our gear. We got smallpox shots in case Saddam resorted to biological warfare, and for a few days we walked around with the telltale scabs on our arms. We followed the news and we waited—but not for long.

From the author's journal, 17 March 2003

As we were eating dinner this evening, everyone fell silent as the TV flashed: LIVE SPECIAL REPORT. The U.S. and Britain have withdrawn a proposed U.N. resolution to establish specific steps for Iraq to avoid attack. The U.S. and Britain are walking away from a Security Council in which some members, especially France, are determined not to get serious about disarming Iraq.

The news said the weapons inspectors are leaving Iraq. President Bush plans to address the nation at eight in the evening, eastern U.S. time, which is five in the morning our time.

From the author's journal, 18 March 2003

President Bush, in his speech at 5:00 A.M. our time, gave Saddam Hussein and his sons forty-eight hours to leave Iraq or face war. Saddam has rejected the ultimatum.

Today, GIs here at Masirah Island, Oman, are running last-minute errands. When the attack kicks off, we expect personal phone calls and e-mails to be shut off. The TCNs, or Third Country Nationals, will not be allowed on base for a while. That means no barber shop or laundry service, among other things.

I was not scheduled to fly today, so I called my wife and parents. I also got a haircut and picked up a uniform I had left at the cleaner's.

Meanwhile, in a revival of an old Air Force tradition, some of us, including me, are growing combat mustaches. The theory is that a mustache makes you bulletproof. We'll see.

Major Chris "Mookie" Walker, navigator

When we started flying into Iraq, that was something else. This was the place that allegedly had all the real weapons that could take us down. It was a little scary for a lot of people at first. But I guess maybe stupidity, youth, or bravado took over, and we just started saying, "Yeah, let's go do it."

From the author's journal, 20 March 2003

The fight's on. This morning, U.S. forces are lobbing cruise missiles into Baghdad, apparently on intel that places Saddam Hussein in a specific location. Air strikes began last night.

Our crew is off duty at the moment. We got back to Masirah last night after a particularly unproductive day. After flying empty to Thumrait Air Base, Oman, we uploaded three fuel bladder pumps. But as we taxied out, oil temperature on the number three engine shot sky high due to a failed oil cooler flap.

We shut down the engine, taxied back in, and waited for maintenance from Masirah to come and rescue us. Another aircraft carried our cargo to Doha, Qatar, and we returned to Masirah after repairs.

We accomplished nothing. But on the other hand, we had a malfunction that could have destroyed a million-dollar engine had we not caught it in time, and we kept that from happening.

Reportedly, Thumrait had an exciting day yesterday. An officer there told us that shortly before we arrived, about four Yemeni nationals tried to sneak into the base. They carried some unidentified fluid. Omani troops killed two and captured the others. That's the story we heard, anyway; I have not read or heard any confirmation. No word on what the hell they were trying to pull.

As we waited for maintenance at Thumrait, we watched a B-1 bomber roar off into a velvet, full-moon night. Its afterburners glowed like four yellow daggers, and the crew kept them lit until the aircraft had almost vanished. Apparently she needed all that power because she carried a heavy load, banking right and heading north.

In 1988, Saddam Hussein's forces gassed to death up to five thousand Kurdish civilians in the Iraqi town of Halabja. Given our enemy's track record, we carry chem warfare kits on every flight.

The kits contain two gas masks. One is for ground use. The other hooks into your flight helmet, and its snaking hoses and wires connect to the plane's oxygen and communications systems, making you look like some sort of alien astronaut. God forbid you actually need to use it.

Then you have something called the Mark One autoinjector kit. That's in case you didn't use the gas mask when you should have. If you feel drooling or convulsions coming on due to nerve gas, take the atropine injector and remove the safety cap. Press the injector against your thigh, and a spring-loaded needle about two inches long will slam into your flesh and pump in the antidote. You have to be careful where the needle goes. A warning says hitting a sciatic nerve can cause paralysis.

Next, take the second injector, the one filled with pralidoxime chloride, and stab the other leg. Now you have chemical warfare at the cellular level, but in theory, you will remain among the living.

As loadmaster John Ratcliffe and pilot Jeff Lane describe, anytime we found ourselves on the ground within Scud range of Iraq, we worried about Scuds tipped with chemical warheads.

Master Sergeant John "Ratman" Ratcliffe, loadmaster

The first night we went into Iraq, we flew into Ali Al Salem Air Base in Kuwait, and there were fighters coming out of there. We were going to load up a bunch of ammo and some Marines and take them to Iraq. It was March 20, right when the war started, and we were like, "Wow, this stuff's real. We're going in."

And a Scud got launched. As soon as we pulled up and we were getting ready to throw the chocks out, the sirens went off. The crew chiefs and everyone out there threw their gas masks on and ran into the bunkers—and left us.

From what I was told, they actually did have a Scud come in that night, and apparently it impacted somewhere around the base, but it didn't blow up.

Major Jeff Lane, pilot, squadron commander

There was a Scud warning and Alarm Condition Red. The war had just started, and the fighters were just constantly moving in and out of there. We had to determine in our cockpit exactly what we were going to do. It was right at the edge of saying, well, do we stay in the airplane, or do we shut down and run to the bunkers? We decided to stay in the airplane with the engines running, and if a chemical attack occurred, we were just going to take the runway and take off.

We had actually just pulled into the area where they were going to unload our cargo. We hadn't really accomplished our mission yet as far as delivering the cargo, so we just stood by on the taxiway. The folks on the ground had put their gas masks on and run off to the bunkers, and so we sat there on the taxiway with the engines running just waiting to see what would happen. After about ten minutes or so they came back out without their gas masks. Then we shut down and they unloaded the airplane.

Master Sergeant John "Ratman" Ratcliffe, loadmaster

We got through that and then we flew up to Tallil. I had saved a Cuban cigar. I said, "The first time I land in Iraq I'm going to smoke this Cuban." So I ran out the back and we offloaded, and I lit this thing up, and I'm smoking my cigar, and then they showed up and said, "Hey, can you take some wounded?"

I was surprised that we already had wounded. I guess it started March 19 and this was the next night. We picked up seventeen litter patients. We just threw up the litter stanchions and put the litter guys on without aeromeds [flight nurses and medics] and just took them back to Kuwait City.

Sadly, the first wounded were quickly followed by the first deaths, as my own crew discovered while flying a mission.

From the author's journal, 22 March 2003

For our crew, the war began in earnest yesterday. We flew empty from Masirah and picked up cargo pallets and five passengers in Bahrain. Then we departed for Kuwait International Airport. As we began the descent into Kuwait, we heard from the Air Force command post there:

"Attention all aircraft, this is Boater Whiskey command post. Kuwait International is under attack. The airport is under Alarm Red."

Iraqi missile launches.

"Well, boys, let the games begin," said the aircraft commander, Major Mike Langley. We requested holding from the approach controllers, and we flew in a racetrack pattern for about fifteen minutes until the all clear came.

On the ground we found a zoo. C-130s, C-141s, C-5s, and C-17s were parked on every available ramp spot and even on the taxiways. Ground crew-men ran around in chem suits, ready to pull on gas masks and heavy rubber gloves if another alarm came. After sitting on a taxiway for nearly half an hour, we got cleared into a ramp. There, we shut down and unloaded our cargo.

As we waited for departure clearance, an Army helicopter with a red cross on the side fluttered toward the field and made a radio call:

"Dustoff Two-Three, inbound, patients aboard."

We learned the war's first American combat deaths had happened that day. In addition, a Marine Corps Sea Knight helicopter crashed in an acci-dent in Kuwait, killing at least eight.

On the way back to Masirah, we removed our sweaty flight helmets once above the range of surface-to-air missiles, replacing the helmets with more comfortable headsets. We rolled up our sleeves, sipped coffee, and tuned to the Voice of America on high-frequency radio for the latest news:

"Administration officials say President Bush is expressing condolences to the families...."

We listened in silence as the sun went down, appearing not so much to sink as to dissolve in the dusty haze.

Master Sergeant Dave Twigg, loadmaster

Soon after the campaign kicked off and we started going into Iraq, we flew into Baghdad, and we had five pallets on board. The first pallet position was aeromeds and their equipment, just in case we had to take people who had been wounded back to Kuwait.

We were inbound, probably about ten minutes out, and we got the radio call that we would have an outbound load, and it would be an aeromed mis-sion with casualties. We offloaded the airplane, and the aeromeds went to get their briefing on what our outbound load was going to be.

When they came back to the airplane, you could tell by the look on their faces that something serious was getting taken out. They came on board and started to configure the airplane, so John Cox [another loadmaster] and I jumped in, and we helped them. We found out, after we got the airplane configured, that we were extracting about thirty people, and out of these thirty people there were twelve who had just been hit in a convoy.

The remaining eighteen were walking wounded. Some were minor acci-dents that were not combat related. But the twelve guys they brought on from the convoy were by far in the worst shape of anybody I've ever seen.

The guy who had taken the direct hit from the RPG [Rocket-Propelled Grenade] had been in the passenger side of the Humvee. He had both legs wrapped with about two and a half inches of gauze, and he had steel pins

A 167th Airlift Wing C-130 on the ground at Baghdad. A pallet of cargo lies in the foreground. The civilian terminal is visible in the background. In the first days of Operation Iraqi Freedom, the temporarily abandoned terminal had a forlorn look (author's collection).

A C-130 crew from the 167th unloads all-terrain vehicles in Iraq. From left to right: loadmaster Roland Shambaugh, navigator Kelly Washington, and on the ATV, pilot Ed Bishop (author's collection).

anti begin.

going into the bones of his legs connected with steel rods to hold his legs straight. Plus, he had chest lacerations and his arm was severely wounded, along with head trauma. He was the worst, and the rest were in rough shape.

We got out of Baghdad and flew back to Kuwait. We hit the ground in Kuwait, and they parked us in a remote spot. We sat there, and we waited and waited. We kept the engines running to keep the airplane cool by using the plane's air conditioning system. These guys were hurting bad, so we figured we'd try to keep them as cool as possible.

Then we got word from tower that we had to shut down; there were no engine-running operations taking place, including the APU [Auxiliary Power Unit], so we couldn't even generate any cool air with the APU. Reluctantly, we shut down.

John and I got the back of the airplane opened up, and we were standing there and still waiting—and waiting and waiting. The sun started to come up; it started to get hot in the airplane, and all these people were in bad shape.

A Humvee rolled up, and out came this chief master sergeant from another unit. He was the aeromed coordinator and was supposed to meet the inbound aircraft and have everything ready when the airplane shut down to get these people off. Well, he rolled up with no support with him other than a lieutenant colonel in the passenger seat.

They got out and the lieutenant colonel walked through the airplane and went up on the flight deck. The chief came on and I said, "Chief, where's the support to get these people off the airplane?"

He said, "Well, I had to come out and see what you had."

I said, "We called inbound and reported the severity of the injuries on board this airplane and said we needed support immediately. These people are in bad shape."

Well, he decided to cop an attitude with me. I thought to myself, "This isn't going to do." About that time the lieutenant colonel came back down off the flight deck, and I saw he had medical wings on his uniform.

I said, "Colonel, we need support out here immediately."

He said, "The chief said he was going to take care of that."

I said, "He gave me an attitude. These guys are not in the shape to have to deal with that. I need support here and I need it now."

He said, "It'll be here in two minutes."

He went out to the Humvee and made a call, and two minutes later they had a bus out there to get the guys off the airplane.

After we got all the casualties off, while the aeromeds were stowing their equipment and putting everything away, this chief came up to me and started giving me more attitude. Well, Jim Powell was my aircraft commander. He came down off the flight deck and said, "What's going on?"

I gave him a brief fill-in on the kind of flak that I was taking from this guy. I had to walk away. If I hadn't I would have said some things I would have regretted later. But I think by the time Jim got done with this guy, he had newfound respect for the way we tried to handle this.

Pilot Shaun Perkowski recalls a fellow flier who became upset at the sight of wounded troops his crew had brought out of Iraq. Perkowski did not reveal the flier's name

Lieutenant Colonel Shaun Perkowski, pilot

I was standing in the back of the airplane at Kuwait City because that's where you brought the injured folks out of Iraq. He was helping lift the litters out. They had the bus ambulances there.

I remember him coming up to me afterwards, and he was somewhat emotional. He said, "They were so young." There was not much you could say.

From the author's journal, 24 March 2003

We are flying in two wars.

Yesterday we went to Kandahar, Afghanistan, which remains a hostile area. Although the U.S. controls the airfield, the base comes under sporadic attack, and U.S. troops have lately been conducting searches for Taliban and al Qaeda sympathizers in Kandahar province.

After picking up outbound cargo in Kandahar, we made a tactical departure, blasting across the desert floor at very low level and around 280 knots. Goats and camels scattered in our path, and in any other situation such flying would have been reckless. But that tactic also made us a very difficult target for a missile, or even for small arms fire.

In this business, we do a calculus of compared risks. We accept the hazards of flying at what the books call Minimum Altitude Capable to avoid something that's even more dangerous.

Later, when we were safely up at altitude and en route back to Masirah, we heard the radio chatter of bombers headed for Baghdad. Regime change in progress.

From the author's journal, 25 March 2003

Thanks to e-mail and snail mail, expressions of support from home keep pouring in. We're all receiving notes and packages from spouses, kin, friends, and churches. All the letters and e-mails help boost morale more than anyone back home can imagine.

My wife, Kristen, just sent me an e-mail saying she's greatly relieved to hear from me again. During the communications lockdown when the war kicked off, five days passed without any word from me. We're spoiled; in previous wars people might have gone five weeks—or five months—without a phone call or letter.

The Air Force has a SERE school at Fairchild Air Force Base, Washington. SERE stands for Survival, Evasion, Resistance, and Escape. The school trains every Air Force member considered "at high risk of capture." That includes anyone who flies.

Part of the school involves a mock POW camp. The instructors, in their roles as interrogators, cannot really hurt you. But they can sure make you wish you were somewhere else.

Some graduates of this school say the main lesson they learned is: "I will not let this happen to me. I'll get as many bad guys as I can and I will save the last round for myself."

But you don't really know what you'll do when faced with that situation. And now it was happening to fellow aviators.

From the author's journal, 25 March 2003

Some disturbing images of captured American fliers on TV today. An Apache helicopter went down in Iraq, and its two pilots fell into enemy hands. Iraqi TV footage re-aired on American networks shows the two men sitting silently with ashen faces, one sipping water from a glass.

God knows what those pilots went through or what lies ahead for them. I only hope we overrun Baghdad soon and free those guys. The stricken looks of American POWs contrast sharply with the smiling faces of surrendering Iraqi troops, who know they won't be harmed.

Marines recovered helicopter pilots Ronald Young Jr. and Dave Williams of the First Cavalry Division after twenty-two days of captivity. The two were found along with five other American prisoners of war.

After we came down from the adrenaline high of the war's first days, we began to realize this would be no hundred-hour ground campaign like the first Gulf War. We started settling in for the long haul.

II

THE SPEED OF HEAT

There is no single, best solution to any tactical situation. The most important concept in developing tactics is to remain unpredictable.
— From Air Force Instruction 11–2C-130,
Volume Three, Chapter 16, Combat Mission Planning

A good C-130 crew has all kinds of tricks and maneuvers to avoid getting shot down. But sometimes nothing beats good old-fashioned hauling ass. Blasting across the desert so low and so fast that the sand melts to a tan liquid. Gone by the time the antiaircraft gunners can say, "What the hell was that?" Below the radar and barely above the horizon. The crews call it flying at the speed of heat.

Captain Brandon Taksa, pilot

When we first kicked off the war in Iraq, the Army was moving faster than they had anticipated. So they were having problems keeping the forward troops supplied. They needed us to go in and resupply those forward-deploying, fast-moving troops.

Because of how quickly everything was developing, they really didn't have an airspace plan, per se, for ingressing and egressing Iraq. There was a lot of traffic.

The first time we went in, it was during the daytime, which is unusual—especially for how we train. We're switching toward a night-oriented mission. This was not that. It was daytime, desert sun.

I saw a couple Bedouins and a couple camels up close. Some of the guys were waving. Which finger they were waving with, I don't know. We were going a little too fast for that.

When we first went into Iraq, you'd see guys there in the desert. I remember thinking they knew what was going on. They might be out in the middle of nowhere, but they knew what was going on.

Master Sergeant Doug Ferrell, loadmaster

The first flight into Iraq was the most memorable because I was the most scared. It was total apprehension. You had no idea what was going to happen. As we were flying up, everyone was calling out, "There's a truck over here. He's stopping. What's he doing? Is somebody jumping out?"

Seeing people in the desert in these little huts, and they're running—you didn't know if they were running from something or to get something. You had no idea. It was a very, very tense time.

In one of those instances I saw a desert nomad, I guess, and he was running; you could see his robes. I tensed up and I said, "This guy is running, and I don't know what he's going for." About the next second as we flew over, his whole flock of goats that we had scared ran right over top of him. I called up and said, "I think we have our first confirmed kill."

During the earliest days of Operation Iraqi Freedom, American aircraft swarmed Iraqi airspace from treetop level to the stratosphere. In theory, all aircraft

A C-130 crew on a desert combat mission. Their combat gear includes flak jackets, survival vests, and flight helmets instead of the usual headsets. The helmets are not bullet-proof, but they guard against banging your head on sharp corners during aggressive maneuvering (courtesy the 167th Airlift Wing).

had assigned routes and altitudes, preventing any danger of mid-air collisions. But in the fluid environment of combat, that's not exactly how it worked. When a lot of fast, powerful machines operate in the same spot, sometimes the biggest danger is each other.

One of our senior enlisted fliers recalls seeing a Marine Corps C-130 a little too closely.

Chief Master Sergeant Billy Gillenwater, flight engineer

It was when we were doing one of our first trips up into Baghdad. We were flying the predetermined low-level route into there, and just in a split second all I saw was the orange and white props of the Marine Corps airplane.

It would have been too late if the two planes had not been at slightly different altitudes. It would have been the largest explosion south of Baghdad since the war started. They flew directly underneath us.

We missed the Marine Corps plane by seventy-five to a hundred feet. You could see the people in the cockpit as they passed under our airplane. That's how close it was.

We were doing 250, 300 knots. I can still see those props to this day. We were just lucky. If we would have zigged, we probably should have zagged that day.

Loadmaster Doug Ferrell flew that same mission, and describes seeing the incident from the back of the aircraft.

Master Sergeant Doug Ferrell, loadmaster

I saw a tail go by. When Karl Levy, my pilot, banked the airplane, I looked out because all I heard was, "Oh my God!" I saw the fin go by. It was underneath and off to the side. Then Karl briefed us real quick on what had just happened.

And then it happened again.

Technical Sergeant Kenny LaFollette, flight engineer

Going in, we normally stayed kind of low. You definitely had to keep an eye out for other airplanes. I do remember there was a Marine C-130—we were egressing and they were ingressing. It just so happened that we were pretty much on the same flight path. The copilot just happened to look out and said, "There's another 130."

Thank God they saw us because they went right and we went right, and I think there were numerous cases like that. There were a lot of close calls.

When we flew into hostile areas, we usually went alone. But sometimes we had help. Loadmaster Dave Twigg describes realizing he had A-10 Warthog attack jets riding shotgun with him.

Master Sergeant Dave Twigg, loadmaster

I guess this was our second or third mission into Iraq. We were going to Tallil [Tallil Air Base in southern Iraq]. We had a load of rolling stock on board. We had bomb loaders, some ammunition loaders; there were a couple of maintenance carts—all wheeled cargo.

We loaded everything up in Kuwait, and we took off probably at nine or ten o'clock at night. We crossed the Iraqi border and we got down low-level, flying pretty good along the desert floor. John Cox [another loadmaster] and I stayed in the troop doors. John was always in the left door; I was always in the right door. [On missions in hostile areas, loadmasters scan for threats through the troop door windows.]

We had just coasted into Iraq. It was dark as all get-out; there was no cultural lighting, nothing. There was no moon that night, so it was very dark.

We were flying along on NVGs [Night Vision Goggles], and I looked out the right paratroop door and saw these two little green dots behind the airplane. If we turned, they were right with us the whole time. I looked at these for a couple minutes, and I walked over to John's side and looked out his door, and he didn't have any.

I told him, "Come over here and look at this."

So he went over and looked out the right paratroop door window, and he said, "What's that?"

I said, "I'm not sure what it is. I'm going to keep an eye on it."

He went back over to his side of the airplane. I called the aircraft commander, Jim Powell, and said, "I'm picking up a signature on the NVGs; there's these two little dots behind the airplane."

He said, "There should be two little dots off EACH SIDE of the airplane."

About that time, John said, "All right, I've got two of them as well."

Jim said, "We've got A-10s with us."

I thought, this is COOL. What we were getting was the heat signature off the intakes of the engines on the fighters. I thought that was the neatest thing. Then I turned the radios up back there at the troop doors, and I heard them talking. I thought, this is awesome. I had never flown anywhere with a fighter escort before.

When pilots fly these low-level missions, they sometimes trim the airplane slightly nose high, and then they push down on the yoke to keep the plane at altitude. That way, if something hits them and they release the controls, the airplane will climb instead of making a smoking hole in the desert. That technique tires them during long flights, but it gives the rest of the crew a chance to live if the pilot gets shot.

Pilot Bill Clark describes the heavy burden of responsibility on an aircraft commander flying low-level to Tallil Air Base, Iraq, in the early days of the war.

Lieutenant Colonel Bill Clark, pilot

How would you relate flying a low-level to a layman? Take an airplane at treetop level, 340 miles an hour for four hours, four one-hour legs, flying in three-mile visibility, hoping nobody sees you. With the air conditioning off in 120-degree heat. [To prevent leaks of pressurized air in the event of a missile strike, C-130s usually fly with air conditioning off while low-level in hostile areas, no matter how warm it is outside.]

Flight engineer Kenny Payne at work in the cockpit. Flight engineers monitor and operate the aircraft's systems, such as fuel, electrics, and pressurization. They also calculate aircraft performance, such as takeoff speed, cruise ceiling, approach speed, and landing distance (courtesy the 167th Airlift Wing).

You would fly at treetop level for four hours, wondering about all the things you saw in the desert—the little dust devil you saw—was that a vehicle, was that a dust devil, was that a good guy, was that a bad guy? Every time something came up on the radar-warning receiver, was that a false indication? Was that somebody actually looking at me?

There was also the issue of not knowing what to expect when we got to Tallil. We were told there were three Rolands [antiaircraft missiles] around the airfield. I had seen a satellite photo of them before I left Kuwait. I knew at the altitudes we were flying that thing could see us. Were they going to be an issue?

All the years we'd spent flying around West Virginia, the type of low-level training we do—was that the proper training? Was that enough training to take care of what I needed to take care of over there?

On these desert runs, it wasn't just the bad guys that could get you. Flight engineer Kenny LaFollete describes a mission complicated by howling desert winds and blowing sand, which made it difficult to see the runway.

Technical Sergeant Kenny LaFollette, flight engineer

We were coming back from Baghdad. We tried to divert into Kuwait; there was a sandstorm coming. I guess it would have been moving southeast. It had started in Iraq and it had moved to Kuwait. We tried to get into Kuwait International, but they had closed the airfield. We tried to go into Bahrain. They were overfilled with aircraft and they turned us away.

So we ended up going into Ali Al Salem, also in Kuwait. That was an interesting experience because this was in the middle of the day, but it was almost as black as night. It was amazing to see that sand could block out the sun as well as it did. You knew the airplane was taking a beating with all that sand.

We descended—and we'd already passed minimums—and they had the runway lights on as high as they went. [When flying an approach on instruments, crews have a minimum altitude at which they must abort the landing if they cannot see the runway.] We finally got down and made out a few of the lights on the edge of the runway. We actually did get to land, but there was an airplane right behind us that tried twice to approach and land and could not get through. They ended up diverting somewhere else. Our situation was that we were getting low on fuel. That was a hair-raising experience, to say the least. If we hadn't been able to get into Al Salem, I'm not sure what our options would have been.

Tactics that worked in Iraq also worked in Afghanistan. In fact, crews might find themselves flying into Iraq on one mission and into Afghanistan on the next.

Flight engineer Steve McDonald recalls flying low through Afghanistan and taking it all in stride.

Senior Master Sergeant Steve "Mac" McDonald, flight engineer

It was mainly into Kandahar, Afghanistan, that I remember the sand dunes, hills just sticking out of nowheres. I thought that would be a good place for the enemy to be because we were below those hills. That would have been a good place for them to shoot down on us.

High speed, low level; it could be a lot of fun. It's like going down the interstate at a hundred miles an hour plus, everything rushing by. I didn't see any fear in it. You were aware there could be bad guys or something, but to me it was more fun flying than anything.

The tactics manuals mention something called the Weapons Engagement Zone, or WEZ. That's the effective range of anything that might shoot at you, whether it's

Helmet on, sun visor down, a copilot on a daylight combat mission. Low-level runs could mean nearly three hundred miles per hour at only three hundred feet above ground (courtesy the 167th Airlift Wing).

*small arms, antiaircraft artillery or surface-to-air missiles. As Colonel Eric Vollmecke
explains, modern-day bombers can operate high enough to stay out of the WEZ. C-
130s, on the other hand, spend a lot of time in it, like the bombers of World War II.*

Colonel Eric Vollmecke, pilot, wing commander

What's great about the C-130 is that you deliver substantial supplies and
forces to the fight, and you do it in a way that's closer to [flying fighter planes],
as far as how you maneuver that aircraft to get in and get out.

Looking back at World War II movies and seeing the bomber crews and
how well they worked together, I feel that C-130s come closer than any other
plane or mission we have today in resembling that kind of crew cooperation.
The bombers today stay up so high they don't have to get down into the threat
zones. But the C-130s have to do that. They have this big plane they have to
operate with, going into a combat area.

From the author's journal, 29 March 2003

Hurtling low-level across the Iraqi desert, fourteen tons of rolling stock
in the cargo compartment bound for Tallil Air Base, now in American hands.
Fighting continues nearby at An Nasiriyah. The desert flows past our wings
at 300 miles per hour.

"Altitude," warns a crewman. We want to be quite low, but not below a
certain height.

"Roger."

Dark objects appear off the nose.

"Possible vehicles, eleven o'clock."

In a couple of heartbeats they materialize as Bedouin tents, the sand outside them dotted with goats and camels.

"Disregard—wait. Vehicle at two o'clock."

A truck rumbles along, its motion given away by the dust plume behind
it.

"Passing on the right."

"Watching him."

The two loadmasters peer out the paratroop door windows, checking for
smoke trails or tracers. They hold red handles that can launch flares manually
if the automatic system doesn't work for some reason. The flares can deflect
heat-seeking missiles. Meanwhile, the truck vanishes behind us.

"Altitude."

"Rog. A few hours of this is gonna wear me out."

II. THE SPEED OF HEAT

More dots in the sand ahead. A moment later, they become camels, light ones and dark ones, running in all directions.

Also another dust plume, ahead and to the right.

"Truck, one o'clock."

"Watch him, loads."

The dust plume rises high behind the speeding vehicle. Then the truck seems to vanish behind the dust.

"He's turning."

"Yeah."

"Keep an eye on that sucker—he just did a 180."

"If you see ANYTHING, punch off those flares."

He dissolves behind us. Maybe he decided our high speed and low altitude made us too hard to hit. Or maybe he just turned because we scared him.

More tents and camels flash by.

"Possible vehicle off the nose."

A black dot gets bigger, then becomes a tank, upside down and in pieces.

"Well, it WAS a vehicle."

I wonder whether the tank was destroyed yesterday or in 1991.

"Something else, two o'clock."

"Vehicle."

The shape grows larger, but there's something wrong with this truck.

"That's a damn missile launcher!"

"On the right, loads."

"That thing is intact, too."

Quickly as I can, I scan altimeters and missile warning indicators.

"Altitude."

"I know it. I'm getting lower."

We won't make it easy for them. No launch takes place.

"Mark the position, nav."

Later, we will report this to intel as a mobile rocket launcher, apparently not hit by anything, possibly abandoned.

"Nothing like a missile launcher to ruin your day."

A few more miles of bare sand, then a major highway.

"Vehicle, eleven o'clock."

"Multiple vehicles."

"That's a big convoy."

Trucks seem to stretch along the highway for miles, all heading north.

"They're ours."

The distance measuring equipment ticks down to two miles.

"Before Landing Checklist."

Touchdown at destination, where some GI has put up a sign: George W. Bush International Airport.

12

COMMAND AND CONTROL

To command is to serve, nothing more, nothing less.
　　　　　　　—Andre Malraux, French novelist and soldier

During part of the time we were flying into Iraq, our mission orders came from our own former base commander. Shortly after Operation Iraqi Freedom began, General Wayne "Speedy" Lloyd worked as the Director of Mobility Forces for the Iraq and Afghanistan theaters. Beginning in May of 2003, Lloyd spent three months in command of all the transport aircraft and tankers in the region.

This job placed him at the highly secure Combined Air Operations Center, or CAOC, at Al Udeid Air Base, Qatar. Although military headquarters don't often look like Hollywood's image of them, the CAOC could come straight out of a Tom Clancy film. Towering video screens displaying feeds from unmanned Predator drones loom over rows of computers, radios, and satellite phones. Commanders can watch battles as they unfold. This provides them with so much real-time information and control that the military certifies the CAOC as a weapons system in and of itself. The CAOC system is called the "Falconer," the word for a huntsman working with birds of prey.

Brigadier General Wayne "Speedy" Lloyd (ret.), former commander of the West Virginia Air National Guard

It was a very difficult job. It was the most intense, difficult job I think I've ever done in my career.

When we got missions down from the Joint Movement Center, we would take those taskings and we would decide what units would fly the missions. We would put those into the Air Tasking Order. So we had people downstairs in Air Mobility Division who would put those missions into the orders and send them out to the various wings.

We got the diplomatic clearances. We looked at the crew duty times. I

Brigadier General Wayne "Speedy" Lloyd during a visit to Masirah Island Air Base, Oman, in 2003. Behind him are four C-130s from his home unit, the 167th Airlift Wing. Planes from Georgia and Texas shared the same ramp (courtesy the 167th Airlift Wing).

had the waiver authority for any operation in any one of the theaters if crew duty times were going to be extended. We had special instructions, SPINS, which I was in control of. We had a website that we used to put information out to all the aircrews that was directive in nature. All the missions flowed through me, and any changes in the missions would come to me for approval.

There was a plan for us to draw down to eighteen C-130s in theater, and when I got there we had eighty-four. When I got over there, they stopped the rotation of Army forces back to the U.S. for the very basic reason that there were still ongoing hostilities. Even though the president had declared the major portion of the conflict over, there was still a lot of fighting going on. There were still a lot of people getting hurt and killed, and the commanders stopped the deployment of the Army back to the U.S.

Planning factors had also been established on the idea that we'd get commercial operations into Baghdad. Once we got the big airplanes landing at Baghdad offloading cargo for the Army, there would be less need for C-130s and we'd be able to draw down. Well, the bad guys shot a missile at one of the C-130s on the eleventh of June, 2003, and I told another of the generals right

A C-17 cargo aircraft as seen from the back of a C-130 at an airfield in Afghanistan. As director of mobility forces, Brigadier General Wayne "Speedy" Lloyd commanded several types of aircraft on missions all over the Middle East (courtesy Chief Master Sergeant Harry "Bud" Martz).

after that happened that the chance of getting more C-130s out of the theater was going to be very slim. Because of the missile threat, we couldn't get the commercial operations into Baghdad and other places.

As the war went on, General Lloyd had to move the locations where his aircraft were based in response to diplomatic concerns and the changing needs of the military. One of the challenges involved closing down operations based in Oman and the United Arab Emirates.

I suggested that we move forces forward because we had three and a half hours of unproductive flight time flying from those bases up to Kuwait, where we picked up most of our cargo to fly into the theater. So I suggested that we go into Ali Al Salem Air Base in Kuwait, but the Air Force was already closing that base up, and I was told to cease and desist.

They kind of gave me an untenable position. They wanted the bases closed down at UAE, but they weren't going to let me establish any more Air Force base operating systems anywhere. I was told that we had four locations that the Air Force was going to support. One was Kirkuk in the northern part of Iraq, Baghdad being the other, Tallil—also in Iraq, and then Al Udeid in Qatar. But we didn't have the parking space at Al Udeid, Tallil wasn't prepared to handle the forces, we didn't have the available space at Baghdad, and Kirkuk was too far away and made no sense. Ultimately, I managed to open up a base at Al Jaber in Kuwait and we put nine aircraft on the ground there.

The one thing I tried to promote when I was there was moving our operations out of Baghdad up to Balad. I supported the Army; I sent in five different survey teams to tell them what they had to do to get Balad opened up. The reason was that around Baghdad you have all these structures—homes and things—where people can hide and come out and fire off a missile at our airplanes. Up at Balad it was open country. If we moved in there it would be easier for the Army to secure the area.

Ultimately, about two weeks before I left, General John Abizaid, the Centcom commander, asked why were we even located in Baghdad, why we didn't move to Balad. General Elder asked me what the response to that was, and I said, "Sir, I've been telling you all along we need to move up to Balad." So all of a sudden the emphasis was placed on scaling down the Air Force operation at Baghdad and supporting the Army up at Balad.

Lieutenant Colonel Mike McMillie served as General Lloyd's executive officer at the CAOC. McMillie decided it was high time to change the name of Saddam International Airport.

Lieutenant Colonel Mike McMillie, navigator

When we first started flying into Baghdad, they abbreviated the airfield name as ORBS. The O was the International Civil Aviation Organization's designation for the Middle East. R was for Iraq, B was for Baghdad, and S was for Saddam.

I said we shouldn't do that. I went over and talked to the airspace guys and they said, "Nah, let's not worry about that."

But one of the Iraqi controllers went over to one of the Australians and said, "When are you guys going to change this? S stands for Saddam."

Word got back up to the airspace guys, and they said, "Hey, do you really want to change that?"

I said, "Sure!"

So I started sending off a series of e-mails. I sent one to General Lloyd, saying, "Sir, this is what we'd like to do." We sent it up the chain.

General Michael Moseley, the region's air commander, said, "Make it happen."

On June 29, 2003, ORBS changed to ORBI. ORBI was kind of my idea, for Baghdad International. I'm kind of proud of that one.

13

THE ROCKETS' RED GLARE

His airmanship and courage were instrumental in the safe completion of combat missions flown into austere locations with minimal ground support and often in marginal weather. These flights were accomplished in the face of enemy threats to include small arms, antiaircraft artillery, and surface-to-air missiles.
—From an Air Medal citation, one of dozens awarded to the 167th.

Winston Churchill said famously, "Nothing is more exhilarating than to be shot at without result." Due respect to the prime minister, it's really not that much fun.

Major Mike Langley, pilot

My two most memorable missions would have to be the two when my crew got shot at with shoulder-launched missiles. One coming out of Numaniyah on April 18, 2003, and the other one May 4 coming out of Baghdad. Because of what happened, those just burned a hole in your psyche. You remember as many details as you possibly can.

The first time, right after liftoff from Numaniyah, we hit a bird. Then we turned to the left and came down through a low area with some streams and running water. We were trying to avoid some of the towns.

Coming down through there, trying to build some airspeed and staying at a reasonably low altitude to avoid line-of-sight detection, we got a missile launch warning off the left front quadrant. I took the appropriate action, and after that was over, I rolled back out, added power, and extended away.

I think the whole crew was trying to get their mind around whether this had really happened. The missile warning system had gone off; we'd seen it go off before just briefly. This time it went off continuously, which was not indicative of a false warning. The flares went out; everything worked as normal. But we were still trying to decide whether it really happened. Kind of like the World Trade Center—is this really going on? Is this really happening?

And then we got a second one on the forward right quadrant. Again I did the appropriate maneuvers. A loadmaster, Brian Beck from Savannah, was in the right window, and he saw the smoke trail and the missile go by the right wing as we did our maneuver. After that, again we rolled out, added power, and descended into the low-level environment.

At that point it got kind of weird because I have never been on an airplane when it got that quiet in my entire life. We're leaving, the sun's going down, the visible horizon is harder and harder to discern. We're at a low altitude and we're clipping along pretty good, and it's just absolutely quiet on the airplane.

I kept asking the crew about every fifteen minutes or so to check in because it was so quiet. I wouldn't hear from a crew member for that long a time, and I wanted to make sure they were still in the game. You can very easily slip into thoughts about what happened, what could have happened, and everything else. And at that moment I needed them to focus on getting out of there. We had to get to the fence [the Iraq/Kuwait border] and get on the other side of the combat exit point.

The second one was on May 4 when we were coming out of Baghdad. I had just lowered the nose and was trying to accelerate when one came off our right rear quadrant. Again, I did the appropriate defensive maneuvers. It was the only time in my twenty-one years in the military that I actually clenched my ass, thinking, "Oh shit." Because when I saw the flares and the bright flash, I thought we might have taken a hit. And my next thought was, "Where can I put this down? Where's the nearest road with any straight length to it where I can actually get it on the ground and maybe save somebody in this airplane? Because we may be going down."

Fortunately it was not an actual hit; it was just the missile and flares going out, and on our night vision goggles it really plumed as we looked out. So we climbed out of there. Again, it was a quiet, surreal moment because everyone was like, "Oh jeez, did it really happen again?"

Senior Master Sergeant Roland Shambaugh flew with Langley during both missions described above.

Senior Master Sergeant Roland Shambaugh, loadmaster

We had a couple incidents of antiaircraft fire. Good Friday near Numaniyah, we had the SA-7 go under us. It was a beautiful evening; the sun was going down and everything was real calm, and then all of a sudden the Missile Warning System goes off. But it does what it's supposed to do. I had full confidence that the system would work, and it did. It proved itself.

Also, it proved itself the night we were coming out of Baghdad, May 4.

It was a Sunday night, and I gotta say Mike Langley did one hell of a job flying that airplane.

Stuff like that you never forget. I remember Mike had just said, "We're building up speed to climb." And just at that time the [missile warning] system went off. We had our goggles on and the airplane was blacked out [flying with lights off]. I was in the left door. Because we were on the goggles, when the flares went out it was blinding. We didn't even have to call for Mike to make the breaks. The second the flares went out, Mike had the airplane rolled up into a sixty-degree bank.

When it comes to dealing with missile threats, the book tells us to remember the four Ds: Destroy, Deny, Degrade, Defeat.

Destroy means having a fighter or gunship take out the missile and shooter. Great if you can get it, but an insurgent with a missile launcher can hide pretty well in urban clutter or in a grove of date palms.

Deny means flying above the threat range of the missile. Fine for a while, but you have to land sometime.

Degrade means classified techniques to lessen the missile's effectiveness.

Defeat means Game On. Getting away from the missile after the damn thing's already in the air.

I flew with Langley and Shambaugh, and I recorded the May 4 incident in my notebook.

From the author's journal, 5 May 2003

A hot time in Baghdad last night. Got another missile shot at us.

We first flew to Tallil Air Base, outside Nasiriyah, where we picked up sixteen thousand pounds of palletized cargo. Then we took off blacked out and on NVGs for the hour-and-a-half flight to Baghdad International Airport.

When we were still twenty minutes' flying time out from Baghdad, we could see the city's lights glowing in the NVGs. That's when we heard the first word of trouble. Another C-130 crew reported to an AWACS [Airborne Warning and Control Station] plane that they had seen antiaircraft artillery fire.

"There's a lot of activity tonight," warned the C-130 pilot with admirable understatement. "Also saw some ground-to-ground tracers."

Our navigator plotted the coordinates reported by the other crew, and he gave us a heading to avoid the area. As we neared Baghdad, the general glow of the city fragmented into individual emerald lights, as seen through green-tinted NVGs.

"Tracers to the left," called one of the loadmasters. I never saw them; they were out of my seat's field of view.

We overflew the field at high altitude, then spiraled down in a tactical approach. The loadmasters continued to report sporadic tracer fire, none of it directed at us.

After an uneventful landing, at least uneventful given the circumstances, we offloaded our cargo with engines running. We then departed the way we came—taking off from a taxiway because the runways were under repair.

On departure we flew fast and low to gain momentum for a steep climb. At about four miles from the field and about 300 AGL [Above Ground Level], we received a launch warning.

Mike rolled us hard right almost instantly. The glow of our flares lit up the cockpit like lightning.

"Anybody see anything?" asked Mike.

"Red light and a smoke trail," answered a loadmaster.

I had a hard time believing we'd actually been fired on again, but the copilot, Ed Bishop, reported seeing the same thing out of the corner of his eye.

Later, loadmaster John Cox also said he thought he saw a vehicle turn on its lights in the spot where the missile came from.

On the mission described above, we flew crew chief Tim Shipway's airplane. To escape the missile, we pushed the throttles up so far that we exceeded certain engine limitations. Tim had to inspect those engines for stress and damage.

Technical Sergeant Tim Shipway, crew chief

My aircraft was one that got shot at. The crew took the correct reaction and managed to avoid the missile, and in doing that they did overtorque three engines. But I'll do an engine inspection anytime if the maneuver saved the lives of the crew and saved the aircraft. That extra work was pleasure for me, knowing they managed to break away from the missile.

Sooner or later, nearly every crew had an incident involving hostile fire. Pilot Carla Riner recalls one such mission.

Major Carla Riner, pilot

I'll never forget it because we were doing a mission to Kirkuk. We were flying Bibles into Kirkuk for the chaplain's office. I just remember thinking it's a beautiful Sunday, and I'm going into a combat zone to fly Bibles.

We had some indications of a missile launch and had to do some maneuvers there on short final approach. That's one of those days that I just remember everybody working together and pulling together and handling the situation, you know, step by step.

A typical experience for an aviator in Iraq: You're flying along at night, lights out, night vision goggles on. A burst of tracers comes up at your eleven o'clock, maybe a half mile away. No big deal.

The next night, you see the little green dot of a rocket-propelled grenade arcing upward at nothing, hundreds of yards from your aircraft. Hmm—you wonder what that was about.

On yet another mission a spurt of antiaircraft artillery blossoms off the right wing, emerald stars spewing crazily up from the ground. A crew member calls it out, but the pilot takes no evasive action because it's not close enough to threaten.

You start to think, "What are those knuckleheads shooting at? There's nothing there."

Then it dawns on you. They can't see the airplane. They're firing at the noise. Those knuckleheads are shooting at YOU.

Staff Sergeant Corey Creighton, flight engineer

I remember my first night flight. We went from Al Udeid [a major air base in Qatar] to Balad [an air base in Iraq]. Going into Balad wasn't bad, and then we had to go from Balad to Baghdad.

Flying over the towns was interesting that night. At first we were all calling out ground fire to let the pilots know where we were seeing the stuff. It wasn't necessarily getting close to us. Of course, we were blacked out [flying with lights off]. After a few minutes it was kind of pointless to call it all out. It was everywhere. Whether I looked left, right, straight, it was coming up everywhere. It was interesting. I even saw some triple-A [antiaircraft artillery] that night.

Most of the tracers were ground-to-air. Of course, we were blacked out, so I think they were just shooting at the noise. It was all over the place, but there wasn't really anything we could do about it because it was coming up from both sides.

When we got to Baghdad, we were watching ground fire arc in front of us. It was still a good couple miles out, so we didn't feel extremely threatened. It was kind of arcing over the approach end of the runway.

Chief Master Sergeant Billy Gillenwater, flight engineer

It looked like Mardi Gras over Baghdad airport. You were always flying around tracers and things like that nearly hitting the airplane. They were just close. You could see it traversing up, and you knew if it were pointed in your direction, it clearly could have hit you. You were just in the right place at the right time. Fortunately the airplanes weren't hit; no one in our unit was hit. We were very fortunate.

Technical Sergeant Lee Deyerle's first experience with hostile fire came in Afghanistan while flying with a mixed crew of Air Guard aviators from West Virginia and Wyoming.

Technical Sergeant Lee Deyerle, loadmaster

We were flying along, we were on NVGs, and we'd just come across the border from Pakistan. We saw some tracers coming up. I called it out on the right side. They were low and not anywhere in our vicinity. I think they were just shooting at the noise.

Jack goes, "Yeah, it looks like they're shooting at us."

We're thinking, "You're kidding. Somebody's actually shooting at us?" So we banked into it and looked.

Jack goes, "This might not be the brightest thing, banking into it. Don't we want to turn away?"

Bruce is like, "Yeah, I think you're right."

So, I thought, "That's cool. I just got shot at. That rocks." Then I thought about it and I realized that it didn't rock.

Months later, Lee got another taste of hostile fire in Iraq.

Coming out of Baghdad, we got an indication [a cockpit warning of an antiaircraft missile launch] and the flares punched. I'm on NVGs, looking out the right side of the airplane.

It happened so quick, I had no time to say, "Break!" or anything. I saw the flash, and I'm just thinking, "That's it. I'm dead."

All of a sudden you realize you're not dead; you're still going; there was no bang. Your NVGs just whited out and you braced up. You never had any time to think about it.

Couple seconds later you're like, "God, why didn't I say 'Break!' or something?"

I think I was shot at about three times over in Afghanistan. Probably two times over in Iraq that we knew of. There were probably a lot of times we didn't know about.

Technical Sergeant Kenny LaFollette, flight engineer

We were sitting in Kuwait one night. It was almost total dark. You could still see a little residual daylight, but not much. We had just finished loading and we were taxiing out, and the copilot said, "Look over there!"

If you looked over towards Iraq, you could see the antiaircraft fire streaming up. It was rather interesting. I didn't even have NVGs on and I could see it with the naked eye.

Another of our aircrews watched as a British aircraft nearly got shot down.

Lieutenant Colonel Rich "Robi" Robichaud, pilot, tactics officer

One flight into Baghdad, about ten minutes out we heard a C-130 that had just departed there report a SAFIRE [surface-to-air fire]. We marked the location of it and said, "OK, we'll stay away from there." So we landed in Baghdad uneventfully.

We offloaded our cargo, and we were waiting for this other C-130 to land in Baghdad before our plane could take the runway. We saw the other aircraft get a SAFIRE. We saw the missile explode right next to the airplane.

He was on about a five-mile final approach to landing, and our loadmaster was the first one who saw it. He drew our attention over there, and by the time I looked up you could see the black puff of smoke next to the airplane.

I don't remember any calls from the tower, but all of a sudden we heard on the radio this high-pitched, shrill voice saying, "ROCKET!" I don't do it justice; it was a lot more panicky than that. I'll never forget that one.

And then we took off right after he landed. We stayed away from where the SAFIRE event took place, but with MANPADS [man-portable air defense systems, or shoulder-fired missiles] they could be anywhere.

Senior Master Sergeant Randall Shafer, loadmaster

I remember Don Jackson, the other loadmaster, saying, "Hey, that plane on final, he's popping flares." So I immediately looked from the left paratroop door over to the right, and I saw the flares going out. The Brit guy was saying something about getting shot at, and we heard somebody call, "ROCKET!"

Someone had their switch in the wrong position, so it went over the tower frequency. I thought, "Man, that dude's pucker factor went up on that one." Then they landed, and we took off the same direction that they were coming in.

Master Sergeant Don "Action" Jackson, loadmaster

I saw the smoke trail leaving the ground. I think I yelled at them up front to take a look. They had time to take a look and see the explosion, too. That's how early we picked it up. It seemed like it exploded right there in front of the British plane.

Then they go, "You're cleared for takeoff," and I'm thinking I don't know if I want to. Is this the best move? I'm going, "What are we doing taking off when they just got shot at? We should wait a half an hour until [the bad guys] change their minds or get tired or something."

Fliers don't usually have to face ground combat, but it can happen if the plane breaks down in the wrong place. In October of 2003, Baghdad was the wrong place.

Major James Powell, pilot

We flew out of Al Udeid to Kuwait City and Baghdad. We got up to Baghdad, and oddly enough, it had been raining on and off for two or three weeks. It was very cloudy in Baghdad that night.

Landed, downloaded the cargo, and got the people and the cargo we were

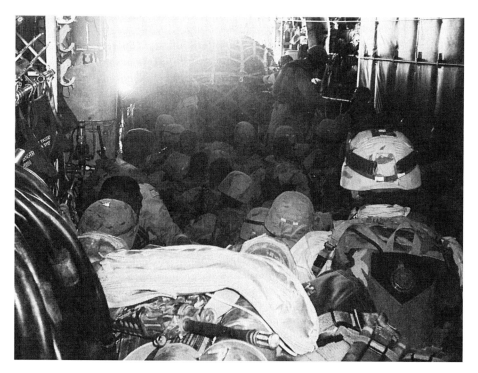

Troops and cargo in the back of a C-130. Flight crews working to avoid antiaircraft fire often had a lot of lives in their hands (courtesy Chief Master Sergeant Harry "Bud" Martz).

going to take back out. We went to start, and we got three of the four engines started. Went to start the fourth one and RPM spooled up really quickly. It just didn't look right. We stopped the start, talked about it for a minute and said, "Let's just try this one more time." Sure enough, got the same thing.

We knew something was seriously wrong. You could spin the propeller back and forth each way with one hand, which was not normal. It was decoupled. [The propeller had become disconnected from its gearbox.]

So I got ahold of command and control, and they said, "We won't be able to get anyone there to fix it for a day or two. We need you to stay with the airplane."

We were an added burden on the camp at Baghdad airport because they weren't expecting us. It was actually a great feat that we got some blankets and some pillows and a towel for the field shower.

Pretty uneventful the first night. We got to our little tent with just a cot and a sleeping bag and went to bed. Woke up the next day and wondered if we were going to get fixed. They said, "Well, not today. Hopefully, we'll have someone up later in the evening."

The second night, the rain stopped. Some of the security forces guys said, "Just beware. We haven't had any incidents in a while. This rain has stopped; it looks like it's going to be clear. Be ready."

Sure enough, just after dark we were sitting in our tent, and we heard what sounded like distant thunder, initially. But within a few short moments we heard the BOOM, BOOM; it was getting closer and closer. Mortars. I had never heard mortars before.

Soon after that started they announced on Giant Voice [a base-wide PA system], "Alarm Red. Seek shelter." Corey Creighton and I had just gone down to the rec center and on the way back, I was walking with him and we were just chatting. Out of nowhere, this flash and this ungodly sound. I'm not sure exactly where it hit, but I heard it and I looked behind me, and I saw all these other people lying on the ground.

Of course, Giant Voice came over again and said, "Take shelter immediately." Corey and I start running for the bunkers.

We, of course, were in the worst possible place, as far from any bunker as we could be, running through pea gravel—a slop of sand, pea gravel, and water. It was probably a good two or three hundred yards to reach the bunker. I remember getting to the bunker and catching my breath and thinking, "That is the loudest thing I've ever heard." I think my ears rang for about an hour. No one was hurt.

Flight engineer Corey Creighton accompanied Powell on that same mission.

Staff Sergeant Corey Creighton, flight engineer

So we were getting ready to spend a night in Baghdad. The first night it was kind of rainy, so it wasn't a real nice night for the insurgents to come out and try to blow stuff up. It was relatively quiet. We heard booms in the distance when we were in the camp.

Of course, they weren't expecting us to be staying there, so we were lucky to have a tent. Originally they didn't think they had a tent. We got a tent that was real muddy on the inside from all the rain. We crammed in there and we scrounged up some cots.

The first night we really didn't have much, just what we had on our bodies because nobody thought we'd be spending the night in Baghdad. But we ended up spending the night there, and they said, "We'll get an MRT [Maintenance Recovery Team] to come up tomorrow and fix you guys; they'll bring an engine."

So the next day we were waiting on our engine, and we were just hanging out and we were ready to get out of there. We watched a couple planes come in, and nothing, nothing, nothing. I guess things got switched around. So then they said, "We're going to have it there by the end of the day." Well, by the time the MRT got there it was already dusk.

They couldn't go out there in the dark on the flight line and fix the plane without any lights. And it was lights-out conditions there. So we were there for a second night, and our maintenance guys were with us. I remember vividly when James Powell and I walked from our tent to a morale tent. They had a concessions place where you could buy sodas and stuff. So we went there and bought some sodas to take back to the tent for everybody.

We were walking right by the chow hall, and it was relatively quiet. It wasn't raining that night. And all of a sudden I heard the loudest noise I've ever heard in my life. It felt like it went off in my head. My ears were ringing. I could hardly hear James talking right next to me. We just kind of looked at each other like, "What now?"

We saw a bunch of people running and we thought, well, they know where to go. So we started running and following them. We came to find out the nearest bunker wasn't anywhere near where we were running.

So that one ended up being the first mortar. There were a couple of them that I heard that sounded like they were going over the whole camp and actually hitting towards the flight line.

By the time we got near our tent, we ran into a security guy who told us to get in our tent and lay on the ground because there were sandbags built up between the tents. So that's what we did. We got in there and lay on the muddy ground in the tent and heard a couple more booms. After that, some sirens were going off. Heard some extra gunfire out there I thought might have been an Apache [helicopter gunship] or something.

After that, all was quiet. The next day, I talked to a security guy and asked if anybody had gotten hurt. He said originally they thought the first one had hit the chow hall, but I guess it fell short. No one got hurt as far as I know.

I asked him where it hit and he showed me. It was about fifty yards from where James and I were walking at the time. He said a couple of them hit the flight line, and a couple of them hit just short of it. I think he told me there were about eight or ten that hit the base.

Mortars and rockets also plagued the bases in Afghanistan, including the Kandahar airport, where Staff Sergeant Michael Seavolt was deployed from August of 2005 to February of 2006. A security policeman with the 167th Airlift Wing, Seavolt offers a different perspective from flight crew members. Instead of running for cover during an air base attack, he's one of the guys telling the rest of us where to run and what to do.

Staff Sergeant Michael Seavolt, security policeman

The rocket attack that was closest to me was on a ramp, a helicopter ramp. We had two rockets come in. One kind of fell short, and one hit really close to a resource, messed up the resource a lot, a jet. It landed relatively close to me, but far enough that the shrapnel fell short. Close enough that I puckered.

I actually saw the thing come in and hit. I was one of the first ones to call it in and go into action that time. We set up a cordon. We went around and made sure all the Air Force guys were in the bunkers and made sure they had the right gear on.

A couple minutes later, somehow, mysteriously—they never did disclose how it happened—we had two fuel trucks explode right outside the gate. Whatever it was, it was probably organized.

It's funny—you always hear war stories about how you go under fire and your training kicks in. When it happens, it's amazing. Your training really does kick in and you just do what you're supposed to do. For a second or two you're thinking about your family; you're thinking about the other guys under you. It may be only for a split second, but it's a powerful second. You're thinking, "I need to do my job to get through this."

For a lot of us, it was the first time we'd ever dealt with anything like that. We sized up the situation and went to work.

When you realize someone just tried to kill you, you deal with the experience the best way you can. Having crewmates to talk with helps.

Major Mike Langley, pilot

This might sound a little strange to people, but probably the highest moments of the deployment were right after both the times we got shot at. We were back at our base, having a beer in the beer tent and we were all together, talking about what had gone on.

The adrenaline was still pumping. We knew what had happened. We were on an adrenaline high. You wanted to talk about it. You kept wanting to talk about it with the guys who'd just lived through it. They were there with you and they knew what had happened.

Although insurgents took an awful toll on helicopters in Iraq, they missed C-130s so often that some of us might have thought we were immune. Our tactics and equipment, we hoped, made us a nearly impossible target.

On January 30, 2005, we learned otherwise. A Royal Air Force C-130 got blown out of the sky near Baghdad, killing ten of our British colleagues. The militant group Ansar al-Islam claimed responsibility and released video of the crash site.

14

ROAD WARRIORS

You just go and do it.
—Staff Sergeant Brad Runkles, 167th AW

When GIs deploy to a tent city, they usually decorate the camp with rough-hewn unit signs made from scrap lumber. When they leave, they bring the signs home and the boards of scrap wood become treasured souvenirs. Some of our transportation people volunteered to drive with Army truck convoys in Iraq in 2004. Their camp sign now hangs in the office, a work of splendid understatement:

The 167th Airlift Wing, Martinsburg, W. Va.
Operation Iraqi Freedom, Camp Speicher, Tikrit, Iraq, 21 Feb 04—27 Aug 04
TSGT Mark Kevin Johnson, SSGT James Wood, SRA David L. Grim II
SSGT Brad Runkles (Purple Heart), SSGT Derek Brown (Purple Heart)
"From Heaven to Hell"

Staff Sergeant Brad Runkles, vehicle operator

They called for volunteers. I'm sure if they hadn't gotten enough volunteers it would have been, "Well, you're going." I asked the chief who had volunteered, and a couple of my buddies had said they'd go. So I thought I might as well go with them now as opposed to getting stuck over there by myself later on.

Once we were in Iraq, we were running gun trucks. We would provide security on the convoys. We'd provide security for the contractors and regular Army convoys.

A gun truck is a deuce-and-a-half with a crew-served weapon—a fifty-cal or an M-249 Squad Automatic Weapon—mounted on the back. [In a convoy] the front gun truck might have a fifty-cal, then you'd have four or five trucks, then you'd have another gun truck and so on. The gun truck would have a driver and a passenger with M-16s, and a crew-served weapon in the back. For most of them I was the gunner.

Mostly we went from Tikrit to Mosul and from Tikrit to Balad. Balad was about two hours one way. Usually that was just go down, drop off, pick up, and come back all in one day. Mosul, it was only once or twice we went up and back in one day. That was anywhere from four to six hours, depending on who you were escorting. We usually ended up going up, staying the night, and coming back the next day.

We were based in Tikrit, Camp Speicher. It was named after Mike Speicher. He got shot down in an F-18 during Desert Storm.

I asked Brad whether he gave much thought to the danger of his job.

Oh, yeah. You think about it a lot. But just like anything else, you don't think it will happen to you.

It's always in the back of your mind. Every time you leave base, you're thinking, "What are they going to do today?" And then, probably four or five days before this happened to me, they hit people in our convoy. Like if we were in the middle, they'd hit the front of the convoy, or if we were in the back, they'd hit the middle. And I remember me and Derek were saying, "How many times can we dodge these things? How many days are we not going to get hit?" And we were the lead gun truck that day and we got hit.

There's nothing you can really do. It's not like you can say, "I'm just going to hang out at the base today." You just go and do it.

We were coming back from Balad. Derek was the gunner, in the back. I was in front. It was June 28, 2004, the day they turned the government over. When we left, they came on the radios and said, "Be on the lookout." There could be people out celebrating and whatnot. We were about halfway back and the roadside bomb went off.

I was in the passenger side, the unlucky spot. I don't remember hearing anything. That's the strange part. Before the mission when we got hit, we'd be going down the road and we'd come across IEDs [Improvised Explosive Devices]. We'd come across six or eight or ten of them [from a distance] before, and they'd explode and you'd hear them. Or they'd call EOD [Explosive Ordnance Disposal] out to destroy them, and we'd be back a couple hundred yards away, and it would be so loud. But I don't remember hearing a thing when we drove by the one that got us. I just remember rocks and stuff coming in, and it felt like my arm was on fire.

By the time the driver got the truck stopped, me and him rolled out the driver's side. I pulled my helmet off and we sat down in the median. It was a two-lane road going both ways. We sat down there between the lanes. The CLS—Combat Lifesavers—came up and asked what had happened. They started their first aid, putting bandages and stuff on. The guy in the truck behind me got hit with a piece of metal through his cheek. I'd say he got it the worst.

The CLS people started bandaging people up, and then they called the medevac helicopter. The medevac came, picked four of us up and took us back to Speicher. They put me to sleep and stitched my eye. I don't remember anything after that.

I had second-degree burns from my wrist down and on my face. Then some cuts and seven or eight stitches over my eye. I remember looking back and seeing the guy from the other truck. There was blood everywhere and his eyes were rolled back. You could tell he was in shock.

The last I heard, they just assumed it was remotely detonated with a cell phone or a garage door opener. In the pictures you can see some mud-brick houses off in the distance, and there's nothing that blocks the line of sight. It would have been easy to set it off from there.

When I talked to Brad, he was back at work at our base in Martinsburg, but still healing. Doctors had him do hand-strengthening exercises.

They gave me some putty stuff. It wasn't really a therapy, but they said make sure you're using your right hand. Since I'm left-handed, with the right one hurt, I'm apt to use my left hand even more now. They said the main thing is to keep using it because with all that skin burned off and new skin growing back, it was real tight to make a fist. They said if you don't make a fist and use it every day, it's going to heal tight like that.

I asked Brad about his immediate reaction after the explosion.

I looked in the mirror and saw my face all burned up. I was sitting there talking and somebody asked, "Are you OK?"

And I said, "Yeah, can you get me a drink?"

I was just happy that everything's fine. Me and Derek, we were just sitting there with bandages on, thinking, "Wow, man, how close was that?"

You're still talking; you're still alive. I guess you can't ask for a whole lot more. There are a lot of people who aren't going to get that. They aren't coming back.

Staff Sergeant Derek Brown, vehicle operator

Me and Brad have been through our whole military career together. Whatever we've done, we've done together. As opposed to one of us getting shipped over without the other one, we just thought we'd both go ahead and volunteer. We went to basic and tech school together—everything.

We were gun truck escorts. We escorted convoys throughout Iraq. We would get up probably five, six in the morning. They'd tell us what we had to do, where we were going. We would just go from base to base, delivering goods and fuel. There were very few days when we didn't go out.

I was on the gun. We were on our way from Balad back to Camp Speicher.

We were the lead gun truck and we were probably about fifteen minutes from Speicher. Somebody detonated the bomb maybe ten yards from our truck—just engulfed our truck in flames and sent shrapnel all through our truck.

I don't remember the blast—the loudness of it. I don't remember that at all. I know it knocked me down in the bed of the truck. There was a tractor-trailer behind us. The blast flattened all our tires, so of course we came to a screeching halt. I remember the driver in the truck behind us took a piece of shrapnel in his face. I stood back up and I looked back there. They were still moving fifty-five miles an hour, and I saw the passenger lean over across the driver, take the steering wheel, and jerk it. They probably missed our truck by a foot, maybe.

Then we just kind of got out and hung out there until a helicopter showed up and took us to the hospital. It was probably about twenty minutes, maybe, before they got there. We loaded up in the helicopter and they flew us to Speicher. They treated me there and they shipped Brad off.

I had burns on my face and my forearm and my neck. It wasn't bad, but it blistered up. I did hear that the bomb was planted in the ground facing the opposite direction from where it should have been, and most of the blast went out towards the field as opposed to our truck.

Derek talked about the training the Army provided for escorting convoys and about the gunner's responsibility for making a split-second decision on when to fire.

Until we got to Kuwait, we had never seen the M-249. We didn't even know what we were going to be doing. We thought we were going to be driving tractor-trailers; we didn't know we were going to be escorts. I guess it was about a week of training on the Squad Automatic Weapon. Before that we'd never even seen one. Couldn't have told you what it was.

There were a couple of times I thought I might have to fire, like if a car would get too close or they wouldn't get out of the way. There were a lot of times where that would happen and you were right there ready, but I never, luckily, got in a situation where I had to shoot.

You're accountable for every round you have. You're nervous because you don't know what's going to go on, but then you don't want to pay the consequences if something does happen.

Derek and Brad received Purple Heart medals on their return to Martinsburg, pinned onto their uniforms by the West Virginia National Guard's top general.

According to Pentagon statistics, U.S. troops suffered an average of fifteen IED attacks per day in 2004, the year Derek and Brad were in Iraq. The following year, that figure doubled to thirty per day. Some attacks use roadside bombs alone, and others use IEDs to initiate ambushes. These devices have taken more American lives than any other insurgent tactic.

Major General Allen Tackett, the adjutant general of the West Virginia National Guard, pins Purple Heart medals on Brad Runkles (center) and Derek Brown (right) (courtesy the 167th Airlift Wing).

The Defense Department created a task force called the Joint IED Defeat Organization to address the issue. The Iraq Study Group Report says Congress appropriated nearly two billion dollars in 2006 for measures to protect troops from roadside bombs.

One helpful measure is to provide better training on how to watch for IEDs. Technical Sergeant Fred Lawrence, from the 167th Airlift Wing's emergency management office, deployed to Balad Air Base from August 2005 to January 2006 to teach troops about insurgent tactics.

When Fred teaches his classes, he sometimes uses a training video made by the British. Drawn partially from terrorist web sites, the video shows IEDs exploding. Fred points out the danger signs before each blast. For background, the Brits dubbed in music from Rammstein, a German heavy metal band. Thunderous power chords blast from the speakers as the singer intones, "DU HAST MICH!" In German, that's a play on words that sounds like "you hate me."

In contrast to the raw emotion of the video, Fred explains technical matters in a matter-of-fact fashion, drawing on both his Air Force training and his background as an Army small arms expert.

Technical Sergeant Fred Lawrence, emergency management specialist

I was the antiterrorism and training NCO, and I was part of the joint vulnerability assessment team for Army and Air Force. After I arrived in Balad, I went to train with the Australians and Brits. Basically it was IED training—how to read markers, how to back out of an area, how to understand how the IED works. It was a "train the trainer" class—to be able to come back and teach the rest of the troops what to be looking for and how to exercise caution.

It was my job to put out what intel we were getting—equipment they were using, materials they were using, and how they were using them.

Fred explains that insurgents often mark the spot where they've planted an IED. That way, when a convoy comes by, they can time when to set off the explosive. Looking for those markers can help GIs stay alive.

We would review with them things like markers. The bad guys were real good at hiding things in what we would consider household materials. They could use foam and create what looked like a rock—with explosive in it. They'd paint it gray so it looked like a rock. Problem is, most of the rocks in Iraq are light tan or brown. So that would be a pretty good marker if you've got a gray rock sitting there.

Markers could be a Pepsi can on a guardrail, maybe a white post on the side of the road. Fresh asphalt was another one. That's a pretty good indicator because they don't fix the roads.

For concealing IEDs, they might use a dead animal, a dog. It's not like West Virginia where people are hitting deer all the time. If you have a dead animal on a road, that's a pretty good indicator. That animal shouldn't be there.

Fred describes some of the insurgents' techniques for making hidden bombs and crude time-delay weapons.

In a car bomb you could have a truck full of 105-millimeter artillery shells, daisy-chained. They'd try to come in the gate with it. They tried this several times. There's a large supply of old weapons still lying around from Saddam's old regime. They'd use 105s with a cell phone strapped to it. They'd dial the cell phone and fire the 105s.

They'd use ice cubes in mortar tubes. The ice would melt and drop the round into the mortar tube after nobody was in the area. They could set this up and leave. When the ice melted, the round would go off.

They would drill out a bicycle frame and load it up with plastic explosive, wire it, strap a cell phone onto it, and put it in a bike rack. They'd put it in an area where it would do the most damage and set it off.

You'd look for anything out of the normal routine. Running into town—normally in the marketplace it would be crowded. If the marketplace is empty, that's an indicator that's something's going to happen. That's when a convoy would exercise caution, maybe change its route. It's really common sense. I'd hate to say you become battle-hardened, but your senses pick up things; you notice something that just doesn't fit.

At the time of the interview, Fred was preparing for another tour in the desert.

15

"CIVIL" AVIATION

When you place the complexities of the work you're doing in the environment of the rocket attacks and your high-speed drives down the highways—you throw that into your daily life routine, and that's Iraq.
                                                          —Major Karl Levy, 167th AW

Two 167th Airlift Wing fliers who deployed with us at the start of Operation Iraqi Freedom volunteered to step out of their traditional flyboy roles. Navigator Chris Walker and pilot Karl Levy both flew airlift missions for several months. But they traded their flight suits for civilian clothes to work in Baghdad with the Coalition Provisional Authority.

First Walker, then Levy, worked as aviation liaison to the Iraqi Ministry of Transportation in an effort to restart Iraq's civilian aviation. They handled matters involving airport operations and airspace management. But they also had side issues to deal with, like staying alive.

Major Chris "Mookie" Walker, navigator, aviation liaison

The job started encompassing things like—OK, now we need to get this airport open. They told me passengers who come in, humanitarian aid people, contractors and such, are all getting crowded into this small building that's meant for cargo. They needed me to supervise getting the passenger terminal open again. So they said coordinate with customs and immigration and security and everything.

I said, "Who, me?"

They said, "Yeah, you."

We had our problems coordinating with Iraqi personnel, deciding how early they could come in and how late they could leave, because these people had to come in by bus. A few times in the beginning, their bus was attacked. The workers said, "I'm not going to come in if this happens anymore."

So the Ministry of Transportation, along with the Ministry of Interior, had to find ways around that. We suggested having them come in different cars, mix it up a little bit. Eventually things started to run pretty smoothly there.

We also had to worry about the nonmilitary planes coming in. The Air Force didn't want to take responsibility for giving them any kind of tactical approaches to avoid enemy fire. So I said, "Well, if the Air Force doesn't, we gotta make up something real quick because the first time something happens, the carriers are going to blame us for not letting them know what's out there."

The AIP, the Air Information Publication, had a statement saying it was dangerous to fly to Baghdad. But we felt we had to give them a little more. So Rob Wayne, who was the senior adviser for civil aviation, and I put together approaches through different corridors, spiraling them down over a certain radius to try to keep them tight within the airfield and avoid hostile fire. It seemed to work because up to this day, none of the nonmilitary aircraft using our approach have gotten hit. The DHL plane that did get hit, we found out he just did a straight departure.

The daily life was waking up early and getting e-mail or phone calls done there at the palace, the Coalition Provisional Authority main palace, and then getting to the airport and getting things done there. So we'd have to drive down the highway all the time, just about every day. The rules were to drive in convoys and wear your flak jacket and helmet and such.

We started noticing a pattern. Whenever vehicles were blown up, they were in convoys. People could see them coming for miles and miles. If you're attracting attention wearing a helmet and flak vest and they put a rocket-propelled grenade into your vehicle, that helmet's not going to do much to help you. The powers that be would have hated us for doing this, but we started adopting a different philosophy of just blending in. Out there they would dispatch vehicles, new 2003 or 2004 GMCs and Fords and such. I said, "I don't think there are many Iraqis driving those." Then they also had what we called "hoopties," little pickup trucks, old Nissans, old Mitsubishi pickup trucks or older Nissan SUVs that you'd see readily downtown. So we said, "The first thing we're going to do is drive only these things. Then we're going to dress ourselves to look as native as possible."

When it got cold, we'd wear leather jackets like the Iraqis wear, maybe have scarves like they have. If a woman was driving with us, she might wear a scarf over her head, and no one looked at us twice. In fact, the only people who looked at us hard were the American soldiers, as if to say, "Who the hell are you?" So we'd flash our IDs and they'd say, "OK." That was a way to stay alive and it worked for us. All the people who got blown up were in obvious vehicles.

I wore civilian clothes all the time and I had a concealed weapon. I carried an M-9 either inside the waistband at the small of my back or on a belt. I'd cover it up with a jacket or a shirt. I'd just wear the regular button shirts that I'd see any Iraqi wear, and I'd wear a leather jacket when it got cold. I never wore desert combat boots. I had a pair of chukka type boots, or I'd wear some brown leather shoes. I'd never wear anything that looked like what an American would wear.

People would say, "You would probably stand out," because I'm black. But no, there are plenty of black people in Baghdad. Locals would always assume that I was from the Basra area. I had no problems blending in as long as I kept my mouth shut and didn't try to stand too tall.

Major Walker says blending in helped, but it couldn't keep people completely out of harm's way.

There were many times when we'd hear gunfire or explosions behind us on the road, and someone might say, "What is that?"

I'd say, "Don't even look back; step on it and drive fast."

Every once in a while in the office, working at night just after sundown, we could expect a mortar or rocket or two to come in—BOOM, BOOM. Those things really shook the ground. We were just lucky that they didn't have good aim, especially with the trailers that we lived in. We lived in small trailers.

Each trailer had two small rooms and in each of those rooms, two beds and one small bathroom. If a mortar or rocket had hit any of those trailers, you might as well have been sleeping in a cardboard box. Sometimes when I was asleep or trying to sleep, I'd hear a BOOM. It would sound so loud. I remember one time I jumped under my bed and pulled the mattress over me. I was under there in all the dust and it felt like it was so close. It turned out it was probably six hundred meters away, but it felt like it was right next to me. I fully expected to come out of the trailer and see the trailer next to me in flames.

The closest call happened when we came back from a meeting in Qatar. We'd heard that the palace was under attack—that we should stay at the airport for a little while until things calmed down. They called us back and they said, "Things are cool now, come on in."

We got there and went to the parking lot. I was pulling my suitcase out of the back of the vehicle and I heard BOOM, BOOM, BOOM. So we started running for the ditches. We didn't see where they landed, but it was so loud that we just put our faces in the mud and waited till it was over.

Another close call I had was coming out of Checkpoint One, going back to the palace with one of the contractors, the president of Blackwater Aviation. All of a sudden we heard heavy gunfire right behind us. He said, "Holy crap, what is that?"

I said, "Let's not try to find out."

I just floored the gas and kept going. He had his hand on his weapon, ready to shoot out the back window if need be. I said, "Whatever they're shooting at, it's not us. But if we stick around, it might be us." We didn't stick around to find out.

It could get pretty shaky at times. It's hard to sleep after that. I just got to the point where I said, "If it's my time to go, it's my time to go." And it'll either happen here or it'll happen back in Hagerstown, Maryland, getting hit by a truck or eating a bad piece of fish or something. So that helped me to rest a little easier.

Every once in a while we'd get adventurous and say, "Let's go to a restaurant downtown." We'd try to keep a low profile and go to certain restaurants that we'd heard were good and the people were friendly. If we went in there and saw a lot of Americans, we'd say, "Time to go." But if we were the only ones in there, then we'd try to sit somewhere in the back, enjoy our meal, tip well, and get the hell on out of there.

Walker's office was in one of Saddam's former palaces, and he recalls being appalled by the opulence.

Everything was totally ostentatious. Everything on the ceiling was decorated to the point where you'd say, "How many man-hours did it take to do that?" It looked like carved wood. Gold plate on certain ceilings, marble everywhere. Just nothing left to look plain. You could tell it took a lot of money to do that. Statues, gold-plated walls. It was to the point where you'd say, "He had people starving, but he had all of this." It boggled the mind.

The pool area was fantastic, the pool house he had there. You'd say, "Why would one guy need all this, or why would ten families need all this?" Incredible.

I asked Major Walker how Iraqis received him.

Very, very warmly, as a matter of fact. For the most part they are very warm people who want to share all they have and all their experiences. I've been invited to people's homes for dinner, and even though they are very poor, they'll put out whatever they can to try to be hospitable. The food was good. Wonderful people, wonderful warm people.

I've even had times when different translators or different friends over there would say, "Since tonight's New Year's or some other event, you shouldn't stay at the palace because they might try and attack there. You should come stay at my house; you'll be safe there."

I'd say, "Thank you, but I have work to do and I have to stay."

They'd say, "The offer is always open."

Most of the people I met were so glad that Saddam's era was over, and they were looking for opportunities to grow and to help Iraq grow. They saw the future they could have. They realize they have oil wealth. They also have agriculture, fruits and vegetables, and livestock. They have historical sites that people would want to see. If they got themselves together, Iraq could be the richest country in that region. They saw the potential for that, and they wanted to make that happen. They were just really disappointed and angry that these insurgents wouldn't let things move forward. It was holding back their lives.

After Saddam was captured, you had people on the street coming up and saying something to you, once they found out you were American. Old men who didn't know any English. The translator would say, "He's saying, 'Thank you because Saddam killed my uncle, my cousins, and my nephew.'" You'd get all these people saying "Thank you, thank you." And you don't hear stories like that on the news.

There were folks who had lived around the airport who said they'd been afraid to look over the three-meter wall because they were afraid they'd get shot if they looked over it. After the liberation of Iraq, they finally did look over it and realized there was a palace there. Some of them said tears came to their eyes because they didn't even know a palace was right there; they were too afraid to look.

I thought, "Wow, that's no way to live." Stories like that made me wake up to the fact that these people did need some help, and if we were to just abandon them now they'd be in a heck of lot of trouble.

Another thing I found was a surprising number of Christians. People think there are nothing but Muslims there, but I met a lot of Christians. They were Catholic. I would mistakenly say, "Salaam aleikum," the traditional Muslim greeting that means, "Peace be upon you," and they'd say, "No, I'm Christian, and we greet each other differently."

In January of 2004, Major Karl Levy took over Major Walker's position as aviation liaison. His background as a military pilot who had also flown for American Airlines made him well qualified to help Iraq get civilian aviation back into the air. Like Walker, Levy graduated from the Air Force Academy. He's the wing's Renaissance man—aviator, scholar, and classical pianist.

Major Karl Levy, pilot, aviation liaison

My job was to help re-establish the Iraqi Civil Aviation Authority. In establishing that CAA, there's a lot of coordination with the military because the military is the airspace master, so to speak. They control Iraqi airspace. You needed someone there who understood military control of airspace, but also understood civil aviation.

We would handle issues such as overflights of Iraqi airspace. We were the coordinating entity to approve or disapprove all the overflights of Iraq. All the civil aviation requirements to bring in goods to support contracts for rebuilding Iraq came through my office. It was an interesting job. You were basically laying down the civil aviation rules and regs for the country at that time.

We tried to use whatever they'd had before, as much as we could, to see what would fit within the current military control. Those items we could re-establish, we re-established. We didn't want to change everything they'd done before and say, "Here's the American way of doing business. You have to do it this way."

The position involved a lot of things. They included reconstructing the airports of Iraq, the contracts that were being let, who the contractors were to provide security, the cargo handlers, the commercial ventures, all these different things.

There never was a typical day. There were so many things happening. When Russia wanted to evacuate their people out of Iraq, you're the one they're calling to ask how to do this. What information do you provide them on how they're going to get in and out of that airport? You receive this word that they'd like to do this within the next two days. Those next two days are chaos as you try to put this together.

Major Levy's responsibilities would have been heavy enough under the best of circumstances. But then there were the roadside bombs, snipers, and mortar attacks.

The highway between the airport and the Green Zone, we nicknamed Ambush Alley. There were almost daily reports of IEDs occurring on that highway and taking out military vehicles. My job a lot of times was to go back and forth to that airport.

We would drive down the highway, and by the time we got to the airport we'd get word that a section of the highway had been shut down because an incident had occurred where we'd just passed. On the way back you could see the burned-out wreck still smoking where an eighteen-wheeler had blown up.

When you're driving down the highway, you're using defensive tactics such as not staying along either edge of the road because the IEDs are usually stuck along the railings. So you're trying to stay in the middle lane.

As you're going underneath the overpasses, you try to change lanes in case there are people standing on the overpass shooting at you. These are running through your head, the defensive driving tactics like weaving. You're looking as you're driving to ensure you're not being followed. You're trying to see any vehicles that look suspicious. You're driving at a high rate of speed because speed is life. You're wearing a flak vest; you've got your issued weapon with you. You're traveling with a driver and a shooter whose eyes are roving outside looking for incidents. This was how you traveled anytime you moved outside the Green Zone.

Then there were the rocket attacks. Your living area was a tent that wouldn't withstand anything, and you'd hear the distinctive sound that rockets make when they're coming in before they hit the ground. Then there's the deafening sound of the explosion, especially if it's close to you, where it shakes and rattles, and you jump.

The smell of the aftermath. You put all that together, the people you know who were killed or injured. You take that on a daily basis and you become very heightened by it. It's like your senses are at their peak. That's what your daily life felt like.

When you place the complexities of the work you're doing in the environment of the rocket attacks and your high-speed drives down the highways—you throw that into your daily life routine, and that's Iraq.

Lowest moments were the losses. You knew people who died. I spoke to the president of Blackwater when his people were killed in Fallujah. [In March of 2004, four employees of Blackwater Security Consulting were killed in a grenade attack. Their charred bodies were hung from a Euphrates River bridge.]

You knew people who were ambushed on the highway. Those moments are the most heart-wrenching. The bombings, the destruction—and you're asking yourself why. Those were the times you were saying, "My God, this is horrific."

Major Levy describes the effort to keep up his guard in such a dangerous environment.

I would strive to never become complacent, never think, "OK, nothing is going to happen right now."

When I was walking back and forth from where I was staying to the palace where I worked, the distance was about a hundred yards. As I was maneuvering through this little walled-in city, a rocket attack came in and I moved up to the edge of the sandbags. There's a moment of fear there. Where do you run? Do you run? Do you just duck for cover and hold?

Even on the walk to work, you're thinking about what you're going to do. Wherever I was, I made sure I had a plan in my head. You're also checking your weapon, checking your ammo, making sure everything is working because your life depends on it. You made sure you had a cell phone, that it worked, that it was turned on, that it was accessible.

That's your thought process, to always engage yourself and be ready: "What would I do if?" One of the security guys made the point that if something happens while you're driving, don't roll down that window to shoot because that first bullet will take care of the window.

I asked Major Levy what motivated him to accept such an assignment.

You join the military for whatever reasons make you join. I came to America as a 13-year-old boy from a small hilltop town in Jamaica. My father's parting wish was for me to be good and join the military to become a better American. I went to the Air Force Academy. I chose the Academy because it was the best way to fulfill that boyhood dream—not just because it was a fine academic institution.

The military deals with conflict resolution. When the military gets involved, it's all about putting an end to something. But this position was not trying to end something; it was trying to create, to begin something, to re-establish civil aviation in Iraq.

So when the opportunity presented itself, I felt like I had a chance to go into the heart of where the issues are, the problems are, but also where the resolution is. So I said to myself, "This is why you came into the military; here it is."

16

DON'T SHOOT THE MESSENGER

Death is a way of life for these folks.
— Colonel Roger Nye, 167th AW

Pilots feel most at home in the cockpit. However, their careers as military officers sometimes require them to take on other kinds of duties, such as Colonel Roger Nye's assignment to Information Operations in Baghdad. Colonel Nye has spent his career as a pilot and air operations officer, but from February through June of 2005, he worked in what amounts to psychological operations—communicating with the Iraqi public. Some of his work was sensitive and cannot be described here in detail, but his experiences show what day-to-day life was like in the Green Zone.

Colonel Roger Nye,
pilot, Strategic Communications staff officer

I had no knowledge of Information Operations. They train Army officers to do Information Operations. The Air Force does not have information officer training. To start out, I did more staff work, but I eventually learned enough that I could contribute something. I was involved in the public affairs side of it, too, in things like helping set up visits for reporters. There was a lot of that type of stuff. Media events—when Secretary of State Condoleezza Rice came over, my organization set up the escorts, the transportation, the press events, and all that.

Typical day, I'd be up at six o'clock, into work by seven. I worked in the former presidential palace. We lived in trailers behind the palace. At one time there were olive groves back there. Each trailer had a room on either end and then a small bathroom in the middle. Two people to a room.

I'd get up, shower, trudge into work. It was about a four-minute walk for me. Usually the first event was a BUA, a Battlefield Update Assessment. This was a briefing given to the four-star general every day. It was a teleconference with Camp Victory, his headquarters at the airport. It was all classified, big screens and everything. You'd go into the strategic operations center, which was there in the palace, and brief the four-star.

You'd come out of there and go to breakfast in Saddam Hussein's former Arab League meeting room. That's where they had the dining facility. Then it would be into the office. I worked in an office called the bird's nest. It was the bird's nest because it was an office for four eagles, four colonels, sitting right there in that room.

There would be varied meetings through the week. A couple times a month we would travel Route Irish from Baghdad's Green Zone over to Camp Victory at the airport for a meeting, or they would make the trip over to us.

My major task every day was preparing the BUA for the next day. We would brief the general on what was being said in the press. We'd have a slide on press opportunities for the next few days. For example, if they were going to dedicate an elementary school or a hospital that had been built, that was a good press opportunity.

Every day but Friday and Saturday my boss would go over and meet with the Iraqi national security adviser, the chief of staff, and the president's press secretary. There were a couple times that my boss was out of town, and I would go and sit in on these meetings. That was kind of cool, to know you were doing these things with that level of people.

I had a sixteen-hour day. It was very routine, except for the occasional boom and rat-a-tat. I was over there when they seated the National Assembly. Whenever they seated the TNA, the Transitional National Assembly, or the elections took place, things like that, they would ramp up security, and we would have to wear our helmets and flak vests anytime we stepped outside.

There were only a couple attacks that really shook us. Probably the first week I was there, maybe the second week, I was still living in transient quarters, which meant that I had just a small cubicle in a trailer. I had to go to another trailer to go to the bathroom and another trailer to shower. I was in the shower one morning—had just rinsed and my hair was full of soap. They blew up a garbage truck downtown and killed a bunch of contractors, and that thing was just over a mile from where I was. That thing rocked the world, I tell you. I don't know what else it affected, but it shut off the water.

Now I'd walked over in my shorts and a T-shirt and flipflops. Are we under attack? My gear was back in the office and I had soap in my eyes. I could hear the automatic weapons firing after that.

A couple times, mortars landed nearby. One time one hit and there was a window right in front of my desk. They said when you hear something, don't go to the window. That's how some of the contractors were killed with the garbage truck. They went to see what was going on, and the insurgents set off a secondary explosion.

There was an explosion of some type and I assumed it was a mortar. I liked to move away from the windows, but as big as the windows were, I could see where the smoke was. It was just beyond the wall, just beyond my trailer.

They got close. One time a couple hit and broke numerous windows along that wall of the palace. I don't think anybody around the area was killed when I was there, but a month or two before I got there, a mortar came through one of the walls and killed a couple guys. It didn't even explode; it was the rocket engine bouncing around that killed a couple guys in the palace.

Small arms fire was not uncommon. One night I walked back to my trailer, and when I stepped into the bathroom, I noticed plaster all over the floor. I thought, "This is weird."

I looked up at the ceiling and there was a hole. I'm thinking my roommate must have been sweeping or something and punched a hole. I had heard stories of expended rounds coming down and hitting people. This hole was just on the other side of the wall from where my head laid. I thought, "I don't see anything, so it must not have been a round." But my roommate came over and said, "What's this?" There was an AK-47 round that had come down through my trailer.

People found them on pillows; people found them on their beds. By the time they come through the ceiling, they're probably not going to do much damage, but they're going to hurt. There was a pool at the palace, and a lot of the embassy folks would sit out at the pool every day. We had a guy sitting out there before I got there—a stray round came down and punched him in the face. It didn't kill him, but he was hurt.

Probably the scariest thing was running Route Irish. Route Irish is dubbed the most dangerous road in the world. It's a highway that goes between the Green Zone and the airport. It's six or seven miles and you don't go out there by yourself. You go in at least a two-vehicle convoy, and they both have to be armed Humvees, up-armored, with either a Squad Automatic Weapon or a fifty-caliber up top. Everybody has their weapons charged.

Before you go, you have a briefing on which is the most important vehicle. If I was traveling with the general, the general would have one vehicle and I'd probably be in the other. If his was hit, I would have to get out of my vehicle so the general could get in, and I would have to wait and try to defend myself. It's a ride. The first time through there was really nerve-racking and after that it never got much better.

The gunners on top—if somebody comes over in a threatening manner, they will fire warning shots and then they'll just rat-a-tat. There have been plenty of civilians killed mistakenly for doing something that looked threatening.

Colonel Nye witnessed the determination of members of the new Iraqi government in the face of constant threats.

They were very professional. I was very impressed with, for lack of a better word, their guts. These are people who know they've put their lives on the line because now they're targets for even being involved.

One day at the end of a meeting, one of the Iraqi security officials said, "I just wanted to inform you that my nephew was killed this morning. He is not a member of the government. He is not active in any way, but he was gunned down because of me."

Death is a way of life for these folks. They see their families being killed because of them, and they know they could be killed because of what they're doing. They believe democracy can happen, and they're working so hard to make this thing happen.

17

THE OTHER WAR

Oh, East is East and West is West, and never the twain shall meet.
    —Rudyard Kipling, 1889, "The Ballad of East and West"

As the war in Iraq dominated the headlines, Afghanistan became the other war. But there was nothing secondary about the risk for 167th Airlift Wing personnel who deployed to Afghanistan while Operation Iraqi Freedom took center stage. For several months in 2005, our wing commander, Colonel Eric Vollmecke, took command of the 451st Air Expeditionary Group at the airfield in Kandahar, Afghanistan. Captain Andrew Schmidt went with him. Schmidt usually works as the 167th Wing's public affairs officer, handling media visits and news releases. However, he went to Afghanistan as Vollmecke's executive officer, or XO.

Later in 2005, Chief Master Sergeant John Alderton went to Kandahar to take a position as superintendent of the 451st. Chief Alderton normally heads our wing's Security Police. But in Kandahar, his job involved working as a liaison between the group commander and about 450 enlisted personnel.

These deployments happened in a year that brought some of the heaviest fighting in Afghanistan since the initial invasion in 2001. The main job for U.S. forces came down to hunting for al Qaeda and the Taliban—a ground mission of boots tracking in the dust, rifles pointing into caves, and brass casings tumbling into the snow. Our unit's people supported the flying in Afghanistan and the flying supported the Army and Marines.

The need for air and ground forces to work closely together meant Vollmecke, Schmidt, and Alderton entered new territory both geographically and professionally. Schmidt even traveled from home to Afghanistan with Army troops. He did not have the relative luxury of flying in one of our own C-130s, with room to stretch out on a bunk. Instead, he flew on a commercial charter flight.

Captain Andrew Schmidt, executive officer

My wife dropped me off at Baltimore-Washington International Airport with five or six huge bags. You're loading up at the AMC [Air Mobility Command] terminal. You're like, "Wow. I'm gone."

You're loaded up in a civilian jet with about two hundred men, arms like tree trunks, almost all soldiers. Everybody's wedged into those seats. Long flight. Stopped in Frankfurt for probably two hours. Got out, stretched our legs, got back in. Stopped in Ankara, Turkey. We weren't even allowed to get out there. Then flew into Manas Air Base, Kyrgyzstan. Spent a night there in transient quarters. The next day we hopped a C-130 and we were gone.

Intense jet lag. Very tired. Very disoriented, trying to think. I remember when we got to Kandahar, we saw the smiling faces of the commander, the XO, and the chief we were replacing. They were there meeting us with the biggest, cheesy grins. They were like, "Ha ha, idiots. We're gone."

They didn't give us time to settle in; they took us straight to the command post. Gave us briefings, just drinking from the firehose. It was so difficult.

When that plane opens up in Kandahar, especially in the sun, you're on a different planet. It's high elevation. There's just that heat coming off. And of course, when you're flying in and you look down, it doesn't look like a twenty-first-century airfield. It looks like an old dirt road that hasn't been paved in thirty years. It was such an intense sensation. I remember thinking, "Where the hell am I? How am I going to survive here?"

The question of survival became quite real. People were still getting hurt and killed in the other war.

Colonel Eric Vollmecke, pilot, wing commander

It was a very harrowing flying environment. In fact, one mission was probably just a millisecond away from the loss of an entire helicopter and crew as they were trying to go in and save a couple of severely wounded Army guys on a mountainside. It actually resulted in a Class A mishap because of damaged equipment. [A Class A mishap is an accident that causes at least one million dollars worth of damage or results in the loss of life.] It was only the skill of the pilot that kept that helicopter up.

There were many instances where planes were coming back with battle damage, and I was looking at it and saying in my head, "There's a fifty percent chance this guy's going to make it." That kind of stuff happened more frequently than I had ever encountered in my experience before—a couple times a week.

A C-130 pilot with a handful of throttles on a mission over Afghanistan. Note that the usual squadron patch on the right shoulder has been removed. Crews often flew combat missions with "sanitized" uniforms. If captured, you want the enemy to know as little about you as possible (courtesy the 167th Airlift Wing).

Even for people in command and administrative roles, hazards could come on the ground or in the air—and out of nowhere. As Chief Alderton explains, a simple schedule change could spin fate's revolver from a loaded chamber to an empty one.

Chief Master Sergeant John Alderton, group superintendent

In my role as group superintendent, I had the opportunity to go to some of the forward operating bases. I had to get on one of the Chinooks. I flew out on a particular Saturday through this certain ridge to the north of Kandahar. We were anticipating somebody being there, so our gunners were ready.

Nothing happened on that particular day, but twenty-four hours later, almost to the exact minute when we had flown through that ridge, they shot down two helicopters. It would have been our helicopter twenty-four hours

An Air Force HH-60 Pave Hawk rescue helicopter, part of the forces under Colonel Eric Vollmecke at Kandahar, traverses the rough terrain of southern Afghanistan (courtesy the 167th Airlift Wing).

earlier. That was the flight pattern we were flying. We were originally scheduled to go on that Sunday instead of that Saturday.

Every day the revolver's chamber spun for someone. During Chief Alderton's time in Kandahar, an air strike controller nearly died in an IED explosion.

We got a call one evening that one of our TACPs had just been hit and the medevac was bringing him in. [Tactical Air Control Party personnel travel with Army units and coordinate air support.] He was out on a patrol at one of the forward operating bases. A Humvee had been hit with an IED. He had burns on seventy percent of his body.

I recall being there at the ER when the helicopter landed and they wheeled him in—seeing his body all charred. They cut his legs and his arms so the swelling wouldn't cut off the circulation.

That's one thing to this day that I look back on. I think quite often about that.

The TACP Chief Alderton saw flown to the emergency room was Staff Sergeant

Israel Del Toro, wounded on December 4, 2005. The attack controller and master parachutist endured a three-month, medication-induced coma, and he lost his left hand and some vision in both eyes. While still recovering, he toured Air Force bases to give motivational talks to airmen.

Vollmecke, Schmidt, and Alderton all say their Afghanistan deployment brought some of the hardest work of their lives. Imagine making life-and-death decisions while running on adrenaline, caffeine, and an internal clock that's not off just a few hours, but sprung altogether.

Captain Andrew Schmidt, executive officer

They operate on Zulu time there. It's very screwed up. Even though your body is on Eastern Time and you're in south Asia, the clocks are all set on London time, Greenwich Mean Time. You just can't figure it out. We used to joke that the whole clock thing was just to get you to work longer. Days were very long.

I was not deployed as a public affairs officer. The XO is the representative for the commander. I basically ran the TOC, the Tactical Operations Center, which is like a command post. I was in charge of the commander's scheduling, his transportation, his security, and logistics. I was the arm, the voice, the ears of the commander. Colonel Vollmecke didn't sleep much on this deployment, and he made a lot of decisions. My goal was to help him out and help him succeed.

Chief Master Sergeant John Alderton, group superintendent

My role was to go out and represent the command staff and see what issues people had before the issues got elevated to the group commander.

Typical day would be to get up at 0500 hours, go into the office, and check the e-mails both on the classified and unclassified systems and see what issues were there for the day. Then we would roll right into our morning report, which had to be sent up to Bagram to the wing commander. That made it all the way up to the Joint Chiefs of Staff.

After that we'd go to breakfast. We'd come back for the day of meetings. Fridays were always the worst day of meetings. You had twelve different meetings scheduled. We worked a minimum of twelve hours a day. Sunday was the only light day; we'd spend maybe four to eight hours in the office. The command staff worked seven days a week.

Colonel Eric Vollmecke, pilot, wing commander

There were a few major challenges I was dealing with. One was to keep the airfield open, given that we were having to reconstruct a forty-year-old runway that was never built to sustain the kind of traffic we had placed on it. On top of that, it had suffered bomb damage during the initial invasion, which caused further erosion and breakup.

In Kandahar, everything except oil and fuel was delivered by air, so it was very important to keep this field open, but we kept losing runway length due to damage. We couldn't repair it fast enough. That was a major challenge every day, to keep that field open.

Also, it was a challenge getting qualified help to work on the runway—in a combat zone. We were rocketed and two contractors from Turkey and Egypt were killed, and the rest decided to quit. We lost all the civilian work-force in just one day. All construction came to a halt. We didn't recover from that, not while I was there. It put the runway construction behind six months.

We had a lot of increased activity because of our offensive operations. We had to conduct a lot of close air support and airdrop missions out of Kanda-har.

We also had to deal with the variety of NATO aircraft that were flying into the airfield, and aircraft from some of the Third World countries—for-mer Russian republics that had airlift capability. There were issues with peo-ple not following appropriate procedures and air discipline.

My biggest concern was failing the Army. They're out there chasing bad guys in the mountains and they need to be resupplied; they need medevac. So I had combat search and rescue, which did a lot of the most difficult medevac missions. I had close air support. I had unmanned aircraft—the Predators—and the air control squadron controlling the battlespace management. There were a lot of functions I had never really worked with that now all of a sud-den I commanded.

Our folks in Afghanistan found themselves in a strange land on the other side of the world, on the other side of the clock, on the back end of the supply system, and sometimes on the wrong end of a weapon. One day might bring trivial inconven-iences, and the next day, mortal danger.

Captain Andrew Schmidt, executive officer

Kandahar is so remote, so far down the supply chain, that weird things would happen. Like all of sudden there's no laundry detergent in the BX. Or for two weeks, guess what? There's no soap. I remember it being very difficult to keep your clothes clean. Very difficult to have a sense of normalcy.

On our sixtieth day there we got rocketed. Somebody low-crawled in close enough and fired some Chinese rockets on us. They went right over our camp and hit a tent full of Kellogg, Brown, and Root workers.

Our personnel chief was an E-6 [Technical Sergeant]. There were 325 people in that squadron. She had full accountability within thirty-five minutes after the rocket attack and that's with people outside the wire. I was amazed at that.

There was another time when we were rocketed and there were a lot of small arms fights, somebody firing stray RPGs. I never personally felt threatened, but ignorance is bliss. What's so abnormal when you're back home becomes the norm.

We were actually on the ground in Kandahar from the beginning of May 2005 until the middle of September. The climate down there in the desert in southern Afghanistan is just brutal, and that's when they fight down there, in the summer months. They put it to sleep in the wintertime when the passes freeze over. When we got there, it was just a short time before there was a lot of enemy activity. There were a lot of casualties. The first week we were there, one of our soldiers got killed.

Chief Master Sergeant John Alderton, group superintendent

We had four rocket attacks while we were there. One landed not too far from us. One did some damage to a Harrier that actually could not be repaired there, so we had to load it onto a C-17 and take it out that way. We had two contractors that were injured in a rocket attack.

The sirens didn't work real great, at least for the first attack. A lot of people didn't know we'd had an attack until it came out in the staff meeting the next morning. It did improve later. When the sirens went off, those who were living in the dormitories would run down the hall and pound on everybody's door. Everybody would fall into the assigned bunkers.

The Air Force's Office of Special Investigations went out into the villages and met with some of the local folks who were able to provide intel on where the rocket attacks were coming from. From the end of November until we left in January, we didn't have any more rocket attacks. They knew they were being watched.

The OSI was one way to deal with rocket attacks. Meanwhile, Schmidt says the Army found another way to stop them—to make them unprofitable for the locals.

Captain Andrew Schmidt, executive officer

We had a thing called hajji-mart. It was a bazaar that was open to our troops on Sundays for a few hours, and you could go over there and buy local stuff. These guys were charging GI money. It was probably a thousand times what they were selling it for on their market. It was a lot of rugs, silver, old pistols and shotguns. There's a nice economy right there, so what the Army did was to say, "OK, somebody from your village attacked us. The mart is shut down until you guys find them and turn them over to us."

If you're going to hit them, you hit them in the pocketbook. If you're going to drive the Taliban out of there, you have to make it economically in their interest.

A watchword you hear in the modern military is "jointness." That means different branches of the service working closely together. The war movie cliché of a bar fight between soldiers and airmen is as outdated as C-rations with Lucky Strikes. To learn more about other services, we even attend each other's classes. For example, an Air Force sergeant who needs a leadership course for promotion might attend an Army NCO school. But as Colonel Vollmecke and Captain Schmidt found, we still had things to learn from the Army.

Colonel Eric Vollmecke, pilot, wing commander

The lowest moment was about three weeks into my command. The threats were increasing. We needed our people to step up and support the Army in securing the air base. I needed volunteers. I asked for volunteers and I wasn't getting volunteers. I was very frustrated and disappointed that our airmen weren't taking on their share of defense of the base along with the Army.

I recognized that in this case the Air Force didn't have it quite right in our training, preparation, and mindset. A lot of our people didn't have that combat mindset and really didn't appreciate the fact that we now were in a real, no-shit combat zone with bad guys trying to kill us. They needed to be woken up to that fact.

At that point I had to put on the black hat as a commander. I called my NCOs in and I said, "This is your job. You have to motivate each one of these people. I can't go out there and just talk to a group and expect things to happen. It's only going to happen if you get in each guy's face, explain to him it's his responsibility and why he needs to do this. Change their attitudes." And they did.

Captain Andrew Schmidt, executive officer

I learned a lot of respect for the Army. I thought four months was a long time in a combat zone. These eighteen- and nineteen-year olds—these kids were there for a year. They were with the 173rd Airborne from Italy. Most of those young men and women had already done a year in Iraq. This was their second tour. And they thought they were going to some rear-echelon quiet post, but every single platoon of the contingent in Kandahar had been in a firefight by the time we got there.

Hey, I'm a coward. I wanted to stay in the wire. Let's be honest. My mission was in the rear with the gear. I wasn't trying to go out there and get medals. I was trying to do my time and do the best I could at my job and get home safe and sound. I'm a married man.

But Colonel V was adamant that we were going to get out to the Army's remote forward bases, or firebases, because his TACP guys were up there. He was in charge of a TACP unit and they were embedded with the soldiers. They were calling in air strikes. I got to do things I never would have done back home as a public affairs officer. We had to get helicopters from the Army. Make sure they were fueled up. Make sure we were all there. Make sure we had enough water in case we got shot down.

Wow. To go up to the Army firebases where they were constantly in combat. You didn't meet anybody who hadn't individually been in a firefight with the enemy. You just didn't.

Schmidt says the Army has a way of making soldiers want to stay out on the tip of the spear, at the forward bases.

The food at the firebases is much better than the food in the rear. There's a reason for that. I found this out—the Army has a policy that when you have places like Kandahar and Bagram where the soldiers come back from their tours on the firebases, you don't want to make it too comfortable. They do PT [Physical Training] all the time and the food isn't that great—wilted lettuce, a fatty piece of roast beef, and a cup full of instant mashed potatoes.

When they go up to the firebases, they eat steak and shrimp. It's brilliant. Because the idea is you want these guys to say, "Can we please go back to the firebases?"

Schmidt says another cultural difference between the Army and the Air Force is the way the Army conducts briefings—or at least the way the Army conducts briefings when shooting's going on. No personal agendas, no touchy-feely, no anything but results. Or, as some special operators say, "The bullshit stops when the hammer drops."

I got to go to the Army's CJTF, Coalition Joint Task Force 76. I used to watch the Army colonel's meetings. I definitely knew to shut up and stay in the corner. You'd have this colonel and his deputy commander, the brass sitting there. Then you'd have the platoon commanders and company commanders, mainly captains. Some of these guys were about twenty-six years old. They're up there just rat-a-tat-tat: "These are my losses. This is what we did with my company. This is how many were killed. These are how many TICs we were in." [TIC means Troops in Contact, or Army jargon for a battle.]

Those guys had to be so on the ball. The junior officers would get up there and give these briefings on big screens showing the different areas, and the brass would just rip into these guys, savagely asking, "Where's that metric I asked for? I asked you for this."

It was like watching an interrogation. I watched how brutal these guys are on each other. The Army's very efficient, and they definitely have a different culture than we do in the Air Force. Man, that's an aggressive atmosphere.

Colonel Vollmecke recalls a similar take-no-prisoners environment in a meeting with General John Abizaid. As the head of U.S. Central Command, Abizaid was the top American general for the entire Middle East.

Colonel Eric Vollmecke, pilot, wing commander

General Abizaid visited in August of 2005, one month prior to the nationwide elections. He was reviewing our planned offense and security operations to ensure a peaceful and successful election.

A major started the briefing with an intel update on each of the five provinces in southern Afghanistan, which was Task Force Bayonet's area of responsibility. The major had studied Afghan history and culture for over a year prior to his arrival in country. This officer was a true expert. I would put him up against any Ivy League professor who teaches about this region of the world.

As we started going through the details of the plans, I was amazed at the focus of the entire staff. There was no room for any organizational, personal, or political bias at that table. Also, incompetence could not hide. If you didn't know your stuff, you would be dealt with harshly and in public.

The general turned to my Army counterpart and asked him as he pointed his finger at me, "Is that man giving you all the air support you need?"

At that moment, I was the Air Force. General Abizaid made it clear he was holding me personally responsible for the Air Force meeting all its taskings to support these operations, whether it was close air support, airdrops, or search and rescue. This is what they call the burden of command.

Colonel Vollmecke also describes witnessing another kind of Army meeting, which impressed him just as much as the session with General Abizaid.

When the 82nd Airborne Division came in to supplement the forces there in preparation for elections in September, I saw a young buck sergeant getting ready to lead his squad out for its first combat operations the next day. After dinner, he had his squad around him and they were reviewing things. I just stopped there and looked for a moment, and I thought, "I'm observing pure leadership in action." Here's this young kid leading other younger kids into battle the next day, and he was exemplifying all the great qualities of our military.

When people say this generation isn't as good—what I saw there was as good as any generation that ever preceded us. I was very proud that I was able to witness that.

As in all wars, the contribution made by this generation of soldiers comes at a dear price. Captain Schmidt says he saw the toll the operations took on the Army and other forces in Afghanistan.

Captain Andrew Schmidt, executive officer

It was really sad because you had suicides. We probably had not quite one a month. These young kids sometimes get a feeling of hopelessness. They're in the middle of nowhere. It's very hard on morale. There aren't a lot of ways to blow off steam.

You had soldiers killed in small arms fights. The Army public affairs officer there was killed. She hit an IED. First Lieutenant Laura Walker. I'll never forget her name; I had a chance to meet her. There was an NCO with her who was killed. I remember when I was there, the youngest soldier on that base was killed by an IED. Private First Class Ryan Tucker. Then there was a helicopter from our base that was shot down. It was carrying eight SEALs and eight Army troops.

We were killing between fifty to a hundred of the enemy every week, and I think we probably lost from our base about twenty-five KIAs [Killed In Action], including the sixteen who were shot down in a Chinook helicopter.

During Colonel Vollmecke's time at Kandahar, his search-and-rescue people launched a mission in an attempt to save some Marines.

Colonel Eric Vollmecke, pilot, wing commander

Two Humvees were going along this riverbank. It was one of those mountain rivers, very cold, and it was very fast water. One of the Humvees tipped over and fell into the river. We were called in within maybe half an hour of the incident. Pararescuemen are equipped to operate in all environments, to include water. They put their gear on the helicopters and they went out.

It was in a hostile zone. The Marines were providing ground security, but still there was a lot of territory to cover and not that many forces. We had overhead support from A-10s and C-130 gunships.

They went in initially to try to rescue these guys. They were going in that river, being exposed to enemy fire, trying to save the lives of these guys. The pararescuemen were trying to see if they'd washed up on the riverbank someplace, hoping there was some way that somebody survived. Unfortunately, nobody survived, so it became a recovery operation. But these guys still exposed themselves to great risk to recover the bodies of their fallen comrades.

The Marines saw how much effort the United States military was putting in to try to save these guys and later recover the bodies. It gave them all a confidence. They were saddened by the loss of their comrades. But they were also boosted by knowing they have the entire United States military behind them. We're not going to leave them out there hanging. They get into a tough situation, we're going to do everything we can to try to save them and bring them back. Even if we can't bring them back alive, we are going to bring them back.

Soldiers and helicopters of Task Force Bayonet, supported by air assets under the command of Colonel Eric Vollmecke, on a mission in Afghanistan. Note the soldier in the foreground has his blood type written on his helmet (courtesy the 167th Airlift Wing).

Like Colonel Vollmecke, Captain Schmidt encountered U.S. Army troops in Afghanistan who demonstrated exemplary military leadership and discipline. He relates an incident when he saw soldiers handle detainees the proper way, and he contrasts that with the troops who abused Iraqi prisoners at Abu Ghraib.

Captain Andrew Schmidt, executive officer

We came up to a firebase because we were giving an award to one of our TACPs. This guy lived with a company of the 173rd Airborne, and he was embedded with them. He was one of them, you could tell. Trust me, there was no blue or green. They were killers.

While we were there, they were swapping out company commanders. The outgoing commander got up there and said a very sincere, emotional good-bye. He said, "I'm proud to serve with you. We lost this many troops; we had these incidents with the enemy."

You could tell these guys had been through something that I hadn't been through. You could just feel it. This was an airborne infantry company that had been in combat. That's probably the most emotional they'll ever become.

I remember walking around that place and seeing Taliban detainees. They were roped up and they had on the sensory deprivation goggles, blacked-out goggles. We're flying out of there on a Chinook. They stop the helicopter and they load these guys up in the back. I'm like, "Holy shit. We're flying prisoners back; we're flying Taliban back with us."

These guys had been out in the field for a year. The worst smell of a human being you've ever smelled. Hey, we'd all smell like that if we'd been in a cave for a year without showering. It was so pungent.

I'll never forget this, and I tell this story because this is what I think about the Abu Ghraib thing, those people abusing prisoners. I know this commander who was flying back with us had just had men who were lost, fighting these guys. I could tell he was seething, and he probably wanted to throw these guys out the back of the Chinook. And I'm thinking, "Holy shit. This is a very tense situation."

And at Abu Ghraib these people said, "Oh, we were just swept up in the moment." I watched these two prisoners get airsick and they started vomiting, throwing up. And I watched a young private first class come over and comfort them and give them water and wipe vomit off them. He really looked after these guys.

That's the right thing to do. If you're trained, you do the right thing. People who do the bad things you see on the front page of the *Washington Post*— screw 'em, they deserve ten years. When you go into a situation like that, you better know who you are and what you would do. I watched a situation when something could have gone really wrong, but the soldier did the right thing.

The year 2005 was the year 1426 in the Islamic calendar, dated from the year of Mohammed's immigration from Mecca to Medina. In Afghanistan, Schmidt found a feudal land of castles and warlords, tribes and families, where bloodlines run as old as the rivers and where currents of the past run through the present.

I heard somebody make the statement that in the Afghan calendar, the year was around 1400, and as far as he could tell, that was about right. Just a different outlook.

I remember we were at this one town, and there was an ancient castle overlooking the town like something medieval. I took pictures of it. And I was asking, "How old is that?"

They tell me, "It's two thousand years old."

And guess what—there's soldiers stationed up there. It's just this weird, Biblical sense of this ancient world. It's so hard to relate—and I don't think people realize how beautiful that country is and how fresh the air is. When you're flying, you'll see the most sparse desert, and all of a sudden you'll see green and valleys and people raising dates and melons and sheep and goats.

Because of all the wars, you don't have a house unless you have your own fortress around it, your own armed compound, and your sons with their Kalashnikovs. You fly over it and it's a whole nation of ancient fortresses.

The Afghanistan deployments allowed for some contact with the locals, from children to Afghan soldiers. In some of Chief Alderton's rare time off, he befriended a local kid working at a bazaar.

Chief Master Sergeant John Alderton, group superintendent

He was out there selling the wares that his family had. He lived in a hut, had absolutely no heat. They built a fire in there, and that's how they prepared their food, as well. His clothes were whatever he could find. Very, very poor. In fact, before I left, I gave him some of my T-shirts.

The kids there loved flashlights for some reason. We had to always wear a flashlight on our uniform. They always wanted flashlights.

Captain Schmidt describes meeting Afghan troops. He says as the country tries to put together a military force, tradition clashes with training when it comes to certain jobs.

Captain Andrew Schmidt, executive officer

Colonel Vollmecke put together a tour with the Afghan National Army. I was impressed with the army they're building. They're really building a professional army. You just have to have realistic expectations in that country. One of the problems is there's just not an economy. How do you build an army? How do you build a department of welfare?

The Afghan army is kind of funny because of a cultural thing. They had a problem building this army because nobody wants to be a cop or a cook. Everybody wants to be a rifleman. Because of their culture, if you're a support troop, that's woman's work. They clean; we kill. So they have to rotate all these jobs. It's hard to build a specialized army because nobody wants to be the finance guy.

The Air Force's main job at Kandahar was to support Army operations. But the enlisted people under Chief Alderton's watch had a wide variety of jobs, some of which involved helping Afghans meet obligations to both God and country. Alderton's stint there included the Muslim pilgrimage to Mecca, and Afghanistan's parliamentary and local elections.

Chief Master Sergeant John Alderton, group superintendent

During our time there we were responsible for hajj flights. We turned over the terminal, which was under U.S. control, to the Afghan government. That enabled them to get their hajj flights out to Mecca. That was a real highlight.

During the parliamentary elections, there was a lot of speculation that the ballot boxes would be sabotaged with IEDs. Explosive Ordnance Disposal would X-ray the ballot boxes to make sure nothing was in there. The Air Force EOD folks played a large part in securing the ballots, while the Army was responsible for securing the polling places.

What an exciting time to be a part of something like that. Here they are electing their government, patterning it after ours to a degree. Voter turnout here in the United States, depending on where you are, can be as low as twenty percent. Very seldom does it ever get above eighty percent. But those folks over there would travel anywhere from a few minutes to several days to reach a balloting place.

That says something. That's how much they wanted to make a difference in their government. And it's not over interstate highways like we have. They had to travel through mountains. They'd put up a tent to sleep overnight. They'd drag their children with them, just to go vote. Just to go vote.

Captain Andrew Schmidt, executive officer

The heart of what we were trying to do was to rebuild that airport, rebuild critical infrastructure so they could have a civilization in that part of the Earth.

You just gotta have realistic expectations of what you're trying to attain there. East is east; west is west. That's what Kipling said.

The goal is to try to provide security, safety, some kind of commerce, some kind of transportation. You're not building utopia. As long as the bad guys are coming across from Pakistan, it's never going to be perfect. But at least in Afghanistan right now they can't build terrorist camps and train people to come over here and fly airplanes into our buildings.

18

FOLDED FLAGS

Requiem aeternam dona eis, Domine, et lux perpetua luceat eis
Grant the dead eternal rest, O Lord, and may perpetual light shine on
them

Our saddest duty was carrying comrades-in-arms on their final journey. Most
of us had never done that job before. As Lieutenant Colonel Steve Truax describes,
many of us were not even familiar with the grim terminology associated with trans-
porting troops killed in action. Truax learned some of that terminology over the air-
craft radios while en route into Baghdad.

Lieutenant Colonel Steve Truax,
navigator, operations officer

You had all these very thick, complicated rules of engagement that you were reading in flight, and all these abbreviations, brevity codes, classified codes, and whatnot. And command post said, "You're doing a Hotel Romeo." I went through all these brevity codes, and I finally called back and said, "What's a Hotel Romeo? You're going to have to tell me, son, what are we rigging for, if you can tell me in the clear?"

He said, "Hotel Romeo is human remains."

I just thought, "Oh my God. We're taking a dead young man home." And sure enough, that's what it was. I saw his picture in the Air Force Times after that. I believe he was a twenty-three-year-old private first class from Missouri: Jeremiah D. Smith. And they laid his remains in there. And then there were a bunch of passengers who wanted to leave Baghdad.

Procedures are that the casket has priority. Passengers can ride with the casket if they don't mind that. Of course, these guys—there were still firefights in Baghdad—and they said, "Hell yeah, we want out of here." So a bunch of people rode in the back with the casket. We flew into Kuwait, which was such

153

a mess. It was so unorganized at the international airport there, swamped with military traffic.

We flew in there and some guys had done this over and over. With a very polished, rehearsed operation, they backed a big old Army truck up to the airplane and loaded Jeremiah Smith's mortal remains into the back of it to take him further downstream for processing.

I stood behind the airplane, and everybody else was already gone, and they just loaded the casket. I came to attention and I gave that boy a salute. I was thinking that if he could see, maybe he'd appreciate that.

Master Sergeant Dave Twigg was among the few of us who already had experience transporting the fallen. He served as a loadmaster on the flight that carried Private Smith out of Iraq.

Master Sergeant Dave Twigg, loadmaster

He was killed in action in Baghdad and that's where we picked him up. That was a somber mission.

John Cox [another loadmaster] and I were not new to this. It's an unfortunate thing to say, but we were not new to hauling this kind of sensitive cargo. I had to do it one time out of South America. It was a peacetime thing. There was a paratrooper who was killed during a jump. We transported him back to Fort Bragg, North Carolina. And John had to do it himself in the first Gulf War. So we knew what had to be done, how the casket had to be positioned, all the protocols that went along with it.

We knew the soldier's name, his rank, and where he had been killed, but we couldn't put a face to go along with it. And I think it was in the *Air Force Times*, they ran pictures and names of all the soldiers killed in action. Stevie Truax brought that down. He said, "Hey, take a look at this. I think you'll find the young private we transported that night out of Baghdad." I looked through and sure enough, we found the kid's picture. He looked like he had just graduated from high school.

Anytime you haul one of your own that's been killed in action, it'll affect you to a certain degree. But it kind of gave me a sense of closure, knowing that I had a face to put along with his name now.

I don't know if he was married or had children or anything, but somewhere out there, there was a mom and a dad, a girlfriend, maybe a wife—I don't know. I'm just glad we could do our part to get him back home where he belonged.

On November 15, 2003, two Black Hawk helicopters collided near Mosul, Iraq. Seventeen soldiers died in what was then the worst single-incident loss of American troops in the Iraq war.

Lieutenant Colonel Bill Clark, pilot

We were sitting Bravo Alert at Al Udeid, and we got launched and we showed up for the brief. We were in a good mood, relatively speaking, and when they put up the frag [fragmentary order], in the remarks it said "HR." None of us knew what HR was, and we were kind of joking around wondering what it was until they came in and told us HR stands for human remains.

There were two Black Hawks that had gone down that night in Mosul. One was shot at and to avoid the missile, he tried to evade and flew into the other Black Hawk. They hit perpendicular and it killed seventeen people.

We were told we were going to pick up seven. We landed in Mosul, and it was back when Mosul was still blacked out. Three deuce-and-a-half trucks pulled up behind the plane with fourteen bodies on them. The bodies were not in coffins; they were still in body bags. We the crew ended up loading them on the airplane; we hand-carried them on.

You just walked up and put your back to the truck and kind of grabbed hold of the bag and pulled it, and the guy behind you grabbed the tail end of the bag as it went by. As I pulled this thing, I had the heavy end of it and as it settled on my shoulder it was still warm. The body was still warm.

We put all fourteen in there, and we carried only fourteen because that's

The flight crew saluting, soldiers carry one of the fallen from an aircraft at Ramstein Air Base, Germany (U.S. Army photograph).

all the bodies you can fit in the cargo compartment of a C-130. That's all it'll hold. We had a flag in the front of the cargo compartment and we had a flag in the back.

These three trucks that brought the bodies were from the unit these guys belonged to [the 101st Airborne Division], and they had a ceremony at the tail of the airplane. At that point I don't think there was a dry eye in the house, including myself. Everybody on the plane pretty much lost it at that point.

We flew from Mosul back to Kuwait that night to drop the bodies off, which was probably an hour-and-a-half flight, and other than checklists, I don't think there was a word said the entire flight. I will never forget that flight. It will never leave me.

Senior Master Sergeant Steve "Mac" McDonald, flight engineer

We got alerted because two choppers had crashed. We flew up there to Mosul and picked up fourteen body bags and transported them back to Kuwait City.

It was a sad time. I remember the loadmaster was crying over it; of course she had to load the body bags in a certain manner. We put some flags up around the cargo compartment.

That was probably the most quiet flight I ever went on, the trip back to Kuwait. I guess it was weighing on everybody's mind that this could happen; it could happen to us.

I couldn't go to the back, into the cargo compartment. It was hard for me to look at them. I guess you see your own mortality. You don't want to end up like this.

Major Mark Ruckh, the navigator for this HR flight, wrote eloquently about the experience in a letter home the following day.

Major Mark Ruckh, navigator, e-mail to friends and family

Folks,

This is not my typical light-hearted rant about the stupidity of the military or the living conditions of the desert. Last night was one of those evenings you hope never comes and when it does, you just aren't prepared for the magnitude of your feelings. Even now, as I write this, I'm having trouble putting it into words, expressing what I want to say.

No, I didn't get shot at, but let me kind of start from the beginning. Our crew was sitting Bravo Alert yesterday. That means you have to get a plane in the air three hours after your crew is alerted. I was working in Ops last night on our redeployment route home when one of the Intel guys walked in and said a helicopter was down in Mosul.

Most of you have already heard about the tragedy of two Army helos colliding in the night, if you have been watching the news. I didn't think much of it other than, "The Army helo force is really taking a beating these days." Rather cold and callous, but we deal with the stuff in our own way.

About three hours later, my crew got alerted for a mission. When we got into Ops, we found out we were going to Mosul, and I assumed it would probably be for a medevac. But another crew had already been launched for that mission. The briefer said, "No, you guys are going on an HR run."

I've been in the military for fifteen years now and never heard the term, so the natural question was, "What's HR?"

HR stands for human remains.

It was a quiet flight up to Mosul last night; we were all pretty tired anyway since it was the middle of the night/early morning. On the flight up, we hung two American flags in the cargo compartment because you can't transport American KIA in an Air Force aircraft without one flying—and our crew wouldn't have it any other way, anyhow. There is actually a regulation about this, too.

After we landed, we shut down and waited for about five minutes for the trucks to arrive. Trucks—plural. We loaded fourteen body bags this morning onto our airplane. We had to leave [some] behind because there wasn't enough room on the floor of the plane.

People, take a look at the inside of a C-130 sometime and remember these words: "There wasn't enough room." I will never forget the sight of the Army troops lined up outside the tail of our aircraft paying final tribute to their fallen comrades—two ranks, saluting rows of black bags on litters that hours before had been friends, guys you might have sat next to in the chow hall or maybe spotted you in a workout at the gym. I read the list of names on the passenger manifest. The families are about to see the one thing a military family hopes they never see—a military staff car driving up to their house with an officer and chaplain seated in the car. The news is never good.

I don't think there was a dry eye on our entire crew last night, and we are still talking about it and trying to deal with the emotions, still crying. I find myself asking the questions, "Was it worth it? Was it worth the lives of those American soldiers?"

I don't know. I don't have an answer anymore. I hope and pray like I've never hoped and prayed for anything in the past that history will say we did the right thing and none of those lives were wasted.

I pray that those fourteen men I carried and the ones we couldn't bring with us are at peace and now rest in God's hands. There are hundreds that have gone before, and there will be those that follow, and I pray they all rest in God's hands. Please remember those that have fallen in your prayers and say a prayer for those of us soldiering on every day.

Immediately following the mission to bring back the soldiers lost in the helicopter collision, Clark's crew had two other wrenching flights.

Lieutenant Colonel Bill Clark, pilot

The mission after the one to Mosul was a trip up to northern Iraq; I forget exactly where, but there was a Black Hawk that went down and they were on the emergency channel, calling for some type of support because they were getting shot at. You could hear the gunfire in the background whenever they keyed their microphone. But the intel report we got after that said there were no survivors on the Black Hawk. So to hear those guys on the radio, knowing that they died very soon after that, was not an easy thing to listen to.

The next time we flew was up to Bagram Air Base, Afghanistan. It was a night mission, and just before we got to Bagram, the base came under attack. We had to hold south of Bagram while the A-10s and helicopters took off to thwart the attack. We were on a northbound leg facing Bagram, and we could see where the attack was coming from; we could see the battle going on.

We saw this huge flash, this huge explosion, and we were all happy on the airplane because we thought our forces had killed a bunch of the guys attacking the base. Maybe we'd defeated some of those guys. But once we landed we found out that flash was a Pave Low helicopter that went down. All the people on it were killed.

That was three missions in a row, the first one being human remains. The second one, we listened to people die on the radio, and the third one we watched one of our helicopters go down. That was a tough three missions in a row.

When we got back to Al Udeid, I went to the scheduler and asked him to take us off the schedule for a while. My crew was pretty much done at that point.

Fallen warriors eventually arrive at Dover Air Force Base, Delaware, home of the primary military mortuary. After the plane parks and shuts down, the aircrew assembles in the cargo compartment and stands at attention while a chaplain offers a prayer. As the honor guard lifts the flag-draped transfer case, the crew renders a salute. This salute comes up very slowly—a measured, final farewell to one of our own. The crew holds the salute until the honor guard places the transfer case into a waiting vehicle.

This flight line ceremony takes place for every service member killed in Iraq or Afghanistan—no matter how late the aircraft lands, no matter how biting the wind off the Delaware Bay, and no matter whether anyone else is there to see it.

19

MORTARITAVILLE

An actual conversation aboard the flight deck of an airlifter on the ground at Balad Air Base, Iraq:

> Intelligence officer: *"The base hasn't been attacked in a while."*
> Crew member: *"How long is a while?"*
> Intelligence officer: *"Oh, several hours."*

Balad's long runways can handle huge cargo planes, which is why the base hosts the biggest aerial port operation in Iraq. Balad also has the largest military hospital in Iraq, and the adjacent Camp Anaconda is a major Army hub.

Because of the high risk of attack, our aircrews were always happy to get out of Balad. For C-130 fliers, it was usually a quick visit: drop the cargo and take off again, often without even shutting down engines. But some of our comrades stayed for the long haul. A number of ground personnel from the 167th Airlift Wing deployed to Balad when the Air Force called for volunteers in various job specialties.

In March of 2004, Captain Tony Henry, a civil engineer with the West Virginia Air Guard, went to Balad to draw up plans for airfields and other sites in Iraq. Master Sergeant Gerry Kendle, a former security policeman turned first sergeant, worked there from August of 2005 to January of 2006. Emergency management specialist Fred Lawrence did a Balad tour in 2005.

Several aerial port specialists from the 167th also deployed to handle Balad's huge quantities of military freight. Their work involves preparing cargo and passengers for shipment, as well as receiving incoming loads and repackaging the cargo for further shipment elsewhere in the combat zone. They load and unload the airplanes, and they even rig parachutes when cargo needs to be airdropped. And at Balad, they did it under fire.

Insurgents attacked Balad so often the troops there called the place "Mortaritaville."

Master Sergeant Gerry Kendle, first sergeant

Of the 134 days I was at Balad, we were mortared or rocketed 116 times. It got pretty hairy. Sometimes it would be far away and it wouldn't bother anybody, and sometimes it would get close. Some of the mortars or rockets would hit housing areas. Most of the time, thankfully, no one was really hurt. There were, unfortunately, several casualties due to the shrapnel wounds. While I was at Balad, there were three fatalities and several wounded.

I was nearby on several of the attacks, close enough to scare the bejeebers out of you. You'd hear the explosions first. Some times you might hear the whistling coming in. Then they would impact. Then several minutes later the base would go into Alarm Red. One of the problems we had was getting people to learn to take cover and stay there. Subsequent mortar or rocket attacks would still occur. That's usually when people were getting injured, because they weren't staying in cover after the first attack.

The attacks were at all different times. Sometimes they would wake you up. Usually the sirens would wake you up. The housing areas were pretty well protected. We had earthen barriers or concrete barriers around all the trailers and the dormitory areas and the tent areas, which actually muffled a lot of sound. A lot of times you wouldn't hear it.

Captain Tony Henry, civil engineer

I was there 170 days and we were attacked 194 times. I had about four rounds land within about 75 to 150 yards from me. One night—I'll never forget it—it was Good Friday. Five or six tents down from me, they took a direct hit and one guy got killed. We got hit, like, five times that night. That was the lowest moment, when we just kept getting pounded and pounded and pounded.

A couple other times, I just went around the corner and as soon as I walked in the building, the corner took a hit. The Good Lord was definitely looking out for me. You think of mortar rounds in John Wayne movies, the big craters and all that. Actually, a mortar round just leaves a little pockmark in the ground, but it throws shrapnel everywhere.

Technical Sergeant Dave Jenness, aerial port specialist

We took incoming fire. It was harassing fire mostly. It's kind of callous to say it, but after a while you just got used to it; it was gonna happen. You just hoped you weren't going to be there when it came in, but you never knew.

It would hit all over the flight line, all over the base. Nobody I knew got wounded, but there were people who were hit.

It was all chance stuff. They would just point it at the base and fire it. The base was fifteen or eighteen square miles. They'd lay rockets on a sheet of plywood on a timer and then get away from it because they knew we had heat cameras and all kinds of stuff. Our guys could see when stuff was launched at us, and they would send helicopters out. So those bad guys didn't stay around and just launch and launch and launch. They would drive by with a mortar tube in a pickup truck. They'd drop a couple rounds and shag ass out of there before something came after them.

You got used to it. Sometimes you'd get scared and startled, and other times it was just more of a pain in the neck because you'd have to stop what you were doing, and we were trying to get aircraft loaded and unloaded to get troops and supplies to the Army.

They hit the tent camp occasionally. Before we got there, they had a round come into a tent where a bunch of Army troops were. Four or five of those guys were killed. The first day we got there, a civilian contractor was walking across an open field. A mortar round hit and killed him. We hadn't been on the ground twelve hours.

The nearest one to me was probably 150 yards. It was at night. Big flash and a loud boom, and it was pitch dark out. It was close enough it would make you flinch.

I think everyone has their own methods for coping. I just basically looked at it as a nuisance. If it was gonna hit you, it was random. There was nothing you could do but take your Kevlar, and if you were sleeping and one fell on your head, that was not your day.

Technical Sergeant Fred Lawrence, an emergency management specialist from the 167th, spent the latter half of 2005 in Balad. Fred says some people dealt with the near-daily mortar and rocket attacks by developing a grim sense of humor about it.

Technical Sergeant Fred Lawrence, emergency management specialist

You could just about put money on when the attacks were going to be, about what time. You knew when you were going to be in Alarm Red. It got real funny. There were days when we'd go to the chow hall early since we knew we would get hit. We didn't want to be standing in line because you'd have to get out of line and come back. On other days we'd go late.

After a while it just got to be a routine. We even had names for the insurgents. We had Mortar Man. We knew he wanted to hit at a certain time. We had Rocket Man, and we knew he usually had four rockets that would come in at one time. They were always rockets, never mortars, so we called him Rocket Man. We had Six-Gun Charlie. He would normally fire six rounds. Usually the attacks were between five and six in morning and in the evenings between six-thirty and seven. You had to make light of the situation or you'd go nuts.

Amid the mortars and rockets, not all the insurgents were outside the base. As Gerry Kendle explains, the bad guys aiming those mortars and rockets got some help from the inside. That's why you had to be careful not to make idle chatter about military matters to the locals working in the chow hall.

Master Sergeant Gerry Kendle, *first sergeant*

A lot of them were civilians that worked on the base. Because there was no mechanism in place to verify exactly who these people were, it was estimated that at any time, ten percent of the Iraqis on the base were insurgents who could have been gathering information. Some of them worked in the dining facilities or doing manual labor jobs. They were always kept under guard. You were supposed to watch them for any suspicious activity, like marking off distances. [Marking off distances between buildings can help insurgents aim mortars.]

Like our other personnel who went to Balad, Fred Lawrence and his people were cautioned to remain wary about civilian employees on the base—and they caught one in the act.

Technical Sergeant Fred Lawrence, *emergency management specialist*

A lot of times we found that the person was not willingly working for the insurgency. A family member would be held hostage, and they'd give information to the insurgency just to save their family member. It's not that the people are bad people. But you put them up against the wall—what would we do to save our family? We might end up doing the same thing.

The local nationals were working right outside our building. There was a senior airman in our office who realized they were pacing off the building. He just happened to be sitting outside smoking a cigarette, and he was watching them work. He realized what one of them was doing. That one wasn't with the group; he was stepping off an area that wasn't being worked on. He had no reason to be in that area. A guy smoking a cigarette saved somebody's life that night.

Fred's job included teaching troops how to detect and avoid roadside bombs and car bombs outside the perimeter. But on at least one occasion, a bomber attacked the base itself, ratcheting up the violence to a higher level. Fred describes responding to the incident alongside the Explosive Ordnance Disposal [EOD] personnel, who defuse or destroy bombs.

The biggest incident we had was a VBIED [Vehicle-Borne Improvised Explosive Device, or car bomb] at the gate. Fuel trucks coming in got attacked. We went out there and addressed the situation with EOD, the Army, and security forces. It was a massive explosion. We had four casualties at the gate: a civilian contractor was killed and three military were severely wounded. It was our job to go back out and make sure there wasn't a secondary device coming through or something that was planted later.

Where it could have been chaotic, it was very controlled. Nothing actually penetrated the base. Everything was handled right at the gate. Though we did have rockets and mortars coming in on a daily basis, that incident at the gate was controlled. They did lose a truck, but it was pretty well handled.

Once EOD did their job, we had to do some reconnaissance—verifying what we had in the area to make sure we didn't have any chemical-type explosive, what EOD would call a "leaker." It was our job to go out and make sure whatever was leaking wasn't a chemical.

Though life on base at Mortaritaville could get harrowing, it was a haven compared to what awaited Americans off base. As a first sergeant—essentially a personnel director—for Air Force troops in several locations, Gerry Kendle's duties took him to Al Taqaddum, Qayarrah West, Tall 'Afar, Al Asad, and Camp Speicher.

Master Sergeant Gerry Kendle, first sergeant

I flew in Army C-23 Sherpas, like a midget C-130, I guess you'd call it. A little boxcar with wings. They would fly tactically at about 100 to 150 feet off the ground, dodging and swerving to fly perpendicular over roadways and over powerlines. It was a very long roller-coaster ride. One time we were flying so low we had a dog chase us. I was looking out the window and saw the dog running after the airplane.

One day we were out to Qayarrah West. We stopped at Al Taqaddum, and at Al Taqaddum we noticed bullet holes in the wing. No one had seen anything on the flight, but the check of the aircraft when we landed showed the bullet holes. That made you kind of think about things.

As a civil engineer, Captain Tony Henry's work often required him to leave the perimeter. He explains that he wasn't trained for traveling the roads in Iraq, but he credits our unit's CATM, or Combat Arms Training and Maintenance section, for showing him how to handle his weapon.

Captain Tony Henry, civil engineer

I lived in the Air Force tent city, but I was embedded with the Army as a combat engineer in the 372nd Combat Engineering Group. I was there for six months.

The Army is geared differently. If it's a regular engineering group, they don't have a design section. So we had a ten-person Air Force detachment that did all the design. We had five officers and five enlisted. The enlisted were the surveyors and draftsmen. I was horizontal design lead, taking care of roads, airfields, helipads, and FARPs, Forward Arming and Refueling Points.

We did some different convoy missions out and about. I got on the ground the first day, like five o'clock in the afternoon. I was out on a convoy the next morning at seven o'clock with no convoy training whatsoever. I had my weapon and I had to borrow ammo for that. Only had thirty rounds. We went down to Taji, which is north of Baghdad, about halfway between Baghdad and Balad.

You're in a Humvee in full body armor. It's 140 degrees inside. You're just shaking and baking. It's pretty much an adrenaline rush and when you get done,

Dining in a rough neighborhood. Civil engineer Tony Henry at a primitive restaurant near Balad Air Base. Henry's pockets bulge with extra magazines for his M-16 (courtesy Captain Tony Henry).

Captain Tony Henry with a civil engineering team outside the wire, away from the relative safety of Balad Air Base (courtesy Captain Tony Henry).

you're full of sweat. You're mentally and physically exhausted because you're constantly on guard. You're looking at everybody as you go by. You're looking everybody in the eyes and watching their hands.

The first time going outside the gate when you put a live round in a weapon with the intent to shoot somebody if need be, it really hits home. The CATM guys had really spun us up good. You don't lock and load until you get outside the gate. As soon as I got outside the gate, my weapon jammed, right off the bat. I had a bad clip. There's no way to raise your hand for help. That's why I try to preach to people that you need to know how to handle your weapon. I was able to clear it real quick.

Fortunately, I didn't have to fire it. I had the safety off a couple times, though. We were coming up to an Iraqi police checkpoint once. Some guy on a moped started pulling forward like he was lunging at us. Everybody was ready to blast him, and a couple Iraqi cops tackled him and took him down. That was at about fifty miles an hour. I think he was just being stupid, but we didn't turn around and stop.

I never got hit on any of the convoys, but one of the lieutenant colonels in our detachment—an IED went up right behind his vehicle. He didn't get hurt or anything. He said they had just passed it by a couple seconds, and it blew up behind them. That's one of the medals I didn't want to come back with.

On September 29, 2005, three suicide car bombers carried out a coordinated attack in the town of Balad, leaving at least sixty dead. The explosions in the mainly Shiite city were part of worsening violence in advance of the October 15 referendum on a new constitution. Gerry Kendle and his people helped take care of the wounded.

Master Sergeant Gerry Kendle, first sergeant

In the middle of the night, I got a phone call from my chief, telling me I needed to have so many people at the hospital. They were rushing forty or fifty casualties into the base. This was probably two o'clock in the morning. I was able to get ten people up and dressed and into the hospital within twenty minutes. These were my logistics people to help move the litters and whatever needed to get done.

It was ordered chaos. The medevac choppers were bringing in the casualties. We had people lined up, and we probably had two hundred volunteers just show up out of the blue to do whatever needed to get done.

The violence erupting off the base—and especially on the roads—represented the core reason for sending members of an airlift wing to Balad. Dave Jenness says it became very clear that anything he and his buddies could send by air meant less exposure for truck convoys on the ground.

Technical Sergeant Dave Jenness, aerial port specialist

Convoys going off the base came back with casualties just about every time they went out. We weren't going outside the wire, so I felt real fortunate that what little bit of fire we were taking was just a nuisance. The Army troops that were going out, and the Air Force cops going out on security detail with these convoys, they were taking a beating. Everything out there was blowing up. Those guys would put an IED in a dead animal and put it beside the road. I felt fortunate that we didn't have to go outside the perimeter.

All the freight would come in for the Army, and we would either ship it on airplanes to the smaller places like Tikrit, or it would go on truck convoys. Our job was to stop the truck convoys because the Army was just getting pounded. Every time they'd go out, something was blowing up, and they were taking way too many casualties. We would try to move everything we could on C-130s. It would come in on a C-5 or a C-17 and we would break the loads and reconfigure them. Certain things were going to the Marine Corps or to different Army units at different bases, and we would set it up to take it out on C-130s.

They told us when we got there, "Your job is to make sure we can stop as much as possible the road movement of freight. If we can move it by air plane, let's move it that way." Anything we could move by air was keeping it off the road because the roads weren't safe.

At certain times, certain areas were taking a lot of harassing fire and getting attacked. So we were just moving food and ammo to certain places in Iraq. Mosul was just getting pounded and they weren't that far away. We sent them MREs and water and ammo for like, two weeks, and that's all they took.

For the crews of airlift planes, Balad was a place to get into and out of as quickly as possible. Fliers depended on Dave and the other aerial port specialists to minimize their time on the ground because a big airplane sitting on a ramp is a mortar magnet.

The highest moment was one night when we downloaded eighteen pallets off a C-17 in less than five minutes with seven guys. The crew was ecstatic that we got them in and out of there in a quick turnaround, in a safe manner. They didn't want to be on the ground. [Planes] were big bags of gas sitting on the ground. The crew didn't want to be there any longer than they had to be. We were doing our job.

For obvious reasons, Balad was a bad place for an airplane to break down. So naturally, that's where some of them decided to break. When that happened, Maintenance Recovery Teams would fly in to do hammer-and-duct-tape repairs just to get the aircraft out of harm's way. Engine specialist Travis Riley describes rescuing a C-130 crew that was wasting away in Mortaritaville with an engine that wouldn't start. Travis explains that when he got the engine running, the pilot didn't realize it was only a quick-and-dirty combat fix and that Travis would have fix it all over again if the crew shut down the engine.

Staff Sergeant Travis Riley, engine specialist

They got stuck in Balad and me and a buddy of mine, Justin Moore, went over there to change their ignition relay. The crew was really new. They didn't have much experience flying, and they weren't familiar with all the aircraft systems. It wasn't one of our crews.

They'd had to sleep on the floor that night. They told us they'd had a rough night, and they said, "Just get us out of here." It took us a couple hours to get them fixed.

This is kind of funny. We started that one engine up, we got it running,

In these two sequential photos, a C-130 from the 167th lands at Balad Air Base, Iraq, in 2003—the early days of Operation Iraqi Freedom. The holes in the runway are where bomb craters are being repaired. The pilot is aiming for a small area to the left side of the runway, where engineers have marked off a section of useable pavement (courtesy the 167th Airlift Wing).

Departing Balad Air Base, Iraq, at low level over the Tigris River as night falls. The aircraft turns onto a course to take it out of Iraq. Note the bank angle reflected in the pilot's attitude indicator, lower left (author's collection).

and for some reason the pilot pulled back the condition lever to shut it down and it stopped running.

I was like, "Aw, man!" So we messed with it some more. We got it running again. He pulled it back again, and it stopped running again.

I said, "Listen, man. If I get this thing going, leave it running until we get back. Don't touch nothing. Once it starts, it'll stay running. Let's get it back and we'll fix it for good back at Masirah Island."

He said, "All right."

It took several times to get the thing running. Me and Justin were so happy. We got back on that plane and got it back to Masirah. We wanted to get the plane back to safety and work on it where it was safer to work on it.

Exhaustion, jet noise, dust, and danger defined daily life at Mortaritaville.

Technical Sergeant Dave Jenness, aerial port specialist

We worked twelve hours on and twelve hours off, and we tried to sleep. There were twenty-four-hour flight operations, and we weren't that far off the flight line, so you had aircraft coming in and out, C-5s taxiing around. You had F-16s on combat air patrols going out every two hours on full afterburner. Those guys didn't roll off the runway like they do in the States; they were combat takeoffs every time. You constantly had that noise. You'd sleep a little bit and wake up, then sleep a little bit and wake up. You were always tired.

Our billets were like real cheap trailers, twelve-by-twelve rooms with two people in them. Then the shower facilities were probably 150 yards away. So you'd walk down there to use the lavatory. The walls were two-by-twos, probably low-bid contract.

There was no alcohol because we were in their country and respecting their laws. You couldn't get a cold beer and relax that way. It wasn't going to happen. You were either in PT [Physical Training] gear or desert combat uniform, so you couldn't put on a pair of blue jeans and kind of kick back a little bit.

The main thing people remember about Balad is the mortars. Then there was the dirt—a powder that easily got airborne and into tents, into aircraft, into lungs. Aerial port specialists Dave Jenness and Roy Brake and pilot Chris Sigler remember it none too fondly.

Technical Sergeant Dave Jenness, aerial port specialist

It was like a fine, tan, talcum powder dust. It blew everywhere and it got into everything. You could not seal it out. You had to clean the filters out in the air conditioners every day or they would just stop up. When it rained, it would turn into the slickest, nastiest mud. It was hard to keep off the vehicles and off the flight line.

Everything was brown. It was terrible. When we got back to the States and saw green, it was just amazing.

Master Sergeant Roy Brake, aerial port specialist

We got there in January and the dirt was like powder, but then it started to rain. When it rained there would just be ponds everywhere. I've never seen dirt like it. You'd get this mud on your feet, and by the time you got from your tent down to work, you'd have chunks of concrete on your feet, just clinging. It was mud everywhere and you couldn't clean it up. You'd try to clean up and it would rain again. That went on for about a month and a half or two months, and then it got dry and powdery again.

Major Chris Sigler, pilot

At night on NVGs, the ramp and the sand looked exactly the same. I remember taxiing out of there; it was hard to tell what was the ramp and what was the sand.

Fred Lawrence saw a bizarre scene at Balad: Iraqi fighter planes that had been hidden in the ground. Saddam Hussein chose to hide his jets rather than have them come up to face American pilots.

Technical Sergeant Fred Lawrence, emergency management specialist

Balad Air Base was Saddam's air force academy. There were MiGs found at the far end of the runway, buried in the sand. I think everybody had pictures of them because everybody was going by to get their pictures taken with the MiGs. There were three found.

Against this strange and dusty backdrop, the fight for the future of Iraq played out, sometimes just outside the base fence. Many of the dead and wounded came into the air base. Balad hosts the Air Force Theater Hospital, one of the major U.S. medical facilities in Iraq. Master Sergeant Roy Brake describes a heart-rending visit to that hospital.

Master Sergeant Roy Brake, aerial port specialist

I was at the Balad hospital one time. I got the crud like you sometimes do, and just to make sure everything was OK, they sent me over there to get an X-ray to make sure I didn't have pneumonia. One of the medevac choppers brought a guy in and they took him into X-ray.

I remember hearing one doctor say, "The bullet is lodged next to his spine and he's probably going to be paralyzed, but let's see what we can do with it."

And I remember thinking to myself, "I really don't know what the hell I'm doing here worrying about pneumonia when this kid just got shot."

Medevac choppers were flying in there all the time. The Balad hospital was a busy, busy place.

Aerial port people are responsible for anything shipped on airplanes. Sadly, that includes the fallen.

Technical Sergeant Dave Jenness, aerial port specialist

The lowest moment was dealing with HRs. It's something you can't get used to. You shouldn't be able to, anyway. Most of the HRs processed in that part of Iraq were brought into our base.

It's kind of cold, but they're considered a piece of cargo. They have to be signed for, but you know who they are because their names are on the paperwork. You take that to the crew chief.

The crew knows when they're going to take HRs out because they have to make sure the aircraft is configured. They always have a ceremony when they take a U.S. serviceman out. They bring the honor guard out, and we load the HRs and make sure they're treated in the manner they should be.

We had to notify any passengers on board. We had to let them know, "Hey, there's going to be HRs on this airplane. If you don't feel comfortable flying with HRs, we'll get you on another flight." Most of our airplanes were configured with seats going down the sides and cargo in the middle. If there were HRs going on board, they were there in plain view.

You saw that more often than you wanted—four or five times a week. It depended on what was going on in country. After sixty-five, I just quit counting because it was hard to deal with.

Master Sergeant Gerry Kendle, first sergeant

As first sergeants, we were responsible for working with what we called Patriot Details, which were the repatriation of human remains back to the States. We would have a cordon of honor to the rear of the aircraft when human remains were put on the aircraft, and we had just a short tribute with words from the chaplain. They were always difficult.

Most often we would get several hundred people to line up on either side to the rear of the aircraft, and we would present arms when the remains were taken off the back of the vehicle and walked up to the rear of the aircraft. Sometimes there would be two or three or more sets of remains. While I was there I did eight ceremonies. There were probably twenty or more while I was there.

Despite the dangers and the heartbreak, many of the personnel who deployed to Balad say they're glad they went. In his fifties, Master Sergeant Roy Brake says it was a good way to close out his military career.

Master Sergeant Roy Brake, aerial port specialist

I felt very proud. I felt very scared. This was one of my last hurrahs. I had very mixed feelings, but I'm very, very glad I did it. It's one of those things they can't take from you. The thing that made me scared was just wondering if I could physically do it—being an old guy compared to the young guys. The mortars—getting used to the mortars kind of bothered me. What made me proud was I felt like I was doing something for my country. I was doing something I had been trained to do. What we do here, maybe it's only once a month in peacetime, but what we've learned we put to use.

Ultimately, service members put their skills to use in Iraq to help create a better future for that country. Captain Henry says during one trip outside the base, he saw Iraq's current problems and hints of potential future all in one mission.

Captain Tony Henry, civil engineer

The highest moment was both scary and good at the same time. We went and did a survey mission right outside the fence for a canal they wanted. It was probably two hundred yards from the perimeter fence. I had three of my Air Force guys with me, and the rest were in four Humvees. I had an Army buck sergeant as the lead NCO. I said, "If something goes down, man, just tell us what you need to do because you guys are trained in this better than we are." So I ran the radios and whatnot. We were out there all day. At one point the base took fire. I turned around and the next thing I know, here's two M-1 tanks rolling out, going where the fire was coming from. That was pretty interesting.

But on the good side of that, we went down the road and here's all these little kids. The Iraqi people really want us there—or did at the time. I don't know about now. But we had some kids come up. We had Girl Scout cookies laying up on the dash of the Hummer there. The kids saw them, so we handed out a couple cookies to each one of them. We had some bottled water, so we gave each of them a bottle of water. One of the parents was there.

We went down the road a couple hundred yards or so, and we didn't think anything of it. The next thing I know, here they come over the top of the canal, handing us grapes and watermelons. We did a little exchange there, right outside of Balad.

As "first shirt," Gerry Kendle's job included encouraging, disciplining, and administering enlisted people at Balad and other forward operating bases across Iraq. Imagine working as a human resources director for a company with hundreds of people deployed far from home. In the desert. Getting shot at all the time.

Kendle says he tried to keep his people focused on the reason they were in Iraq.

Master Sergeant Gerry Kendle, first sergeant

We were there during the parliamentary elections and the voting on the Iraqi constitution. Several of the Iraqis showed me their fingers with the dye.

That was a mechanism put into place to limit voting fraud. After a person voted, their finger would get dyed so they couldn't go somewhere else and vote again.

A lot of them would walk around and show you the ink on their fingers to say, "Hey, I voted." That left a very strong impression on me. That made a lot of it worthwhile—hey, we're here for a reason; this is why we're here. It was very important for me to get that word out to the troops, especially the younger airmen, to explain this is why we're here. A new country's growing. This is the first time a lot of these people have ever had a chance to vote in their lives.

If I could go back—well, my wife would kill me. But it was definitely a rewarding experience.

20

HEALERS

He is the best physician who is the most ingenious inspirer of hope.
—Samuel Taylor Coleridge

If you ever run across an Air Force medical officer on flying status, look closely at the center emblem on his or her wings. Flight surgeons' wings feature the ancient physician's symbol of the serpent and staff. Florence Nightingale's lamp appears on flight nurses' wings, symbolizing the responsibilities of the nursing profession. Spreading out from these emblems are the traditional Air Force eagle wings. Wings represent flight, the core mission of the Air Force. And medical wings represent flying the wounded out of harm's way.

Working alongside the nurses and doctors are flight medics, radio operators, and other enlisted technicians who treat and transport sick and injured troops. Our aircrews and medical people served in Iraq, Afghanistan, Pakistan, Uzbekistan, and other locations in a military medical system that spans the globe. A soldier wounded in Iraq or Afghanistan receives initial treatment in country, then might fly to Kuwait or Uzbekistan for further treatment, then go to Germany or the U.S. for long-term care. In all of these locations, doctors, flight nurses, flight medics, and aircrews faced some of the most emotionally draining work demanded in wartime.

Though war was new to most of us, even the youngest medical people had at least some idea of what to expect because of their hospital training. But most of the front-end crews—pilots, navigators, and flight engineers—had never seen much of blood and pain.

Lieutenant Colonel Steve Truax, navigator, operations officer

We took some very badly injured people. I remember the smell of it, the smell of the medications and things. Some had been hit; there was an appendicitis attack; there were some badly injured guys whose Humvee had been hit with an RPG [Rocket-Propelled Grenade]. One guy was deaf; you had to holler into his good ear or he didn't understand what was going on. And one of them flinched every time the airplane hit a bump. As soon as we landed and they got him off the plane, they put more morphine into him.

Captain Brandon Taksa, pilot

I don't have a strong stomach for that stuff. To see it is just not pleasant. We were transporting guys out who were critical. I remember blood. We were hauling guys out from Baghdad when Baghdad was still being overtaken. There were quadrants of Baghdad that had some stronger resistance and there was fighting going on. It was a particularly bad time. We hauled some of the guys out. I remember them just being quiet, eerily quiet, lying on their litters. A lot of blood.

When wounded troops get moved, aeromedical crews watch over them in flight. The flight nurses and flight medics, also known as "aeromeds," monitor their vital signs, administer anesthetics and, when necessary, render emergency treatment. Aeromeds also have ground assignments, prepping patients for flight or receiving them on the other end. Most aeromeds are guardsmen or reservists; of the Air Force's thirty-one aeromed squadrons, only four are active duty.

In October of 2001, Lieutenant Colonel Sandie Duiker went to Incirlik Air Base, Turkey, to head up aeromedical operations for troops wounded in Afghanistan. If you don't think a hundred-pound woman in her fifties can exude command presence, you haven't met Sandie Duiker. When you speak with her about her work, two things come to mind: "This woman knows exactly what she's talking about." And "If I ever get hurt, I want her there."

She explains how she had to coordinate nurses, medics, and flight crews, often with little guidance from higher headquarters.

Lieutenant Colonel Sandie Duiker, flight nurse

When I called to ask Air Mobility Command what they expected of me, they said, "Your equipment and your people will be there awaiting you."

Right.

Got there and my equipment was my personal laptop, nine sheets of paper, and my own printer.

I stayed up all night, called AMC headquarters and said, "Gee, I'm here; you assigned me by name. Where is the con ops?" [Concept of Operations, the game plan, the script]

There was this long pause. Then they said, "Well, execution is six weeks ahead of planning." I said a very unladylike word and hung up the phone. So I was really on my own.

It was the Wild West and cowboy country. You did the best you knew how to get the mission accomplished, and obviously you didn't do things that would break regulations, but at that initial stage you went by the seat of your pants.

Lieutenant Colonel Duiker describes the challenge of getting cooperation out of groups of people who had not worked together before.

I had a number of people, to include C-141 crews, C-9 crews, and a crew management cell. There were also active-duty aeromeds in the theater already at Kandahar and Bagram.

So it was a bit of a challenge. We worked out of the lobby at billeting until we could find a place to meet. I could already see these little attitudes— well, I'm guard and you're reserve and you're active duty. They didn't play well with others. The bottom line is I got 'em all together and told them, "This is not acceptable. We're all wearing blue, we all got a single job, and we're going to do it, and God help you if I hear you're causing problems."

That being said, I had a good team. They just needed some ground rules to know how to behave.

Lieutenant Colonel Duiker eventually relocated from Turkey to run aeromed missions out of Uzbekistan. Operating from Karshi Kanabad Air Base, the aeromed crews would move patients from one location to another in Afghanistan, or out of the theater altogether. She describes treating patients during Operation Anaconda, an effort to encircle Taliban and al Qaeda fighters in a remote location in Afghanistan.

I was there for Anaconda. In fact, my number three son [Sergeant First Class Ben Duiker, light infantryman] was one of the Tenth Mountain Division that was in the caves and doing things, which made it a bit stressful. I really didn't want to look at the names we were pulling out.

He did fine. Managed to meet him for about a minute and a half in Kandahar while I was doing an air evac mission. He came home in good shape, for which I'm thankful.

In Afghanistan we moved a lot of children. I don't know if anybody knows that. We did a lot of kids that were burned, kids that got hurt by makeshift bombs. Firefights, the Taliban tearing up villages, just kids being in the wrong place at the wrong time. And they had lived all of their very short lives like this. For us it was a culture shock; for them it was business as usual.

Because they were Afghanis, they couldn't be moved out of the country. But we were responsible for moving them; Kandahar was a hellacious place. So we'd move these kids from there to Bagram.

Bagram had a Combat Support Hospital, or CSH [pronounced "cash"], as the Army calls it. They would take care of these kids—and adults. And then

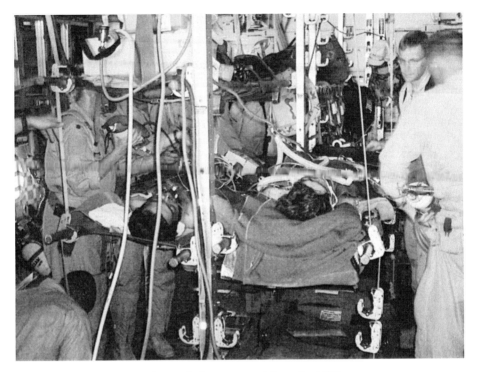

An aeromedical team that includes personnel from the 167th prepares to transport two wounded Afghans in the back of a C-130 rigged for medical evacuation (courtesy Chief Master Sergeant Harry "Bud" Martz).

we had to move them, once they were stabilized, back to Kandahar to send them home. Obviously you aren't going to fill up the Army CSH with foreign nationals to the detriment of the care of the Coalition. So it was a fine line to get those people the best care you could and then move them.

And little kids—when I got back to Turkey, there was a kid in the passenger terminal, and that kid laughed. It was one of those things that just turns you around because I hadn't heard a kid laugh or smile or do anything like that for so long. You didn't even realize you hadn't seen it, but you sure did notice it when you heard a kid laugh.

During this assignment in Uzbekistan, Lieutenant Colonel Duiker and her people treated a civilian journalist wounded in Afghanistan.

There was a Canadian news unit; a lady was the reporter. It was a husband-wife team; I don't know the husband's job.

They were driving along and someone tossed a grenade into their car, and it did significant damage to the lady. It probably doesn't sound very complimentary, but the lady was rather hefty and that's what saved her life.

The grenade did great damage to her buttocks and thigh and took a lot of tissue and destroyed a lot of things. But it didn't get major organs because she was well padded.

When they brought her in by chopper to us, essentially the lady was dead. She had no vital signs, and my team worked like dogs and they got that lady revived. They got her into surgery and did a great amount of tissue debridement and brought her back. [Tissue debridement is the removal of tissue that cannot be saved.]

I just found it very interesting. Here was a civilian, which caused all kinds of State Department issues getting her out. That was very remarkable: someone was dead when she was brought to the pad, and the people in the air evac made sure she lived.

I asked Lieutenant Colonel Duiker about how combat shows both the strength and fragility of the human body.

What you probably saw the greatest of was the strength. People who should have been dead, who should have just given up and been gone, took great strength from their teammates or comrades-in-arms and survived.

Duiker says she witnessed inspiring dedication—including that of a rescue medic who became one of the heroes of the Afghanistan war.

You saw people do their job—Jason Cunningham was a PJ [Pararescue Jumper, not from our Air Guard unit]. I can't say he was a friend of mine, but he was somebody I knew there at Uzbek. He was lost because he got into a firefight. He was shot up seriously. The man was a medic; he knew he was shot badly. Ultimately he was lost because he bled out.

He was an unassuming young gentleman. Just like one of the boys your kids grow up with. Being an old lady, most of these guys looked like kids to me. Just a very unassuming, pleasant young gentleman.

Senior Airman Jason Cunningham posthumously received the Air Force Cross for his actions March 4, 2002, in the Battle of Roberts Ridge in Afghanistan. The citation accompanying Cunningham's medal reads, in part, "In a display of uncommon valor and gallantry, Airman Cunningham braved an intense small arms fire and rocket-propelled grenade attack while repositioning the critically wounded to a ... collection point. Even after he was mortally wounded and quickly deteriorating, he continued to direct patient movement and transferred care to another medic. In the end, his distinct efforts led to the successful delivery of ten gravely wounded Americans to life-saving treatment."

Lieutenant Colonel Andy Wolkstein commanded a Mobile Aeromedical Staging Facility at Baghdad International Airport for several months in 2003. During this time, the MASF personnel handled not only American troops who were wounded, but also the civilian victims of several terrorist bombings.

On August 7, attackers bombed the Jordanian Embassy in Baghdad, killing at least fourteen people. On August 19, a bombing hit the U.N. headquarters in Iraq, killing at least twenty-two people including the top U.N. representative, Sergio Vieira de Mello. On October 27, a car bombing at Red Cross headquarters killed a dozen people.

On each occasion, 167th flight nurses and medics treated some of the survivors.

Lieutenant Colonel Andy Wolkstein, flight nurse

We operated twenty-four hours a day, seven days a week. Most of my personnel were on nights because the patients were on nights, but sometimes the planes would have a day flight. If there were any patients left over from the night, we would take care of them and get them ready to fly out during the daytime. During the day we'd clean up from the previous night mission and get everything ready to be available because we never knew when there would be a mass casualty.

Our patients were supposed to go to another facility before us. We were just a holding area. A MASF is like a passenger terminal for patients. So these patients were already being treated by the Army's Combat Support Hospital or the Air Force's Expeditionary Medical Squadron [E-MEDS].

The patients would come in. We would make sure they were taken care of for pain medications, make sure their IVs were flowing properly, make sure their vital signs were stable. And then we would wait for the plane.

Once the plane landed, we would talk to the medical crew director for that plane, tell them what kind of a patient load they would have. Then we would load the patients on Humvees and take them over to the plane and load the plane up.

We had a couple of bombing incidents. We were there during the U.N. bombing. We were there during the Red Cross bombing. When the helicopters came in, we would be the first medical group to meet the helicopters and offload the patients.

What would happen during a mass casualty is that the bomb would go off, and then of course the first responders would get there and call for medevac. Helicopters—the Black Hawks—or ambulances would take the casualties to the closest facility.

Well, after a while the closest facility to your mass casualty can take only so many. You'd have twenty or thirty patients, and they could handle only two or three or maybe five at a time. So the Black Hawks would then take the patients to different areas. The helicopters would come. Even before we knew anything was happening unless we saw it on CNN, a Black Hawk would be incoming. And then we would go out and greet the medevac with our Humvee,

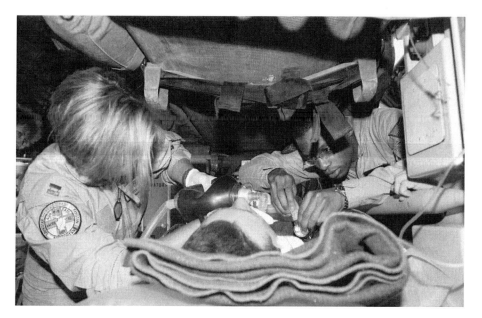

Aeromeds prep an Army Special Forces soldier to fly from Afghanistan to Germany in April 2003. This patient took gunshot wounds to his right side and right hand, and another round grazed his head. Despite a punctured lung, a perforated diaphragm, and a destroyed kidney, he survived. Two of his teammates died in the ambush, and they traveled to Germany with him on the same plane, in flag-draped transfer cases (U.S. Army photograph).

Loadmasters tie down transfer cases containing the bodies of an Army Special Forces soldier and an Air Force tactical air controller killed in an ambush in Afghanistan. The two fallen servicemen traveled from Afghanistan to Germany in the same aircraft as their wounded teammate (U.S. Army photograph).

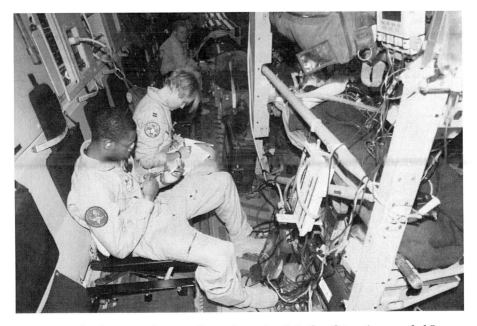

Aeromedical personnel wrap up last-minute details before flying the wounded Special Forces soldier out of Afghanistan. Note the tubes and wires of medical monitoring equipment. Badly wounded troops can be flown out of combat zones while still in intensive care (U.S. Army photograph).

offload the patient, and if it was a patient that had not been seen at any facility, we would take them to E-MEDS immediately. E-MEDS was only about two minutes away from the flight line.

E-MEDS would stabilize them and take them to surgery if they needed surgery for amputations or whatever, or take them to the critical care area of E-MEDS. In E-MEDS they could stay overnight or weeks at a time if they had to.

One time there was a military intel sleeping tent that got mortared, and two people were killed and thirty were injured. The night shift at the MASF, all they heard was "medevac incoming." The flight medics went out to the medevac not knowing what to expect, and they found these were seriously wounded Army personnel.

Staff Sergeant Kerri Faller, flight medic

We opened up the side door of the helicopter, and it was just blood everywhere because they had a mass casualty. There was a mortar that hit a sleeping tent. Four guys were brought to us, and a couple of them were already dead when they came off. When you don't know what's coming and you open the door and you see all these people, that's pretty startling.

Flight medics like Kerri are enlisted personnel with extensive medical training. Their skills make them approximately the military equivalent of a Licensed Practical Nurse, and they receive an Emergency Medical Technician certification that's recognized nationwide. Their flight training covers aviation physiology—for example, how patients with certain wounds or illnesses will react to reduced cabin pressure. They work with doctors and flight nurses to prepare the wounded for transport and care for them in flight.

Flight medic Scott Holcomb, like Kerri Faller, worked at the Baghdad MASF. He recalls the attack on the United Nations facility.

Technical Sergeant Scott Holcomb, flight medic

I remember with the U.N. bombing it was weird because I went into the MWR [Morale, Welfare, and Recreation] tent to work out. As I walked past the movie tent, they had CNN on. It said there was an explosion. It didn't even dawn on me we would get tasked for that. I was working out, and my medical crew director came and grabbed me right about fifteen minutes after the headlines were on the news. Said, "Come on, we gotta go." We sent four or five planes up right away that day to evacuate the patients.

With the U.N. bombing there were a couple people with broken necks, and there was one guy, I don't think he was in the actual bombing, but he was in a Humvee accident or something. A piece of the windshield came through underneath his chin and up into his eye and blew his eye out. He was on a ventilator and they had a CCAT team with him. [A CCAT, or Critical Care Air Transport Team, consists of a physician, a critical-care nurse, and a cardiopulmonary technician. The team operates what amounts to an airborne intensive care unit.]

One of the other guys in the U.N. bombing had the whole side of his head flattened. He had sutures and stuff and he kept trying to grab his head. I asked my medical crew director if I could somehow restrain his arms because he was pulling at everything, and she wouldn't let me. Sure enough, the minute we turn around to help load patients, he's got his IV out, and he's got everything off his head. Looking at his wound, I don't see how he couldn't have severe brain damage.

Staff Sergeant Kerri Faller, flight medic

One of the hard ones was a big Marine who was, I think, thirty-five or thirty-six. Had three kids at home. His wife was a stay-at-home mom. All his life he's been this invincible Marine, and he had a double amputation of his arms. Both his arms were gone and one of his legs was gone.

He's laying there crying and sobbing, saying, "Who's going to take care of my kids? Who's going to take care of my wife?" He's crying and he realizes he can't even wipe his own tears.

That was hard for me. All those guys who were in such agony and pain and had some kind of dismemberment were looking for you to say the right thing and make it all better. And there's nothing you can do. You can just try to listen and be supportive, but other than that there's nothing you can do.

That was harder for me than seeing the actual injuries. We got some mass casualties, and as startling as that is, the emotional side was harder for me.

Master Sergeant Bob Phillips, an aeromed supervisor, looks like a senior NCO from Hollywood central casting. Gray hair, square jaw, straight talk. He calls anyone younger than himself, enlisted or officers, "the children." His patients are "customers."

When I visited him in his office, he showed me a black-and-white photo of himself taken in Vietnam in 1966, during his Navy days. A younger, bearded Phillips wearing a boonie hat leaned on an M-60 machine gun aboard a gunboat. Then he showed me a color photo of himself behind the same type weapon, posing on an Army vehicle in Iraq. Clean-shaven this time, he looked a little older but just as strong, with his ever-present K-BAR knife on his web belt.

Phillips describes his work with Lieutenant Colonel Wolkstein and the flight medics in Baghdad.

Master Sergeant Bob Phillips, flight medic

We were serving sixteen hundred a month through our facility—wounded, psychological and physical. Some were really badly torn up; some were just mildly wounded. We took care of the Jordanians when their embassy got hit, and we took care of the U.N. personnel when their place got hit. Took care of the personnel in the raw, you might say, when they had an incident at the Army firing range and when the prison got hit.

I use the word "in the raw." Normally we got all our patients from the CSHs, the Combat Support Hospitals with the Army, and they were already prepped and prepared. On those two incidents, they were not. Unfortunately, one of them didn't survive that came through us.

We worked hand-in-hand with E-MEDS on the post. We filled up their facility very quickly. Got them shipped off to safety.

We'd just go out and greet the helicopter and fall into what we knew we had to do, whether it would be continue to provide air, reset the dressings to keep them from bleeding out, whatever was necessary.

On occasion we would go out and give the chopper pilots and the crews cold water. They were very appreciative of that. I found out later the flying they were doing was very dehydrating, even though they weren't at high altitude.

I spent nineteen months in the jungle in Vietnam. I didn't see anything at Baghdad I hadn't seen before. For me, my biggest thing was worrying about the children, those who were quite younger than myself. Those who hadn't been afield and didn't know what they were looking at. Didn't know what they were dealing with. It's a bit of difference from an emergency room or a civilian emergency helicopter to what we were facing in Baghdad.

Bob explains that his experience in Vietnam made him a mentor to other health care providers. He also knows how to shortcut bureaucracy to make medical supplies appear where they're needed.

I consider that part of my job, the mentoring, taking care of the personnel, making sure they have what they need, finding what they need. After this many years, most of my officers know better than to ask where things came from.

Some of the officers had never been afield, had never seen these things. Some of the children—we had to sit down and talk to them when they saw some of the customers coming in younger than they were. They were dealing with things like helping the fire department clean blood out of helicopters or the back of a Humvee.

As a whole, we seemed to maintain morale without lows sneaking in there. I tried to keep that from happening. I can't expect anybody to do their job taking care of a customer if they can't take care of themselves. We tried heading it off before it got that far.

Some of them took it rather stoically. Some, as I mentioned, because the soldiers coming were younger than they were, were bothered a little bit. The usual stuff of seeing what people can do to other people bothered them somewhat.

A situation came up a number of times where the patient would talk to one of our children with the attitude of, "You weren't there, how the hell do you know, don't talk to me." I told them if that happens, come see me.

I would wander in, and I would sit down and say hello. He'd start the same spiel and I'd just cut him off and say, "I spent nineteen months in Vietnam. Now, what do you want to talk about?"

After Lieutenant Colonel Sandie Duiker's deployment to Uzbekistan, she took another assignment, this time to Jacobabad, Pakistan. Medical crews based there normally handled stabilized patients who had been wounded in Afghanistan. But on one occasion, the war on terror came straight to their camp.

Lieutenant Colonel Sandie Duiker, flight nurse

We were sitting around the office, and we had just walked in after having our twenty-seventh straight meal of chicken and rice because that's all there was to eat. I swore I was going to stand up when the sun came up and crow after eating all that chicken.

Heard a chopper coming into the flight line and that was unusual. So I kind of drifted to the door. Didn't stand out and make a target of myself, but I drifted to the door. It was a Pakistani chopper and it was coming down right from the tower. Very obviously, something was wrong.

We took the Humvee out because we could see there were people coming in, and when we got the Humvee there they started putting people on the back of it. They had been thoroughly shot up. They were PJs [Pararescue Jumpers] we knew and that added to the emotional stress.

By the grace of God, we had gotten one of these CCAT [Critical Care Air Transport] teams into our location. Many of the higher-ups laughed at us when we requested the CCAT team, and we said, "You don't understand—there are many other things going on besides Baghdad. Don't short us."

Anyway, long story short, we grabbed the CCAT people. They were at chow, so we had to run and bring them. Brought them to the E-MEDS. The E-MEDS was just a little place. They had a family practitioner as their physician. They had a veterinary and several medical technicians, but they were not set up for this—chest tubes, major trauma care. Within thirty minutes from the time that chopper sat down, we had them stabilized enough.

We weren't supposed to use the PJ aircraft at Jacobabad. That C-130 was supposed to be doing other things. But we pirate airlined it and they were ready to go. After all, it was their people. Got those people on board, got the aeromed crew, and those three men lived.

I guarantee you if they hadn't been delivered to us as fast as they had and if the CCAT had not been on site and if the aeromeds hadn't configured that plane and got ready to rock and roll in less than thirty minutes, we wouldn't have saved them.

The pararescuemen were wounded over Pakistan while on board a Pakistani helicopter.

Yes, this was kind of interesting and caused some serious diplomatic discussions. Jacobabad was a Pakistani air base and we were guests there. The Pakistani forces and our PJs had been doing some training. There was a little nondescript village on a little bluff; they did a fly-by, and there were two or three villagers out there. Came around and did another pass, lower this time with the back end of the aircraft open. The Americans were standing in the aircraft, and the personnel on the ground opened up. I assumed it was AK-47 fire; there were multiple holes.

Chief Master Sergeant Harry "Bud" Martz, flight medic

The PJs went out on a rappelling kind of thing. It was supposed to be a simple little training exercise and they got ambushed. They got all shot up. The Pakistani helicopter just made it back to where we were in Pakistan. They had come in from near the Afghan border where they got hammered.

We had an E-MEDS in Pakistan, but it was just a small thing with a doc, a nurse, and a couple of med techs. They would have been totally overwhelmed with these PJs that got shot up if it hadn't been for the CCAT team. The E-MEDS doc said if he hadn't had the assistance of the CCAT team, chances are those PJs wouldn't have made it.

They were hovering, doing a rappelling kind of thing, from what I understand. They were zooming around and when they stopped to hover, that's when they got hit.

When troops get wounded in the field, an on-scene medic or Combat Lifesaver usually provides the first treatment. Then a medevac helicopter flies them to a Combat Support Hospital or Air Force Theater Hospital for more extensive care. If necessary, the wounded continue to travel farther from the combat zone to a major hospital, such as Landstuhl Regional Medical Center in Germany. All these transfers can happen as quickly as one day, under the care of flight nurses and flight medics. When the patients travel to a major facility, they go through a CASF, or Contingency Aeromedical Staging Facility.

Lieutenant Colonel David Porter is chairman of the department of pathology at Marshall University School of Medicine, and he's a physician with the 167th Airlift Wing. As a flight surgeon, he monitors the health of flight crews, gives us our physicals, and puts up with our lousy jokes. But in the first half of 2004, he served as senior flight surgeon at a CASF at Ramstein Air Base, Germany, receiving troops wounded in Iraq. Most of these wounded were on their way to the nearby Landstuhl hospital.

Lieutenant Colonel David Porter, flight surgeon

During Vietnam and post–Vietnam in the Cold War, the whole scenario was to move medicine forward as much as possible, to have field hospitals set up near the front lines, as you remember the MASH hospitals. As we've transitioned to the way care is given now, we evacuate the wounded back to a facility, perform surgery, stabilize them, and immediately move them clear out of theater way back to Landstuhl or some other major medical center.

We were getting people who were injured, operated on, and received in Ramstein within forty-eight hours. We would receive those who didn't need surgery, say a burn victim, within twenty-four hours.

The ability to move those patients immediately after surgery has become quite an art. We would get patients straight out of surgery, say in Balad, where they'd been operated on, still on respirators, still in need of intensive treatment. Oxygen respirators, suction pumps, IV pumps, all of that can be mounted on a typical field stretcher and carried by four men. So they would mount all this equipment with a patient and load him on a C-141 with an intensivist to monitor him during the flight. They'd move him halfway around the world while he was under critical care, right out of an operating room, right into another intensive care thousands of miles away, and never miss a beat. That is a phenomenal step—very, very impressive to watch. Some of these patients were very seriously critically ill and would never have made it out of theater as recently as ten or twelve years ago.

It was a very tough time because I don't think I'd worked that hard since I was an intern. During Fallujah we were getting approximately eighty sick and wounded a day, and each one of those patients was litter moved up to four times. And then we had planes leaving, so we would be receiving eighty and moving eighty on any given day and moving each one of those a couple times each day. It was very, very busy. We went long hours without sleep, and then, of course, we had the emotional trauma of dealing with some severely traumatized war injuries.

But yet, the bright side was the quality of the young soldier. Here you had a lot of soldiers who were losing eyesight in one eye or losing a limb or being disfigured in some manner, and yet they were very upbeat, very proud, and basically more upset about having to leave their buddies than they were about their own injuries. So I was very impressed with the character of the American soldier that came out of there.

The most common wounds were the Improvised Explosive Device injuries, and these were shrapnel wounds. A trend that we saw was leg, arm, and head injuries because of the use of body armor. We saw a lot of eye injuries because eyes were exposed. We saw a lot of wounds to the arms, and amazingly, we saw a lot of rifle or gunshot wounds to the thigh for some reason. I don't know why. But there were a lot of eye injuries and a lot of extremity injuries because body armor was protecting the torso. We saw some burns, as well.

[Some reports say insurgents target soldiers' thighs because body armor doesn't cover thighs, and a bullet through the thigh can cut the femoral artery.]

I think the body armor is protecting them from the isolated wound. The ones that are not surviving are probably head injuries and massive wounds, massive explosive injuries in which the body armor doesn't protect them.

You saw some guys come through with some really horrible injuries, such as a young man who was paralyzed from the waist down, but yet had a phenomenal attitude about life. At the same time you had those who really hadn't suffered a lot of trauma and probably hadn't even seen a lot of trauma, but just from the exposure of being away from home and so forth, suffered severe emotional and mental difficulty. That's not to say they weren't strong individuals; it was just how that affected them as opposed to someone else.

Then you would see some people come who had absolutely remarkable pain tolerance—massive injuries and phenomenal pain tolerance and others who had small injuries with a lot of pain. So everybody's different.

There were a lot of emotional and psychological problems coming out of the desert. It's very emotionally tough to be away from home, in a new environment, especially in 130 degree temperatures, living in the dirt with no facilities and so forth. So there was a lot of that.

I think the majority of it was just severe depression. But yet you had others who had, basically, clear psychotic breaks—loss of touch with reality. There were several episodes of soldiers who got up and armed themselves and had no idea whether they were amongst friends or enemies and clearly had a break with reality. But I think the most common thing was just depression to the point that they could no longer function, and they became a danger to themselves and others because they could not concentrate on the task at hand.

Dr. Porter recalls the look on the face of a wounded soldier when he realized he was finally out of harm's way.

One of the most emotional times that I had was during Fallujah when we were getting so many soldiers in and out of there. The first thing we did when the C-141s landed with rows of stretcher patients was to walk the rows and make sure that nobody was in acute distress, nobody was suffering from uncontrollable pain.

We usually just commented, "Welcome to Germany," or whatever. And I looked down at this one kid who was on the bottom row, and you could just tell the kid was still afraid, still afraid of his wounds, where he was going or where he had been, and what was happening. I looked down to him and said, "Welcome to Germany, soldier." And his face just instantly changed. You could just see the relief for this kid. He was now in a definitive health care environment outside the confines of Iraq, and you could just see the relief instantaneously, and I'll never forget that reaction. Of course, that was repeated many times, but the first time that happened, it was very impressive.

Dr. Porter explains that his time at the CASF in Germany was like nothing he'd encountered in civilian medicine.

The emotional trauma of seeing large numbers of wounded soldiers every single day begins to wear on the health care provider. I've been in medicine for thirty-something years and have dealt with a lot of trauma. But usually in the civilian world, you get a trauma and then you get a break. You get another trauma and then you get a break. But in this instance you just had trauma upon trauma upon trauma and large numbers of it, and there was never a day without it. Over a period of time, that begins to wear on even the strongest health care provider. When I came back I was a different person than when I went over.

I think when I came back, a lot of people noticed I was a lot quieter and quick to anger. I had a very short fuse for about two or three months. A lot of people just seemed to have a shorter fuse, a lot quieter, a lot more introverted when they came back. But then, with the other guys as well as myself, we all commented that after another two or three months, you just kind of gradually went back to your old self. The bad moments became distant memories.

Though medical missions can be exhausting and emotionally draining, those who take part in them often look back on them with a sense of accomplishment. Pilot Shaun Perkowski recalls those missions as the most fulfilling flights of his career.

Lieutenant Colonel Shaun Perkowski, pilot

I've carried generals and congressmen. I carried Sandra Day O'Connor on a 737 out of Hartford into D.C. That's all important stuff, but when you take injured people who are fighting the war and you get them out safely, you complete the mission, you do it well, you do it on time, that's the greatest satisfaction. When you're helping folks who need help and you're using every skill you've got, that was the most satisfaction I felt over there.

Flight medic Kerri Faller says the gratitude of the patients made it easier to handle the hardships of her deployment. Faller had recently completed a lot of medical training, and she says her war experience brought the big picture sharply into focus.

Staff Sergeant Kerri Faller, flight medic

One thing that was surprising to me when they came into the MASF was they kept saying, "You guys are so nice." We didn't wear our fatigue overshirts, and you never knew who was an officer and who was enlisted. A lot of the officers would walk up to the patients and say, "Just call me Jason; just call me by my first name."

We didn't really use official titles. It's kind of like, they've done their job and they're now in pain. They're away from their real family; they're away from their military family. You just kind of got into what you had to do to comfort them.

As hard as it was being over there, the best time I've had in the Guard was being deployed because you feel like you have a purpose. You know, all this training, everything you're learning, and all the schools you go to count for something. There's actually a reason why you go through all this. You get there and you see their faces, and they're so happy that someone's kind to them and someone's willing to help them. It was worth it to me.

21

ARABIAN NIGHTS

No current obstacle data. Engine running offload not permitted during sand storms.... Exercise extreme caution when landing/taking off Runway 15R/33L due to ... bomb damage crater repair.
—From the Airport/Facility Directory,
Baghdad International Airport

Quick scan of the panels now. Fifteen thousand feet and descending at 2,000 feet per minute. Airspeed 260 knots. Oil pressures and temperatures good. Antiaircraft missile countermeasures on AUTO. The tiny green light on your helmet microphone illuminates your watch; it's 0200.

A flash on the ground, just in the corner of your eye. Grenade? Car bomb? No time to think about it.

The Combat Entry checklist is done, but you touch the external light switches again anyway. Dear God, you don't want to get shot down because you're so tired you left a strobe on.

You're too busy to get scared, but your mouth is dry. It's the air in these planes. Just another night in Iraq.

Major Mike Foley, navigator

I remember seeing things burning. Buildings burning and with the night vision goggles, you could see it for miles and miles away. You could tell where the war was being fought because you could see the explosions.

I also remember just being real careful. We had corridors to fly and I had to make sure we were doing that right. If you get too far off the corridor, you're considered an item of interest to both the friendlies and the enemy. You don't want everybody looking at you. Stay where you belong and the friendlies leave you alone.

A C-130 from the 167th as seen through night vision goggles. NVGs turn night into broad daylight, as if viewed through dark green sunglasses (courtesy the 167th Airlift Wing).

Chief Master Sergeant Billy Gillenwater, flight engineer

In those environments, anything could have happened. The places we went, as low as we flew and the places we got into, you never knew when the Bedouin guy was going to pull out his SA-7 missile.

You could have crashed in the desert and ended up being *The Flight of the Phoenix* all over again. I tried to think about all those things. It's not that I was trying to get myself scared or excited, but I just really wanted to be prepared so when it does happen, I've already thought about it.

No matter how much you prepare, in a combat environment, something will surprise you. It happened to loadmaster Dave Twigg on departure from Balad Air Base.

Master Sergeant Dave Twigg, loadmaster

We had about forty-five or fifty ground troops with their baggage pallet and a smaller pallet with their equipment. We were taking them to Balad. We landed at Balad; we got turned around and offloaded the troops. We onloaded about twenty people and some aircraft parts.

When we took off out of Balad, the sun had just started coming up, and I was sitting in the right door with the pistol grip in my hand to launch chaff and flares if needed. [Loadmasters scan for missiles or other threats, and they can fire countermeasures to help decoy antiaircraft missiles away from the airplane.]

We had just broke ground and we were climbing through about 600 or 700 feet, and the pilot started a right turn on departure to pick up our course back to Kuwait. About the time he started this turn, I was sitting in the right-hand door with my nose about four or five inches from the glass, and the outside pane of glass cracked right through the middle, forward to aft. The sound was like a gun went off right in my ear.

When that thing popped, I came out of my seat at the door. I don't know to this day what kept me from launching flares with that pistol grip in my hand, but I dropped the pistol grip. I came out of the door. In the blink of an eye I was standing forward of the troop doors with my comm button in my hand, and the first thing I yelled was, "Holy shit!"

About the time I yelled, Dougie Hilliard was sitting up in the engineer's seat, and we had a TIT rollback on number three [Turbine Inlet Temperature rollback, an indication of a possible engine failure]. They had a real engine problem to look at, and I came out of the door, hollering on interphone.

I looked to my left and there was this sergeant first class Army guy sitting there, and all I saw of him was the whites of his eyes. They were as big as teacups. He saw me come out of the seat, and when he saw that, everybody else looked at me. I was standing there, my chest heaving, out of breath. Of course when I yelled into the interphone I must have yelled loud enough for the people around me in the troop seats to hear me because they all looked at me.

When I looked back at John Cox [another loadmaster], he was doubled over in his seat, laughing at me.

The rest of the crew kind of prioritized things. They didn't know what had happened in the back when I came out of the seat and yelled. So the aircraft commander, Jim Powell, said real quick, "What's going on back there?"

I said, "The paratroop door window just shattered in my face. It scared the hell out of me."

He said, "All right, you're OK. We got to deal with this engine problem now."

I don't know what the deal with the number three engine was, but the turbine inlet temperature rolled back, and then it came right back to where it was within limits. So we pressed on; we climbed out and headed back to Kuwait City.

As pilot Brandon Taksa relates, the strangest cargo could show up in your airplane.

Captain Brandon Taksa, pilot

One of the missions we flew into Baghdad was cash in small bills. The country was extremely unstable, and we were pumping a lot of cash into the country to try and stabilize it.

Thirty million dollars in small bills. It seems to me it was three or four pallets of cash. What's the size of a pallet? Ten by ten feet on the floor, six feet tall, all cash. And we weren't the only ones doing it. There were other airplanes flying that same amount of cash in. I think it was to pay Iraqi workers, to help stabilize their economy.

I think most of us have a souvenir of the Iraqi money. It had a picture of Saddam on it. Worthless. One of the basic needs of society is a way to trade, and we just brought in our money.

And then, sometimes NO cargo would show up in your airplane. Due to the inevitable miscommunications of war, crews would occasionally arrive at airfields to find nothing to carry. Fliers call it "hauling sailboat fuel" when they have nothing in the cargo compartment but air.

Technical Sergeant Kenny LaFollette, flight engineer

A lot of times you would get to a certain location and offload cargo, and you'd be waiting and waiting for outgoing cargo, and they'd come out and tell you they had nothing. You'd take off and continue your mission to another airfield. You'd land and they'd have nothing for you. You weren't accomplishing anything that night. When you were empty, it was rather depressing.

Master Sergeant John "Ratman" Ratcliffe, loadmaster

What was funny was carrying sailboat fuel, as we called it. We'd get a mission, for example, "You gotta go to Thumrait." [An air base in Oman.]

I'd call them up, "What do you guys have for us there?"

"Nothing."

Well, we gotta fly it anyway. Air Mobility says we gotta fly it.

We'd say, "Hey, we're going to get sailboat fuel." We hauled a lot of that. That just boggled me.

Master Sergeant Les Morris, loadmaster

Our crew got to haul five senators. That was pretty cool because I got one-on-one time with U.S. senators, and they were real nice to talk to. I was talking to them face-to-face. They asked me my own personal opinions of what was going on and what could be helped and what things were going right. I got to voice my opinion and I thought that was a real cool thing.

They asked a lot about morale. Are things getting done in a timely manner? Personal stuff like, are you getting your mail, are you getting to contact home? There was a lot about the military, too, like how the C-130 works, and how the operations work, and how much do you fly, where do you go? I showed them all the night vision goggle stuff and the capabilities of our aircraft. They got a thrill out of that. Most of them had seen NVGs, but they hadn't got to fly with them.

Senior Master Sergeant Roland Shambaugh, loadmaster

When the ground war was going on, we were doing the live stuff, flying low and fast. I remember the first time we went into Tallil, I had twenty-five thousand pounds of Meals Ready to Eat.

On another mission we hauled out half a company of the Third Infantry Division, and these guys had been in the fighting that took the airport. There were about forty-seven of them and they were coming back to Kuwait City to catch a plane home. They'd been there almost a year. The Third ID's dear to my heart because my dad served in it back during the Korean War.

One particular young guy had a sniper rifle, and he looked like he was about eighteen or nineteen years old. He had notches cut in the stock of his rifle, and he was just as proud as a peacock of the contribution he'd made.

The day we went into Baghdad and brought these guys out, they had live grenades hanging off their web gear and they had live magazines in their weapons. They were all excited to come home, and I said, "Whoa, whoa, you guys can't get on the airplane with live fragmentation grenades and loaded rifles." They brought a big barrel out and they filled it with grenades and live rounds.

I recall them talking about how they thought some of the enemy troops might have been hopped up on PCP or some other kind of drug. They said in some instances it took several rounds to put them down.

I remember the looks on their faces. Most of the guys were young; they looked like they weren't old enough to use a razor on their faces. Their attitudes were generally good. They all believed in the cause.

During the first several months of 2006, an intelligence specialist from the 167th volunteered to fly with the Nevada Air Guard. Staff Sergeant Tony Dunnigan worked as a sensor operator on C-130s equipped with the Scathe View advanced surveillance system. Scathe View provides optical and infrared imagery to units on the ground, giving commanders and troops a bird's eye view of what's around them.

Tony likens the mission to that of the unmanned Predator reconnaissance drone, except the C-130 crew can more quickly move to different targets as priorities change on the battlefield.

Staff Sergeant Tony Dunnigan, intelligence specialist

We were supporting the guys on the ground. This program was supplementing the Predator with a manned aircrew up in the air. We were retaskable, a little bit more than the Predator at the time.

I was an equipment operator in the back. We operated the FLIR [Forward-Looking Infrared] and also manned the radios. We could talk to the guys on the ground or other aircraft in the area.

The most fulfilling part of the mission was to help the guys on the ground, like convoys. Looking at places or buildings or whatnot to make sure nobody was going to jump them. We'd keep an eye on them and make sure everything was kosher in the area around them. If something came up, we could say, "Hey, check this out. It looks like something's coming your way." There were a few times when we saw something that was kind of out of the norm, and we called it in.

We were tasked to watch over our guys and the Coalition partners. They were very appreciative of us. They said it felt great to know there was somebody there to talk to and also to look down on them.

You were able to make out what was happening on the ground, but not in explicit detail because most of the stuff was at night. You were able to tell what was going on. With the equipment we were using we could see the flashes of gunfire. That's how we were able to discern the direction of fire. Knowing the location of our guys and knowing the location of the bad guys, we were able to say, "OK, that's not friendly fire. You need to pay attention to this area here."

World War II aviators tell stories of flying when they were so tired they'd crush a cigarette and put tobacco in one eye so the pain would keep them awake. Fewer of us smoke now, but on those long night missions, one might see crew members slapping themselves or biting their lips in a losing battle against fatigue.

Flying through half the day and all the night might make tactical sense, but it hurts like hell. The rules said maximum flight duty period was sixteen hours. And that could be waived.

Master Sergeant Doug Ferrell, loadmaster

You're very nervous. You're very scared, and you don't know what's going to happen. It may not be a missile that gets you. It could be crew fatigue that crashes the airplane because we were all tired. It was long days; it was hard days. A lot of times you'd be praying, "Please, just get me home."

Lieutenant Colonel Mike McMillie, navigator

The low moments were coming back from missions, having flown a mission into the northern portion of Iraq, coming back through Kuwait to get some gas, and you're just dog tired because you've been at it for sixteen hours or whatever the case might be. You're halfway across the Persian Gulf and the sun's coming up, and you're absolutely tired as can be.

You're thinking, "I just don't have the discipline I need because I'm just so tired." Very, very depressing.

Lieutenant Colonel Shaun Perkowski, pilot

When you get fatigued is when you start making mistakes. I've never seen fatigue called causal in an accident, but your judgment is affected when you get fatigued. I was always really cognizant of how long our day was going. It was always toughest when the sun came up. When the sun came up, the eyelids started going down for some reason.

Major Jeff Lane, pilot, squadron commander

There's a couple challenges. One is physical stress and the other one is operational considerations. The stress component comes in. Just the long days—flying ten to thirteen hours every other day is a shock at first. You kind of get used to it after a few weeks. But duty days going up to eighteen hours—most people aren't used to working that much, so that comes as kind of a shock.

Meanwhile, operationally, particularly when the war first starts, everything is not spelled out for you on the mission. So you go into a field that we've recently taken over, they may not have an operational tower, a radar, instrument approaches. There are limited procedures for coming in and out. So the crews and the aircraft commanders have to do some good preflight planning, and they need to think about what they're doing.

Wartime flying tested us intellectually as well as physically. Navigator Steve Truax describes lively debates over how best to get the job done.

Lieutenant Colonel Steve Truax, navigator

We took our laptop computers there and by the time we were done, I was using some of the more advanced computer flight planning functions to help me to draw approaches and draw orbits and depict the restricted operating zones around different places. We had some discussions about tactics that were never resolved. We argued passionately about what was the best way to go into Baghdad, what was the best way to go into other places.

I formed strong opinions about what you should do, and part of that was predicated on not running into friendlies. Some people were so afraid of getting shot at that they were doing things that made it more likely they'd hit other airplanes or Army helicopters.

Friendly aircraft were a common sight during missions over Iraq. Down low, helicopter gunships fluttered along like lethal wasps. At middle altitudes, transport planes like our own C-130s droned through the clouds, along with fighters and tankers. Up high, the Stratofortresses rained destruction on an epic scale.

Master Sergeant John "Ratman" Ratcliffe, loadmaster

There was the night the B-52s flew over us. They were called Doom flight. Mark Ruckh was our navigator and he was a prior B-52 nav. We heard them call in Angels four-zero or something like that [40,000 feet]. They were way up there.

Mark said, "That's Buffs out of Barksdale. They're going in to bomb something."

With our NVGs on, after we heard them, we could see a short time later the sky just lighting up. I don't know what they were bombing, but they were bombing the crap out of something.

I saw it for only a few seconds. We were turning, and I looked out the troop door and saw it. I called up front and said, "You gotta see this." It was just lighting up out there.

I also remember seeing a lot of tracers. I specifically remember one night, going to Balad, I saw a small amount of tracers going this way, and then I saw a LARGE amount of tracers going back. I thought, "Well, that's got to be the Americans because there's a lot more firepower." Then, BOOM, something blew up.

When you're spring-loaded to look for threats, everything looks like a threat. Loadmaster Doug Ferrell describes his crew firing defensive flares in reaction to what they thought were heat-seeking missiles.

Master Sergeant Doug Ferrell, loadmaster

The one that sticks in my head was actually pretty funny. The Army had convoys that they were rolling out of Baghdad, and these convoys were extremely long. Intelligence had neglected to tell us that they fired flares at the head of the convoy to signal that they were ready to go. Then the back part of the convoy would fire flares to say, "Roll out."

In Baghdad, anything coming up at you was considered hostile fire. As we circled into Baghdad, we saw what we thought was a missile coming up at us, and I heard the other loadmaster start screaming, "Break right, break right!"

As we turned and punched flares out, the C-17 that was taking off below us saw our flares go. He punched flares. We punched MORE flares and then we landed, scared to death, thinking we'd just been shot at.

The intelligence officer on the ground proceeded to come up and yell at us, "What the hell you all think this is? The Fourth of July?"

Lieutenant Colonel Rich "Robi" Robichaud, pilot, tactics officer

The mission that stands out for me the most, I would say, was not long after American forces had captured Tallil Air Base. There was still some fighting around Nasiriyah, about ten miles away. We weren't the first C-130 crew to go into Tallil, but it was our first trip there. We went to Ali Al Salem Air Base in Kuwait and we picked up General Moseley, who was the CENTAF [Central Command Air Force] commander. He showed up on our airplane and said, "Let's go to Iraq, boys!"

That's the only word he said to us and he sat down on the bunk. It was about sunset then, so we all got down to business and started our engines. We had a couple of A-10 escorts that took off right after us, joined up on our wing, and escorted us all the way from Kuwait to Tallil.

We flew at 500 feet. It was total darkness. A lot of desert haze and low visibility due to blowing sand. There was no moon, no stars, and no cultural lighting, so it was kind of like looking at nothing, basically. The occasional nomad tent was out there, and when we'd see those coming, we'd stay a good distance away in case there was a bad guy in there who wanted to get lucky.

When we saw those lights, the A-10s would speed up ahead a little bit and check them out and make sure there was nothing there.

Squadron commander Jeff Lane also flew on the mission to transport General Moseley.

Major Jeff Lane, pilot, squadron commander

Probably the most memorable mission for me was when the war had actually started and I flew along observing with Robichaud's crew. We flew General Moseley up to Tallil Air Base in Iraq, 300 to 500 feet at night on night vision goggles. When we were flying the low-level route up there, we could see the flashing lights of the battle at Nasiriyah.

Major Carla Riner, pilot

Everything looks the same in the desert. I just remember thinking over and over, there are no lights. There's nothing to look at. There's no cultural lighting from towns and cities. In the United States as an airline pilot, you're pretty hard pressed to go somewhere where you're not going to see a light. I remember flying over the Arabian Peninsula, where you cross over the water to Masirah, and you could not tell the difference between the sky, the water, and the land. It was all black until you saw the stars. It was just unbelievable.

From the author's journal, 11 May 2003

Another all-nighter into Iraq last night. We flew empty to Al Jaber Air Base, Kuwait, where we picked up six all-terrain vehicles for the USAF Security Police.

At Al Jaber we parked next to a hardened aircraft shelter that had been hit by a bunker buster during the first Gulf War. The concrete building had a huge hole in the roof, and concertina wire had been placed around a hole in the floor. It's hard to imagine that anything in that building could have survived.

We departed Al Jaber late in the evening and flew at relatively high altitude, 14,000 feet, until we reached Kirkuk uneventfully. We spiraled down to an NVG landing at Kirkuk and offloaded the ATVs with only about thirty minutes on the ground.

We were due for an uneventful mission and we got one. No tracers or missiles came up at us. However, we did hear AWACS clearing a kill box for some fighters; apparently the F-15s and F-16s were trying to light up something.

Master Sergeant Doug Ferrell, loadmaster

I remember a run into Numaniyah. We took three pallets of Meals Ready to Eat to the Marines. That was interesting because the flight was totally blacked out, on NVGs. The loading crew was on NVGs, no lights whatsoever.

A photo taken through night vision goggles shows a 167th crew unloading cargo from the back of a C-130 at Tallil Air Base near Nasiriyah, Iraq, during the first weeks of Operation Iraqi Freedom (courtesy the 167th Airlift Wing).

You could look underneath your NVGs and it was pitch black. You pulled them back down and you'd see vehicles behind the airplane. There were people everywhere; there were helicopters landing. It was incredible.

When you took off on even the most routine mission, you never knew what kind of circumstances you'd face. Doug describes how sometimes those circumstances required throwing the rules out the window—including the rule that says aircrew members should not give blood.

One night in Kuwait we landed and they had brought wounded in, and they were short of blood. We almost got to spend the night in Kuwait City because they were asking all the aircraft coming in, "Does anybody have O negative blood?" They needed it for a guy they'd just brought in. He needed blood desperately. So [aircraft commander] Karl Levy polled the crew.

I was the only one on the crew with O negative blood. They were actually going to take me off the airplane and plug me into this guy until they could get him stabilized. I had volunteered to do that. They finally came back and said, "We found somebody else. Go on your way." But we delayed a half-hour in Kuwait to see how that would play out.

When you're getting shot at, it's easy to forget that flying has inherent dangers that have nothing to do with the enemy. Mechanic Travis Riley describes seeing a plane from another unit land at Masirah Island after getting hit by lightning.

Staff Sergeant Travis Riley, engine specialist

We saw it come in with no lights on except for one little one underneath the plane. We didn't know what was going on.

When we talked to the aircrew, we found out they'd been struck by lightning coming out of Iraq. They wanted us to look at their plane, so we gave it a general look-over. They said they'd been shot at with two rocket-propelled grenades. One went under the wing and one went over the wing. Then they said it was even scarier getting struck by lightning. They said it shut off all the electrical equipment temporarily. Everything just shut down. They said it was probably only a minute or two, but it felt like forever.

It messed up a lot of avionics, but it wasn't actually too bad. It didn't fry everything. We worked a couple days on that plane. Day shift changed a radome on it. The engines were pretty much OK. Lightning hit the front and came out everywhere.

I felt sorry for that crew, getting shot at by RPGs and getting hit by lightning all in one trip. That's a bad trip.

From the author's journal, 16 May 2003

Returned early yesterday morning, around 1:30 A.M., from a night run into Baghdad.

At our first stop at Al Udeid Air Base, Qatar, we picked up fifty-two infantry troops from the Florida Army Guard. They'd been in Jordan for two months, and they were posting to Baghdad for an undetermined length of time.

After a max weight takeoff from Al Udeid, we had an uneventful cruise north. However, we could hear an AWACS plane coordinating fighters to provide close air support for ground units in contact with the enemy.

Once we began our descent into Baghdad, night had fallen and we were on NVGs. It happened to be Mohammed's birthday, and once again Baghdad was hot.

Here and there we could see ground-to-ground tracers, along with the occasional fire directed upward. Usually, one projectile would rise to four or five thousand feet, then appear to burn out.

We suspected these were rocket-propelled grenades. Antiaircraft artillery would likely appear as a burst of several rounds, and a missile would go much higher. The fire did not seem directed at us—or at least it was not directed very well. Since most aircraft were flying blacked out, I suspect the bad guys were randomly shooting at the sound of planes.

A long, sleepy midnight run back to Masirah.

Lieutenant Colonel Steve Truax, navigator

As we were flying at night, sometimes we'd get on the same frequency with our other planes flying that night and talk. Especially as we were calling for deviations for weather and whatnot, we'd recognize each other's voices and talk. You'd run into friends where you'd least expect it.

22

WHEN YOU LEAST EXPECT IT

SEVERE TURBULENCE: Turbulence that causes large, abrupt changes in altitude and/or attitude. Aircraft may be momentarily out of control. Occupants are forced violently against seat belts or shoulder straps.
—Aeronautical Information Manual,
Turbulence Reporting Criteria Table

In the dynamic environment of the sky, a routine flight can turn into a life-threatening emergency in an instant. Our worst incident during the war took place thousands of miles from the combat zone, on the most routine of flights. Personnel who had deployed to Puerto Rico for airlift missions in Latin America were flying home in one of our C-130s. They were to spend a few days with their families, then go to Masirah Island, Oman, to take part in Operation Iraqi Freedom. As the crew diverted around a thunderstorm off the coast of Virginia, the aircraft hit severe turbulence.

Lieutenant Colonel Joe Myers,
pilot, Puerto Rico mission commander

July 12, 2003—Black Saturday, I came to call it. That was my first group of people that I sent back, and the purpose was for them to spend a few days at Martinsburg and then relieve some of the fellows who had been over in the desert.

I believe we had thirty-three people on the airplane, and I was the supervisor of flying that morning. I went out to the airplane to say goodbye to everybody. I stood there and watched them crank engines. I actually had tears in my eyes as they were taxiing out. Of course, I had no idea what awaited them, but just that they had been "my people" for so long, and now my people were having to leave me.

It was not a very enjoyable process, selecting who was going, but of course at that time it didn't matter a whole hell of a lot. It was going to make only a couple of weeks' difference.

Later in the day, [Lieutenant Colonel and safety officer] Don Magners called down and told us basically what had happened. The airplane had diverted into Oceana Naval Air Station in Norfolk with injured on board. He needed some information from us, crew orders and various other things to begin the investigation. That made for one hell of an afternoon and evening, worrying about them and how many were injured and how badly.

I believe it was thirty-three on board, nineteen injured. I don't remember how many were hospitalized. None of the injuries were life threatening. Had some broken arms, some back problems, bruises, and a broken pelvis. Curtis Surratt had a broken pelvis.

Strong turbulence can happen in a variety of circumstances. It can extend for miles from thunderstorms, as in this case. Although rare, the most severe turbulence can rip the wings from an airplane. No instrument on board can directly detect turbulence.

Master Sergeant Les Morris, loadmaster

The first indication we had, and this was all in a matter of seconds, was a little bump, just enough to get your attention. And then the next thing we knew, everybody was against the ceiling. And then everybody came crashing back down. The first thing that went through my head was, "Are the wings still on the airplane; are we still flying?" And then after that I realized we were flying straight and level.

I wasn't belted in at the time. I was sitting near the wheel well. Matt Bennett and Barry Schatzer were the primary loadmasters, so I was just on for the ride home. There were about six guys strapped in and the rest were not.

It took a couple minutes for everybody to realize what was going on, just picking yourself up off the floor and looking around. There's people bleeding and people screaming in pain, and I had landed on another guy who broke his hip, so I was taking care of him.

Meanwhile, I had hurt my knee and head and I was in a little bit of pain. There were a couple people up and moving and helping others. We flew for forty minutes like that getting the plane ready to land, making sure everybody had things tied down and making sure nobody else was going to get hurt on the landing.

The loadmasters still up were me and Troy Smith and Matt Bennett and Dave Hoffman. That's because Barry was hurt. We were getting everything ready because we couldn't unload the people until we got the cargo off the plane. We had to make sure the ground guys knew, so we took care of that in the air.

Matt, Dave, and Troy took care of the cargo in the back to make sure everything was tied down, and then as soon as we landed and opened up, I went to the cargo locks and everybody else got the cargo out the back.

Then we assisted the medical teams that were coming on. There was a very large group of medical technicians. There was Navy and there were civilian EMTs who helped get everybody off the plane.

There were several broken bones, a lot of bumps and bruises, and a couple cuts. There was some bleeding from the cuts and the head injuries. The most severe one was the broken pelvis because of the potential for internal bleeding. That was Curtis Surratt.

That's the only thing that ever made me think about doing something else for a living. You're seeing your friends get hurt, and even though it wasn't a wartime thing, it was something in the line of duty that could happen at any moment. Seeing your best friends hurt on the job, and there really isn't a lot you can do about it, that was my lowest moment.

One of the injured was flight engineer Corey Creighton. He wiped the blood from his eyes and continued doing his job until properly relieved. Corey explains that he remembered to check oil pressures because in severe turbulence and negative G forces, oil pumps can cavitate and starve the engines of oil.

Staff Sergeant Corey Creighton, flight engineer

We were deviating around some thunderstorms, and I don't remember too many details about how far we were or anything like that. I know that pretty much as far as we could see in front of us, it was clear sky. I had my seat belt off because I had my chair back a little bit. I had pulled the seat belt off to reach forward to the fuel panel. I had my head up under the overhead panel when I felt the first couple little bumps.

I finished flipping the switches and I went to lean back and put my seat belt on. I had both ends of the seatbelt in my hand; that's when we hit the big bump. The plane dropped, so I ended up testing the airplane's durability with my forehead.

When I ended up coming back down and basically falling into my seat, I actually thought I was going to die. I thought there's no way I can hit my head on a panel full of switches and not die. Then when I fell back down in my seat I was like, well, I'm alive. That's a relief.

But then I just kind of felt this stinging on me, so I knew it was pretty bad, but ... I pulled myself together after a few seconds. I made sure, for one, that the pilots were still conscious and they were OK and somebody was flying the airplane. The second thing I did was check oil pressures. After we got on the ground, I thought I don't know how I even remembered to check oil pressures. But I did.

I never would have thought I would have done that. But you know, it came to me. You hear stories and they pound it into your head in school, the things you need to know, and your job comes first. They teach you that in a wartime situation when everything's going to hell, you need to do your job. I guess that's what happened. In the back of my mind, it just took over and said, "Hey, you need to do your job."

Luckily, [flight engineer] Pat Cook was in the back of the airplane and he was fine. Since I was bleeding from my forehead, somebody went back and saw that Pat Cook was OK, so they sent him up and I went back and sat on the bunk. He jumped in the seat for the landing.

I took some stitches and it wasn't really as bad as I thought it was going to be. It was some bad timing, but I definitely learned something from it. Now I hardly ever take my seat belt off unless I absolutely have to, and when I trim fuel, I slide my chair all the way up and leave that lap belt on because that two seconds it takes to click it on could be valuable.

Technical Sergeant Christopher Barrow, engine specialist

We were an hour outside of Norfolk and I had my legs up, stretched out. We hit just a little bit of a bump and I brought my legs down. I had my seatbelt on and a second later I'm looking, and all I could see was everybody's shoes. Everybody's all up in the ceiling and then BOOM, everyone hits the floor.

Jay was right beside me and he landed right between my legs, so if I hadn't put my legs down I'd have been really screwed up. People were yelling, screaming, broken bones. Stuff just falling everywhere.

More than a dozen people were hurt, with six hospitalized. Avionics technician Curtis Surratt suffered the most serious injury.

Master Sergeant Curtis Surratt, avionics specialist

It was a few minutes after 12:30. I remember Barry Schatzer telling everybody to buckle up. I handed my buddy his seat belt and I reached for mine. Before I reached mine, I remember going up into the ceiling, and I saw the air duct up in the ceiling at about face level.

The first thing that came into my mind was, "This is not good." As quick as I went up, I came down. I hit the floor. I was looking around to see what was going on. There was really no panic at all. People kind of looked around at each other like, "What's going on?" Then for a few seconds you wonder, "Are we going down?"

I remember I saw Larry Eggleton, and he was kind of all tangled up and he was really hurt. I saw another guy holding his arm, the one who broke his arm in three places. I couldn't get up at the time just because it was too much pain to move, in my pelvic region. I wasn't sure what was going on, and I was lying there and they started asking, "Should we land or not?" I said, "Let's land as quick as possible. I can't make it back to Martinsburg. Let's land now."

I couldn't get up, so the loadmasters strapped me to the floor. I remember that landing was rough, very rough. We landed at Oceana Naval Air Station. That was fortunate because when we landed there, they had some Navy doctors and some pararescue guys there. They were right there on the spot. They had heard about the emergency and they were on the aircraft right away.

There were people on the aircraft there who were doing a real good job of taking care of people. We had one individual who started going into shock and they were taking care of him.

The pararescue guys and the Navy doctors got everybody else off and I was the last one. I just remember being in the aircraft and it was so hot. There was this one guy standing over me trying to stick a needle in my arm, and it was so hot he was sweating all over me. The urinal was behind me and there was that smell back there. I wondered if I was laying in urine and then I thought, "Well, it don't matter anyway." I really wasn't too worried about that.

Another guy came in and he finally got a vein, and then they pumped morphine in me. It was like a warm sensation all over my body. Then after that, they put me in a neck brace and a backboard.

They flew me to the hospital in a helicopter. I remember they had me on a gurney and my feet were sticking out. The only time I lost it was when a guy ran my foot right into a door, and it hurt so much. I screamed and everybody cleared away after that.

They did a CT scan there at Hampton Memorial Hospital. I was there about two or three days. After that they moved me over to Portsmouth Naval Hospital. They had to put a plate in my pelvis. It was broken in two places. There was also some internal bleeding in there. They ended up putting my pelvis back together with a plate and four pins.

I've been in some places where you've had turbulence and it was bad. But nothing was as bad as this; the bottom just dropped out.

Curtis made a full recovery and remains on duty with the 167th Airlift Wing.

23

METAL HAS MEMORY

Desert operation generally means operation in a very hot, dry, dusty, often windy atmosphere. Under such conditions, sand and dust will often be found in vital areas of the airplane such as hinge points, bearings, landing gear shock struts, and engine cowlings and intakes. Severe damage to the affected parts may be caused by the dust and sand.
—From the C-130 Flight Manual,
Chapter Nine, All Weather Procedures

Mechanics will tell you airplanes never forget. If you overheat a turbine, it is forever weakened. Let sand pit your propeller blades and you've instantly shortened their service life. Electrical circuits don't tolerate dust and dirt. Neglect or abuse an airplane and she'll always hold a grudge. As the maintenance guys put it, metal has memory.

In an unforgiving environment, our mechanics kept our unforgiving machines running beautifully. Somehow they even kept them fairly clean.

Crew chiefs like Tim Shipway, John Grimm, and Mike Miller, all in their forties, have years of experience working on airplanes. On any given day, you might see one of them up to his elbows in an engine, or perhaps sprawled under an avionics compartment, invisible except for his feet. If a crew chief has no repairs to make, you might find him painstakingly cleaning dust from an instrument panel with a brush or a cotton swab.

His responsibilities involve the overall mechanical condition of the airplane assigned to him. When something needs fixing that's beyond the crew chief's general knowledge, he arranges for specialists to work on his plane. The aircraft's fuselage bears the crew chief's name, and the plane belongs to him; the aircrew just borrows it to fly.

Technical Sergeant Tim Shipway, crew chief

I'm basically a jack of all trades and master of none. I have to know just about all the systems of the aircraft, and I get support from the different shops

A 167th Airlift Wing C-130 before launch at Masirah Island Air Base, Oman. In the background, crew chief Mike Rice checks his watch for an on-time departure. The bags in the foreground contain the crew's chemical warfare kits. The kits include gas masks, protective suits, and antidote syringes with spring-loaded needles (author's collection).

to work on the aircraft. We work on engines and props and landing gear with the help of specialists.

When we're on the road with a flight crew, we're the first level of maintenance. When a problem happens or something goes wrong, we're the first ones to identify it or to work on it. My day would start out getting an aircraft ready for a mission by doing a set of inspections and going over the equipment to make sure it was serviceable and ready for flight. That included servicing fuel, oxygen, and oil, and making sure the aircraft was in shape.

Flight crews like the C-130 because it's easy to fly, and as Shipway explains, mechanics like it because it's easy to fix.

The C-130 has been a workhorse for the Air Force. Its history goes back to the 1950s with the A-model. I have worked on the B-model, E-model, and H-model.

It's been a good aircraft. I compare the C-130 to the Boeing 737. In size it's similar. The 737 is a workhorse for the passenger airlines, and that's the aircraft I worked for U.S. Airways. I compare the two; they're good aircraft for a mechanic. It's easy to get to the different components.

The planes held up very well. [At the start of the Iraq war], we took four aircraft, our later models, the '95s. They showed the work that we've done in the past. We keep up a piece of equipment and it will perform for us. We're good managers and we have the parts we need. We can get things fixed in a timely manner so we don't lose reliability. All of the planes did quite well, and we put a lot of flight hours on them.

During our initial deployment for Operation Iraqi Freedom, we often flew night missions, returning before dawn to our base at Masirah Island, Oman. We taxied into parking during the small hours, weary and hungry, welcomed home by the sight of Shipway and other crew chiefs waving electric wands, marshalling us to a stop.

In the harsh white glare of portable floodlights, the mechanics would swarm the airplane. They opened engine cowlings to check fluids, scanned wings and tail for damage, and climbed into the cockpit to debrief the crew about how the machine had performed.

I did have the privilege of working night shift, so we had a different light on things. We weren't out in the heat like the day shifters, but there were long nights. When the aircraft came back at night, we had to do turns on them, to go over everything, to get it preflighted and ready to go for the next mission.

Of course it was hot, and we were on an island with water all around us, so it was humid. But I enjoyed working the nights and seeing the falling stars. There was limited light on the island, so the night just sparkled with all the stars and constellations.

In the military, there are some rules you never break. Then there are the rules you're allowed to break sometimes, especially in wartime. Then there are the rules you're technically not allowed to break, but if you do it safely and to accomplish the mission, you get away with it. As Technical Sergeant John Grimm explains, that's called "taking care of business."

Technical Sergeant John Grimm, crew chief

Even at night it was hot. You'd go to work and sweat. As far as challenges, you did what you had to do to keep the airplane flying every day. You took care of business, basically. If the airplane was scheduled to take off and ATOC [Air Terminal Operations Center, which includes personnel who load cargo aboard the airplanes] didn't show up and the K-loader was sitting behind the airplane, we'd load the airplane. We'd become ATOC. Stuff that you wouldn't be able to get away with on a normal basis.

Grimm says the challenges ranged from desert wildlife, which could give you a scare, to desert weather, which could cause engine temperatures to spike during startup. That required mechanics to inspect the engines and start them again.

Crew chief Garey Diefenderfer conducts a postflight inspection on a C-130 following a desert mission. Immediately after engine shutdown, maintenance personnel swarm the airplane, checking for fluid leaks, bird strikes, and battle damage (courtesy the 167th Airlift Wing).

It was dirty, dusty. Trying to take care of the airplanes, trying to keep them clean was the main thing, inside and out. We had a lot of hot starts [engines exceeding temperature limits on startup]. We did a lot of engine runs to diagnose hot starts, which were caused by the breeze blowing up the tailpipe. Everything was a little rougher because you've got an airplane sitting on a metal pad with nothing but thick gravel all around it, and you're trying to move maintenance stands around to work on engines and do inspections. Plus, dodging camel spiders at night, not knowing what you're going to find when you crawl up in the wheel well after the plane's been sitting there for an hour or two. So you had to be a little cautious on that. Especially working night shift, there was usually a camel spider about once every couple weeks and it would give you a little surprise.

While at Masirah, we were shown pictures of a cobra that had crawled into the wheel well of a Chinook helicopter in Afghanistan. Luckily, the snake didn't bite anyone before somebody killed it.

Meanwhile, Grimm explains how crew chiefs learn to work problems created by the environment and problems created by the supply system.

I've worked on C-130s in the jungle and in the desert, and you get your little quirks in different places. You get them in a wet environment, you might have more electrical write-ups. You get them in a hot and dry environment and you've got your hot starts. Brakes were an issue over there because of some of the runways, the short strips, and dodging mortar holes and stuff like that.

Parts were a big issue. There were several times we would have parts we wouldn't tell anyone about. Kind of like, "Well, where did you get that brake assembly?" We kind of had it stashed away. We kept our airplanes flying.

Master Sergeant Mike "Hawg" Miller, crew chief

The sand, the desert dirt, got into everything—the ballscrews of the landing gear, the flap jackscrews, all the bearings on the flap carriages. We did a clear-water rinse every fifteen days. Also, every time the flight crew was coming down the road getting ready to launch, we'd see the vehicle coming and we'd have somebody jump up and wash the windows real quick. You'd always have a film of desert dirt on the windshields.

In addition to crew chiefs, who are general mechanics, the maintenance team includes specialists in hydraulics, avionics, structural maintenance, and other fields. Fortunately for all of us, structural maintenance specialist Steve Smith had little to do in terms of traditional battle damage repair, which means fixing bullet holes in sheet metal.

Technical Sergeant Steve Smith, structural maintenance specialist

There was little sheet metal work, per se, because we weren't taking rounds. If we had been taking rounds through the airplanes, more like a World War II setting, there would have been more of my kind of maintenance.

However, Steve had plenty of other work to do, and in the desert environment, it sometimes involved making judgment calls on when to leave well enough alone. For example, a component normally protected by a sealing compound might just have to go without it.

A lot of times, you wouldn't be messing with sealant and those kinds of things. The sealant can cure too fast. It's not worth opening a whole tube of sealant when you maybe have only five tubes. You're going to save your materials for the absolute necessities. So many things are, "What can we live with?" Unless it's really falling off, you're going to leave it be. That's because a lot of times you can create more problems getting in at damage and then not having sufficient tools and the support to make a complete repair.

When the specialists have nothing to do in their specialty, they help other mechanics. So when a sheet metal man helps an engine man, rank gives way to expertise.

What I would do was tell the young guys, "Don't worry about the stripes. Don't worry about my age. I'm here to help you. If you need something, forget the etiquette. Let's just get the job done."

In these situations, the kids know more about the engines. They may be younger than me, but they've been through engine school. I'm holding the ladder for them. I could either be holding the ladder or sitting over in the hangar reading a magazine.

There are situations where we need to follow military protocol. Other than that, we're all just people trying to get the airplane going. That seems to work real well. If you get most of that overbearing BS stuff off the people so they can really do the job, then the job gets done. It makes a safer product; it's a win-win situation.

We have a small, hometown group of people who get along and party together. Also, a lot of the people grew up together and went to high school together. Some go on to do the officer thing. Others like the hands-on enlisted role so much that they want to stay with it. Some people even have college but choose not to do the officer role. So we have total interaction without the boundaries. We have the capability of having respect without it being forced.

Master Sergeant Curtis Surratt, avionics specialist

Working on the aircraft there, especially up in the flight deck, it was probably the hottest I've ever been. You'd just walk up there and start to sweat profusely, right off the bat. They did have an external air-conditioning unit up there, but it broke in about the first week.

We'd do a work-rest cycle. Basically, get up there and work, then take a rest. We tried to do a lot of our work at night if we could because it was a lot cooler.

For the first few weeks, a lot of electronic stuff was breaking down. I guess if it was on the verge of breaking down and the heat got to it, the heat took it over the edge. So once we started swapping out parts and getting new things in there, [the planes] seemed to start doing real well. It's almost like the aircraft had to get acclimated to the weather, too.

Surratt and other avionics specialists maintained our defensive equipment, the systems that warn of antiaircraft missile launches and help confuse heat-seeking missiles by firing flares. Our lives depended on those things working right every time.

Your main concern is that the systems are working correctly, so we have a way of double-checking with each other to make sure everything's good. I don't care if you're a master sergeant or an E-1, I want somebody to come back and check me just as much as I want to check them because with systems like that, you don't get a second chance.

Whenever you hear the systems worked, that feels real good. But most of all, if I don't hear about a missile launch, that's the best thing. Some people say, "Yeah, I want to see how the system works." But if I want to see the system work, I'd rather it be out at China Lake or someplace where they do the testing, instead of a real-world mission.

Aircrew members try to take care of the aircraft and not make extra work for the maintenance people. After all, it's not your plane; it's the crew chief's plane. If you break it, you have to answer for it. But sometimes things happen that you just can't help.

From the author's journal, 7 April 2003

Today we hit the biggest damn seagull in the world. It splattered just under the copilot's swing window. Our copilot, Ozzie, actually ducked in the split second before the sickening WHACK!

Normally, when you have a bird strike on takeoff, you return for landing to inspect the plane. However, we decided the threat from missiles made returning more risky than pressing on.

As it happened, we suffered no damage, but we had to fly all the way back to Masirah with blood and viscera smeared across the right side windows, where it all froze and dried at high altitude.

When we taxied into parking, I could see one of the crew chiefs standing with his arms folded, shaking his head and looking at the mess as if to say, "What have you idiots done to my airplane?"

Turning wrenches may not seem like a glamorous job. But when maintainers do that job well, they get something more important than glamour: they get respect.

Senior Master Sergeant Steve "Mac" McDonald, flight engineer

Maintenance did an outstanding job. The C-130 had the highest in-commission rate of all the other airplanes there. Actually, the Guard and Reserve had the highest rates of all of them. I think that was due to our maintenance.

The airplanes were used constantly. They'd come back, turn right around, and go out again. They seemed to work wonderfully. Our guys, I could trust them [to have properly inspected the plane before the flight crew inspects it]. I'd sort of do that quick combat preflight inspection. I'd trust our guys and ask, "Hey, is it good to go?" There were a lot of challenges — the heat, the dust, the sand. The planes held up quite well.

Senior Master Sergeant Roland Shambaugh, loadmaster

Our maintenance guys are the best in the world. I'm apprehensive about flying on a commercial airliner, but when I go out here and get on one of our C-130s, it never, ever crosses my mind to worry about maintenance.

24

THE AVIATOR'S PRAYER

There's an old joke about a World War II aviator's prayer: "Dear God, please don't let me screw up. But if I do, don't let me screw up and live."

People might tell the story with a grin, but the sentiment is real. Aircrew members are not folks who take counsel of their fears. When you can get them to talk about fear at all, they usually don't talk about fear of getting hurt. Almost invariably, they worry about letting someone else down, either crewmates or family members.

Staff Sergeant Corey Creighton, flight engineer

My own personal worst fear was not knowing what to do. Flying is a dangerous business and things can happen anytime. You're flying along and you think, "What if we take small arms? What if we take a missile?" There are so many "what ifs." My worst fear was that something would happen and I would not know what to do.

Whenever we were in cruise and things were kind of in chill mode, I would tend to sit there and think to myself. I'd look up at my panel and say, "OK, what if this happened?" I'd give myself little challenges and scenarios and say, "What would I do?"

That's actually a little tip I learned from Rich Talbott [an instructor flight engineer]. We were there in the desert at the same time, and sometimes we'd sit around outside the tent and talk about things: "Hey, what do you think about this?" or "What would you do if this happened?"

Colonel Eric Vollmecke, pilot, wing commander

My greatest fear when I was flying combat missions was that I would do something to let the crew down, or that I wouldn't perform to the standards. I think that's a healthy thing to be concerned about. You don't want to let down the guy next to you. I never felt concern for my own personal safety. I felt we did everything right to mitigate risk, but at the end of the day, it's a risky business, and you accept that.

Lieutenant Colonel Bill Clark, pilot

I guess my biggest concern at the time was not necessarily myself. I looked at the crew before I left. My concern was that I got them home to their families. The potential of not seeing my own family again did not cross my mind. My thoughts were getting Jerry Stuck home to his family, getting Scottie Wachter home to his son, getting Jimmy Blackford home to his kids. The thought of me being in the same boat never crossed my mind.

Captain Curtis Garrett, navigator

You're dealing with professionals; you want to get the job done. You want to be on time. You don't want to let the crew down. I didn't want to have any surprises as far as information, something that I should know. That was my biggest fear. Stuff's going to happen that you can't control, but my biggest fear was not knowing things I was responsible to know.

For me as a nav, that was the type of environment I was trained for. Going down to Charleston, you really don't need me on the airplane, but over there I was an indispensible part of the crew. I had two pilots who had to rely on me for certain parts of the job. Two couldn't get it done; you also had the flight engineer who had to do his part of it.

The team had to do everything. If one person was messing up, no matter how small the detail, it would just throw a wrench into the chain of events. I didn't want to be that person.

Lieutenant Colonel David Porter, flight surgeon

I think my personal worst fear is meeting a plane with a patient who is crashing [vital signs dropping] and not having the knowledge or the equipment or the support to save his life. Didn't happen, but I think that's an underlying fear that all medical providers have. I've been around long enough to have been in situations where people are crashing and you don't have the equipment, you don't have the medicines, you don't have the knowledge or the skills. I think that was my greatest fear and fortunately it didn't happen.

Senior Master Sergeant Roland Shambaugh, loadmaster

Leaving my kids as orphans. You really don't like to think about that, but it was part of it. I regret the time I missed with them, but that's just part of the price you pay for wearing the uniform. And then, something happening to one of our guys. It was just a big relief when everybody made it home safe to their families. And my heart goes out to all the other military families. All the casualties we've taken, every one of them had a mother and a father and a sweetheart, and a lot of them had kids.

Major Mike Langley, pilot and aircraft commander

Well, it wasn't dying; it never was. I think my greatest fear was losing someone, because I am responsible not just for the aircraft. I'm responsible for all the people who are on that aircraft, and that means their extended family. So, not to be melodramatic about it, but I take that very seriously. If I had lost anyone, whether they stepped off the tarmac and stepped on a land mine because I had not briefed them appropriately, or I'd not stayed on their butt enough about doing the proper procedure, then I would consider myself responsible. I consider myself extremely fortunate to have gone and to have come back with all my crew members making it back.

I never felt fear for my own life. I never even really felt fear for our lives because I really believed in what we were doing, and I believed our training would get us through it. Maybe that's why we do what we do, because we do believe it. But the fear of losing someone by my own fault—I think I would have carried that guilt with me for the rest of my life.

Lieutenant Colonel Andy Wolkstein, flight nurse, commander of a medical detachment at Baghdad International Airport

Personally as the commander, the officer in charge, my biggest fear was not knowing what I would do under attack. Or not knowing whether my orders would be appropriate. Would I say the right thing, do the right thing, be the right person? I'll say this, even though it might not be politically correct: You get to know God very, very well. You get to know yourself very well. You get to know your limitations very well. Luckily I had a lot of good supporting people around me who would help when I wavered.

I felt like I met the call. I went with twenty-six people; I came back with twenty-six people. That, to me, is an accomplishment and I felt good about that.

Now, one of my crew members had a heart attack and we had to air evac him out. He's fine now and I had to get a replacement.

I remember one mission when a C-130, our crew, was coming in with patients from Balad or somewhere, bringing them to the MASF [Mobile Aeromedical Staging Facility]. We were going to offload them and then another plane was going to take them to Landstuhl. Before the C-130 could land, we came under attack, and this was mortars. They thought someone had penetrated our perimeter. They weren't sure. So they locked everyone down, and then we heard a C-130 landing with patients on board.

In a lockdown we're not supposed to get out of our tents, because they're doing a search of the area. We thought since we were under attack that the C-130 wouldn't land, number one, and number two, if they did land, they would take off right away so they could get out of the area since there was a potential suicide bomber.

Turns out that the C-130 wasn't going to take off. The patients were in this plane. The patients were in the plane for about twenty to thirty minutes. After a while, I didn't hear any mortars hitting, and I made the decision to get the patients off the plane and bring them into the MASF. While all this was going on, we were in our "battle-rattle," our flak vests and helmets. We took all those patients off because they were getting hot in that plane.

Brought them in and then after everything was all clear, the C-130 took off. The patients stayed and eventually we got them out to Landstuhl.

Making a decision under fire. One thing I remember is that a Vietnam vet came up to me after I made that decision and he said, "Good job."

Major Jeff Lane, pilot, squadron commander

Your worst fear is that there will be losses. To a certain extent, we all mentally prepared ourselves in case that happened.

Also, we didn't all deploy to the same location, so selecting names of people who are going to go to a more dangerous place or a less dangerous place could mean somebody getting hurt, some people not, so it's very serious. As it turns out, none of our planes were hit over there, so you have to feel good about that.

In a combat environment, sometimes you don't have time to get scared. But as navigator Mike McMillie explains, you get around to it later. He describes one mission into Iraq.

Lieutenant Colonel Mike McMillie, navigator

Going into Baghdad, we're about eighty miles west of Baghdad and coming in from the west. We're landing on the taxiway because the runway's been bombed. We're seeing all sorts of gunfire and tracers going up, mortars and things like that.

It's surrealistic because you're watching all this stuff take place from the airplane. You're doing so many different things, trying to get into an unknown field and all that, you really don't have time to fear anything. You have time to do your mission.

Once you land, you kick everything off that you have to kick off, put on a couple passengers, take off. Of course, this is at night on NVGs, blacked-out runway. You take off and you see some more of this gunfire, but you're already above what's going to happen.

Then you have a chance to actually think about what you just did. You're going, "Man. We coulda got shot down!"

Captain Brandon Taksa, pilot

During an off day, I was playing some basketball. I didn't know it at the time, but I ended up tearing my ACL [anterior cruciate ligament, the major stabilizing ligament of the knee]. My knee swelled up; it looked pretty heinous. I couldn't walk on it. Had to have crutches.

I was off flying status for about a week. During that week the doctors fed me anti-inflammatories, took a good look at it, said I didn't really do anything to damage it. They assumed it was just a severe sprain.

A week later it seemed like that would be true. The swelling went down. I could walk on it. I was running on it, working out on it. I could run on it, but only on flat, even terrain, and my ability to cut left and right, forward and back, stopped all of a sudden. My knee was very weak.

Based on that, my biggest fear was, for whatever reason, having to egress the airplane or, Lord forbid, being shot down and having to evade and not being able to. It wasn't so much for me but for the guys who were my crew members. I didn't want them to feel obligated to wait for me or carry me. That would mean everybody would be captured.

That was my biggest fear. Not so much the fear of being shot down, but the fear of not being able to take care of myself after being shot down. Bringing harm to others, in that respect.

Major Carla Riner, pilot

I didn't let myself think about it very much, but probably my worst fear is capture. A lot of people are afraid of dying. I do not fear death at all. The idea of dying in any capacity, much less in the service of my country, I really don't mind that. The idea of being captured, not just for me and what I might be subject to, but also watching those that I know and love in my squadron, that would probably be the hardest thing.

It's sad to say you'd almost rather die than live. It depends on the circumstances, of course, but that was probably my biggest fear to face.

Occasionally, troops will write The Letter. The one you put away for someone else to mail for you in case you don't make it back. Pilot Shaun Perkowski says it helped him get past his fears and get on with the mission.

Lieutenant Colonel Shaun Perkowski, pilot

At some point it either drives you crazy or you just give it up to God. You just say if it's my time, I hope I'm right with You and I hope I'm right with my family. Otherwise, it just drives you nuts.

I really didn't want to [volunteer for dangerous missions]. But if the commander tells me I'm going, then I'm going. There's other guys who want that Air Medal. My uncle's got five Bronze Stars from the Battle of the Bulge. He did what he was asked and that's fine. I did what I was asked.

I wasn't out there volunteering, because I knew my wife would kick my butt. My biggest concern was hoping to do everything right to bring my crew home and bring me home too.

One thing I did to help me get from that point of the fear was I sat down and wrote The Letter. I didn't write it to my wife; I wrote it to my kids. The letter that people would find if something happened to you. I still have those. Those are tough letters to write. I sealed them up and took them home with me. I don't know what I'll do with them.

I bought a nice guitar when I got home, a couple thousand bucks spent on a nice, big old Martin acoustic guitar. Those letters are sitting there in that high-dollar guitar case. I don't know if I'll shred them someday or what.

From the author's journal, 16 March 2003

Went to a chapel service this morning. The PA system suffered from radio bleed-through, reminding us even during a hymn of just why we're here:

Amazing Grace, how sweet the sound
    "Scorpion Ops, Reach Six Two Yankee, radio check."
That saved a wretch like me
    "Read you five by five."
I once was lost, but now am found,
    "Pace Two Four requests positive launch."
Was blind, but now I see.
    "Positive launch approved."

25

NEVER OPEN YOUR WALLET IN A SANDSTORM

If there ever was a good thing about being deployed to the desert, it was how simple life can be there.

—Major Chris Sigler, 167th AW

The hot wind feels like a hair dryer blowing in your face. The sand stretches beyond the horizon, and after you've looked at it long enough, it expands in your mental horizon until you imagine the whole world must be wasteland. Thermometers brought from that green and cool fantasyland become worthless, pegging at 120 every day. Dust storms block out the sun. If you don't keep drinking water, the haze will become fuzzy, then go black. The next thing you know, a medic will be waking you up and inserting an IV. If you're lucky. In conditions like this, you learn to make the best of it.

Lieutenant Colonel Steve Truax, navigator

For the first couple of weeks, I was deadly afraid of sun stroke, which I perceived could get you very quickly there if you didn't know how to take care of yourself, so that was one of my priorities. I knew I wouldn't do anybody any good in the infirmary with heat exhaustion. So I took care of things; I got a lot of sleep. The squadron commander laughed at how much time I spent sleeping, but that was part of how I learned to recuperate and operate in the desert.

Then I would look at our Life Support people and the maintenance guys out on the ramps there, working for hours at a time in that kind of heat. That was when I really began to appreciate some of the ground personnel we have. Especially maintenance, but also Life Support and the Security Police and others. They faced very adverse conditions and accepted them very stoically and still did outstanding work.

Captain Brandon Taksa, pilot

The thing I really remember is the heat. As soon as we stepped off the air plane over there—I really hadn't been to that part of the world before—the thing that struck me the most was the heat, the unrelenting heat. Even in the evenings it didn't seem to get down below eighty. Even in the evenings you were just sweating nonstop all the time. The heat was what really impressed me.

Senior Master Sergeant Roland Shambaugh, loadmaster

I remember walking out of the tent the first morning and I thought to myself, "I need welder's glasses," because the sun was so bright and the heat was so intense. I'd never encountered anything like that. With the heat and humidity—we were close to the water there—you're just wringing wet all the time when you're outside.

You acclimate in a few days. But that was the biggest challenge, just getting used to the harshness of the environment and the intense heat.

When you go as a unit into an expeditionary wing like that and you're about eight thousand miles from home in a very harsh environment, flying long, long missions, all you really have is one another. You really get close with the guys. Everybody's attitudes are good and everybody's bending over backwards to help one another. It really brings out the best in everybody. That was my favorite part of it. You draw close to the guys you serve with. You get some understanding of the older veterans and you see why they're the way they are. You get close just like family.

Overall, we had it much, much better than the Army or the Marines. We had a really good mess hall; you could take a hot shower every day; you could wash your clothes. We had a clean, cool, dry place to sleep. It wasn't that bad.

The biggest adjustment for me coming home was getting used to the quiet again. That's because in the desert it was constant chaos between the air conditioner running, aircraft maintenance engine runs at night, and you're living on top of one another with no privacy. You can't expect everybody to be quiet all the time. I remember the first morning I woke up at the house it was so quiet. It was just so eerie before I opened my eyes, I thought for a few seconds I was dead.

Major Chris Sigler, pilot

If there ever was a good thing about being deployed to the desert, it was how simple life can be there as opposed to working at the base with the phones ringing off the hook. In the desert, it was pretty much eat, fly, sleep, work out, drink three beers at the beer tent.

The crew would tend to get into a routine together. When you weren't flying, you'd either work out or sleep. I think I watched more movies in the desert than I ever had. I normally don't watch many movies, but there wasn't much else to do.

You'd have maybe an eighteen-hour duty day. Then you'd get back and even if it was five in the morning, you'd just sleep straight. Sometimes I'd sleep ten hours, through planes taking off, the hot tent with people coming in and out. I don't think anything could have woken me up. It was some of the best sleep of my life.

Sometimes the simple life becomes a little too simple—especially if you go to a dentist who's running out of supplies.

Technical Sergeant John Grimm, crew chief

I got fillings done without Novocain in Masirah. I figured I'd get a little dental work done while I was there, and of course, the dental clinic consisted of a tent with what looked like an old World War II dental chair in there. The dentist got me in there and he had this big, bulky assistant. The assistant kind of held me in the chair while he was drilling on my teeth because they didn't have any Novocain left. Once I got home they had to remove all those fillings and redo them.

Senior Master Sergeant Mike Bayne, flight engineer

I read a lot. In two months I read at least eight books because that's how many I took with me, and I read one or two some other people had. Played a lot of dominoes. Our crew played marathon domino games for hours at a time.

In the midst of the heat, sandstorms, and separation from family, you learned to pass the days with some sort of distraction or you went nuts. As crew chief Tim Ship-way explains, some folks found a way to have some fun and cool off at the same time.

Technical Sergeant Tim Shipway, crew chief

The best was the water gun battles between maintenance and operations, getting commanders involved, soaking officers. Good sport, a good game to pass the time and break some of the tedium there and add some fun.

A group of ops people once was playing miniature golf, and we had a van and everybody had water guns, and we sneaked up behind them and soaked them. Of course, we knew what was going to happen then. We had to watch our backs; the next night they attacked us. We had the van door open, and they threw a bucket of water and doused everybody inside the van.

Master Sergeant John "Ratman" Ratcliffe, loadmaster

We were not as prepared as the maintenance guys. Those guys brought water guns with them, Super Soakers. Brian Hensell and I came back from a mission one night and went to the chow hall. It was one of those flights where you get back and you think, "I'm so tired I don't know if I want to eat or sleep, but I'm hungry, so I think I'll eat, then I'll sleep." We came back up from the chow hall, and those guys had that little white van and they drove by us. I thought, "What's this?" They threw the door open and just soaked us. I was so tired I didn't care.

That was fun because we started getting creative. We were getting condoms from the medical people and using them as water balloons.

You might call it "tactical humor"—a water fight to blow off steam, or a well-timed joke to keep spirits up. Sometimes a natural entertainer could make you laugh when you wanted to snarl.

Major Carla Riner, pilot

Karl Levy, one of our pilots. When we first deployed, he said he was deployed to the wrong location. That's because when you flipped over your orders, there was this weird code, something that nobody had ever paid attention to, and ours all started with, let's just say, PXJ. Well, Karl's said RLN, or something. And he's kidding like, "Wait, I'm not supposed to be here; I'm supposed to be in Puerto Rico. I'm only going to be here two weeks."

We just got the biggest kick out of him, and he was just so wound up. It was really funny because we were in this briefing we didn't want to be in after we had landed and we had flown all night. It was, like, bleah. So he's kind of laughing and trying to get everybody to loosen up. And he said, "By God, if I'm here in two weeks, I will run around this camp in nothing but a red dress." And I remember thinking, hmm. And that was day one, hour one.

I had to go home about three months later. Guess who brought back a smashing red dress? He lived up to his word. He actually did put it on and run around the camp in nothing but the red dress. And I have photos to prove it.

Sometimes the partying could get a bit out of hand. The details are little fuzzy.

Major Mike Langley, *pilot*

Somebody spinning records with a Kevlar helmet on and buck naked—we won't get into who or anything like that. Oooh, I don't know who....

Even the local wildlife could become a source of amusement if you got desperate enough.

Lieutenant Colonel Bill Clark, *pilot*

We were in Masirah, and my tent was directly across the way from Scottie Hostler, and Scottie Hostler found a camel spider in his tent. He shooed it out in the alleyway between our tents, and he thought it would be the funniest thing on the face of the earth if he could shoo that camel spider into our tent.

So I start coming across the street, and it became a hockey match out in the middle of the road—he and I and a camel spider that was really pissed off and wanted to bite the two of us really bad. I was trying to shoo it to him, he was trying to shoo it to me, and we were both trying to keep from getting bitten by it.

Lieutenant Colonel Sandie Duiker, *flight nurse*

Going into Incirlik Air Base in Turkey, we got a building that had been condemned since the first Gulf War. We had roaches that we painted with whiteout so we could have races. You know, like my roach had a whiteout diamond and your roach had a whiteout stripe, so we knew who was winning.

Also, we found this enormous toad. An enormous bumpy, brown and green toad. I made her the mascot and threatened anybody's life who killed her. She was good for eating at least three roaches a day.

When the maintenance crews were off duty in the desert, what did you have? Guys who were good with their hands, good with tools, smart about improvising, with time to kill. Don't tell them they can't do something. Mike Miller put to work his natural talent as a painter.

Master Sergeant Mike "Hawg" Miller, *crew chief*

We were at Masirah Island, Oman, on June 20, 2003, and that's the birthday of West Virginia—June 20, 1863. So we decided to fly the West Virginia

A long way from home: Signpost at a desert air base, Camp Snoopy, in Doha, Qatar, 2002 (author's collection).

flag. But it was against Omani rules to fly your flag in camp. The maintenance commander made us take it down.

I decided to draw one on wood. Tim Shipway had a West Virginia flag and he let me borrow it. I looked at it and painted from there. We had a maintenance bulletin board right in front of our row of tents. We mounted it on the back side of that platform.

By the way, when the maintenance guys build something—don't steal it. Bad idea.

Master Sergeant Dave Twigg, loadmaster

The maintenance guys built a wooden soapbox derby car. Three of the pilots decided to get together and steal this car and hide it in the females' tent. The way they went about it was classic.

All the maintenance guys were sitting in front of their tents, and the car was inside one of them, on the front porch. [Troops built porches in front of their tents, which often had camouflage netting or canvas around them for shade.] Well, Jon McCullough crawled around the corner of the tent; he crawled in on the porch, wheeled the car inside, and unzipped the back end of the tent, which was usually kept closed. The pilots carried it through the tent, out the back, and then carried it into our tent row and hid it in the female tent. The execution of that plan was awesome in that our maintenance guys didn't catch them.

About an hour and a half later, I was on my bed reading a book. Here came crew chiefs Robbie Webb, Dickie Long, and Jason Collins. Robbie was a high school wrestling champ. The first thing he did was to pin me on the bed.

He got in my face and said, "Where's our car?"

I said, "I don't know." I didn't find out until after the fact. I had an awful time convincing him I didn't know where it was because they were ready to tie and tape me to my bed.

After about fifteen minutes of begging and pleading and trying to convince him I didn't know, he said, "I believe you."

They left the tent and I don't know where they went next. They were scouring the camp looking for that car. They finally found it. After it got around, no one could keep it quiet.

In the middle of a desert war, the smallest luxuries mean a lot.

Lieutenant Colonel Andy Wolkstein, flight nurse

The little things make a big difference. You really appreciate home when you go away. You really appreciate the butter that you don't get for two weeks because the convoy was ambushed. When the butter comes, you really appreciate that. You look forward to what you're having for dinner. You look forward to the routine. I enjoyed a cup of coffee and reading the paper. Of course, I didn't have a paper for a month. It was a month-old paper. I'd get a cup of coffee and sit down and read the outdated paper.

Major Carla Riner, pilot

One of the most interesting experiences, not in flight, was when I went over to the tower at Ali Al Salem Air Base in Kuwait, and I took tea with the Kuwaiti gentlemen in the tower. They were in their full wraps and the whole thing. And they were so excited because a blond-haired, blue-eyed, light-skinned girl came in with them. They were also very proud of themselves that they could offer me peanut M-and-Ms. It was just a huge luxury that they were very excited about.

One day some of our people at Masirah Island did get a break from the heat and dust.

Captain Brandon Taksa, pilot

Of all things, the desert got a rainstorm. Not just a small rainstorm, but a BIG rainstorm, to the point where I woke up in the morning to rain falling on the tent. At least I thought it sounded like rain falling on the tent. You gotta say that because the air conditioners were running in those tents all the time, and you had dreams where you'd hear water falling because I guess it's something your brain misses.

The more I came out of my sleep, the more I realized this really did sound like rain. So I got up and looked out, and sure enough, our tent was starting to flood. I went back to the lowest corner, which happened to be my aircraft commander's part of the tent, and said, "Hey, you might want to start moving your stuff. Watch where you put your feet."

I still remember sitting out on our front porch, watching the rain fall, enjoying it.

Life in a tent can present other little challenges, as well. For example, there's home maintenance.

Captain Tony Henry,
civil engineer assigned to Balad, Iraq

We had to build our tent's blast walls twice because some supply idiot ordered biodegradable sandbags.

Members of the 167th Airlift Wing deployed to Camp Snoopy in Doha, Qatar, in 2002. The rock garden reads: "167 AW Mountaineer Pride Worldwide" (author's collection).

Technical Sergeant Jay Barrow, engine specialist

At night, our tent was the coldest tent in the friggin' place. I had a little thermometer, and it would get down to forty-five degrees at night with the air conditioner running.

On the nights we would have off, we'd be in there watching movies or playing cards. We were playing cards one night and I'm like, "To hell with it. I'm going to turn this air conditioner off." It would never shut off. It was just full blast cold.

Everybody says, "Don't mess with it, because it won't come back on."

I go out there, and I turn the knob just that far and that air conditioner shuts off. So I turn it back to where it was and it won't come back on. I'm thinking, "Oh, crap. I'm not going back in 'cause there's ten guys in there." I'm like, "Come on, kick back on." I turn it one more time and it comes on. I thought they were going to kill me.

At some deployed locations, troops could leave camp and go into town. For example, at Al Udeid Air Base in Qatar, you could wash up, put on a pair of slacks, and visit the fine hotels in Doha. There you could swim in the pool, sip cappuccino in the lobby, or shop for souvenirs. But you had to watch your back.

Staff Sergeant Clayton Atkinson, aerial port specialist

At Al Udeid we were allowed to go into town. It took a lot of coordination; you had to have people who were certified to drive in Qatar and had taken the driver course. I went twice. It's an interesting experience, the culture there.

Anytime you'd go to eat in a restaurant or something, first thing you'd make sure all the vehicles were locked up. When you came back, you'd have to do a thorough inspection, checking tailpipes, wheel wells, behind the grille.

Most everybody we encountered was nice and polite, happy to see us and talk to us. There were a few instances when you could sort of tell we should leave. The eyes were the biggest thing. We couldn't understand what they were saying, but we could see them whispering and watching us. That's when you'd say, "All right, we need to go somewhere else."

To get through a desert deployment safely and sanely, you needed to stay slow to anger and quick to laugh. You had to enjoy small pleasures and ignore big discomforts. Sometimes you needed to keep your eyes open and your mouth shut. And navigator Steve Truax learned one more thing....

Lieutenant Colonel Steve Truax, navigator

Never open your wallet during a sandstorm. I went and had a beer at the rec center at Masirah Island. I stepped out and the winds were kicking, the sand was stinging, and papers were flying. I decided to go back and have another beer, and I wondered if I had enough money. So without even thinking, I reached into my pocket, pulled out my wallet, opened it up, and POOF, two seconds later, all I had in my wallet was sand. And it was dark. I chased bills all over. It was like sixty or eighty dollars I had in my wallet, and downwind they went. They disappeared instantly.

26

TWICE THE CITIZEN

The reservist is twice the citizen.

—Winston Churchill

This job makes us a bit cosmopolitan. You might see a flier fumbling through his wallet, thumbing past the dollars and euros, looking for that five-dinar note he knows must be in there somewhere—the one that says, "Central Bank of Kuwait, We Seek God's Assistance."

We live our lives across great distances, through all twenty-four time zones, plus those weird little half-hour time zones. Our sense of time and place becomes tied to the prime meridian and the equator, and some of us keep watches set on Greenwich Mean Time. When we first get back home, we can't sleep.

The travel attracts some to the job. Others just love airplanes. Still others mainly want to serve their country. Some come from families with generations of military service. The reasons for joining are as varied as the people.

Major James Powell, pilot

Part of it would be the dream I had as a kid. My mom could tell you, my dad could tell you, the Boys from Syracuse [a New York Air National Guard fighter squadron] would fly over the family farm, and I'd drop whatever I was doing and just watch them until they were out of sight. I'd think, "I'd love to do that someday." Thankfully I was able to go do that. Love of flying was the big thing.

I told my wife when I first went to the desert, "I can't explain it, but something tells me, not that I'm going to do anything heroic, but something tells me I need to be a part of this. Maybe me being there may save somebody's life unknowingly. I feel I need to be a part of it." I love what I do.

235

HE SPEED OF HEAT

Lieutenant Colonel Rich "Robi" Robichaud, pilot

It's a fun job. I like the people you work with. For the most part, it's just top quality people. And also service to country. Our country gave us a lot; we have a lot to be grateful for.

It's all I've known all my life. Just going to the same office every day five days a week pushing paper doesn't seem like it would be as much fun as what we do.

Senior Master Sergeant Roland Shambaugh, loadmaster

I was raised up to be patriotic, to love my country. And like my wife always says, it's going to be a terrible change when I quit doing what I do. Just this past Saturday night, in the wee hours of the morning, I was on a crew that was dropping equipment and dropping jumpers. The airplane was completely blacked out; we were on NVGs. Where else in the world can you get a job like that?

The job just gives you so much flexibility. I enjoy the part of the job getting out once or twice a month and talking to the schools, working with the recruiters, telling kids about what we do, how we live. It's something different all the time.

We got the best damn C-130 unit in the world. I mean that. But everybody who serves in the military should feel that way about their outfit. We can bust on our leaders and our management, and we can bust on each other among ourselves, but to the rest of the world, we fly the C-130 and we're the best at what we do. We train hard and we're very well prepared, and we've proved it over and over.

Staff Sergeant Corey Creighton, flight engineer

When we go away, it's not just another day at the office. It's real-world stuff. And we have a lot of camaraderie, a lot of pride. Even people who talk about how much they hate leaving their family, even the people who say that— you can tell they have a lot of pride in what they do.

I'm proud of that. The way I look at it is we're like one giant family. Because when we go away, each other is all we have. You can get on the phone and you can write letters and you can send e-mails back home, but when it comes down to being able to interact with people and enjoy people's company, we're family.

Staff Sergeant Michael Seavolt, security policeman

My grandfathers were in World War II. My father and uncles all were in the Army. I was instilled with a great sense of national pride. I could be one of these guys who just kind of sits around and lets other people do stuff for them. I'm not like that, though. There's other ways to make money; there's other ways to have an easier job. But what's that going to leave you in the long run?

Technical Sergeant Lee Deyerle, loadmaster

My wife really digs my flight suit.

No—with all the check rides, schools, currencies, trying to keep a full-time business going, I don't do it for the money; I know that. I don't think one of the guys in here does it for the money.

I love the military. I missed it when I got out of the Army. You're held to a different standard. There's a reason we might be perceived as cocky sometimes. I've gotten to do things most thirty-year-old men haven't done. I've seen the world.

I love flying. I love the little problems that come up. I love being under the clock and knowing that we gotta get it done. I played football a lot in high school; it's like that final push to the end zone.

Afghanistan was a growing point for me. I learned a lot there. I definitely was a different person when I came back. It put a lot of my life in perspective. They say war changes guys. We were really getting shot at. You'd be there when somebody got killed. You knew somebody who knew somebody who just died.

I wasn't Joe Dirtbag anymore. I felt like I had done my part.

Deyerle recalls feeling his heart touched by the sight of another loadmaster greeting him and his crewmates when they returned from their first Iraqi Freedom deployment.

Ray Sheldon had gotten real sick. He had a heart attack. Ray's just one of those guys who's a very spiritual person, very upbeat about everything, and a very easy guy to love as a friend and a mentor.

He was standing there friggin' saluting the airplanes as we all came in. Just seeing him salute us, knowing how much he had wanted to be over there, it was very humbling. It was one of those moments that just gets you right there in the chest.

Ray Sheldon greets his squadron mates as they return home from a desert deployment (courtesy the 167th Airlift Wing).

Lieutenant Colonel Steve Truax, navigator

I worked in the public schools as a school psychologist, and it's very different, the mentality of people working in the school system versus people in the military. People in the school systems should be the picture of dedication and selflessness, and some of them are. But for an awful lot more of them, it's punching a clock, it's getting health benefits, it's having summers off.

In the military, on the other hand, it tends to be a lot of irascible, disagreeable people. My God, we got some cantankerous people in here. But when the rubber hits the road, they are just the hardest-working, most disciplined, most organized sons-of-bitches, the most innovative and the best at taking initiative of any profession I have been around. I just think, God love 'em, even the guys I butt heads with.

Technical Sergeant Steve Smith, structural maintenance specialist

You're flying over the desert for five hours. Then you fly over Mount Sinai. And then you fly over the Pyramids. How many people get to see the Pyramids?

And you're paid to go see them. Wow. How many people get to snake up the Nile?

Even the worst trip I've ever had has been a great adventure. Stuff that other people wish they could tell their kids about.

Major Mike Langley, pilot

What motivated me to want to be in when I first signed up? Part of it is that I come from a military family. My dad was in for forty-two years; my brother is also in. But I think more than that is having grown up in the South, there's a big sense of responsibility for holding and cherishing the things that were afforded to me by my forefathers. If I can do nothing else but to make sure my children and my friends' children and their grandchildren get the same opportunities that I had, that motivates me to continue to do what I do. They deserve to have at least what I've been given.

Master Sergeant Les Morris, loadmaster

I grew up playing sports, playing baseball, football, and basketball. You get used to that teamwork mentality. Then you become an adult and you don't have that anymore. This is probably about the closest you can get to that team spirit. When you're out there with six guys on a crew, doing a mission, you form a bond together and it's hard to let that go.

That's why I keep on doing it. I feel pride in doing a job and serving the country, but the biggest part is working with the other guys and doing something you really like doing. You start out doing it for your country and for yourself, then you get to a point where you're doing it to be with your squadron mates.

Major Carla Riner, pilot

Oh, the people. Everyone told me that when you get into the Air National Guard, you're getting into a new family. That has proven so true it's almost unbelievable. 'Cause when you see people on a weekend here and there throughout the year, you go, "Oh, you guys had that baby—Oh, you got that job—Oh, you went on vacation."

Let me tell you, that's one thing. But when you pack up and move in with them for five months, that's a whole other thing. You really learn what people are made of. And you talk about surprises of the deployments. I was very surprised at how some people could handle it and some people couldn't, to no fault of theirs. It's just personality traits, or whatever situations they were dealing with that we may not have known about.

It's like your family. You love 'em and sometimes you can't stand 'em. But by God, they're still your family.

Technical Sergeant Tim Shipway, crew chief

What motivates me is pride. I've always loved aviation; I've always loved working with aircraft. You do the inspections, you get the aircraft ready, and then you see it fly. On those flights a lot of times there's no problem, but then they may come back with a write-up [a notation of a malfunction]. So now it becomes a challenge and you're using data to fix the problem. I'm a researcher; I like to dive in and try to solve a problem. The biggest satisfaction is when you achieve the goal, when you fix the problem. And you've learned something. Every day I learn something new about this aircraft and I've been working on it twenty years now.

Senior Master Sergeant Mike Bayne, flight engineer

I did sports in high school and I had a partial scholarship for cross-country and wrestling, but it wasn't enough to go to college. I'm the oldest of seven kids and my family didn't have the money to pay for me to go to school. I was kind of tired of school, anyway, so I joined the Marine Corps. I was seventeen when I signed up. Then I went back in and finished the last semester of high school and then went to boot camp.

I've had a really interesting career. I've gotten to travel all over. I've been to twenty-some countries and once I started flying, I just liked it. In terms of real-world missions, I've done more here in the six years I've been in this unit than in the fourteen years I was active-duty Marines.

Lieutenant Colonel Bill Clark, pilot

I do this so that my kids and their kids and their kids' kids someday can go to the store and buy whatever they want, go watch whatever movie they want, go and eat at whatever restaurant they want, and study whatever they want.

Major Chris "Mookie" Walker, navigator

What motivates me is saying we've got a job to do now. We've gotta get it done and if I don't do it, who's going to do it? There are plenty of people who'll say they'll volunteer to do it, but if these are people off the street, it's going to take a while to train them. If I already have all these skills and I can do my part, then let me do it now. Because if we don't do something about it, it's going to continue to plague us and grow.

I don't care if we pulled out of Iraq right now and offered apologies to all of them, they would still keep coming after us. So the only way to deal with terrorists is to get rid of them. That is going to be a monumental, Herculean task. So I figure I just have to add my little bit of strength to the task.

Lieutenant Colonel Andy Wolkstein, flight nurse

You do this for one thing and one thing only, and that's for love of country. You have to do it for love of country. The pay is not good. Of course, I'm a lieutenant colonel now, so the pay is not bad, but when I was a first lieutenant, second lieutenant, you could make more money as an agency nurse. So this is not the place to make money. You do it for a sense of duty, a sense of giving something to this country.

I think everyone in this unit does it for that reason and that's what keeps us going. I could have retired last year if I'd wanted to. I could retire now if I wanted to. But for some reason, it just keeps you coming.

Master Sergeant Bob Phillips, flight medic

I was dropped on my head as a kid.

I could do the usual spouting you normally hear about patriotism, love of country. It just seemed like the thing to do. I grew up in a family where Dad was a lifer, thirty-eight years in the Navy. To me, it's just something I had to do. I won't say had to do—that I wanted to do.

It's a brotherhood. No matter where we go, it's a brotherhood. [Even across the branches of service] we're still brothers-in-arms. It's someone we can talk to about what has happened.

Lieutenant Colonel Mike McMillie, navigator

Obviously a love of country is probably the biggest motivator. Everybody's got a motivation as far as love of country goes. We're there to do a mission; the mission's gotta get done and we do it because our fellow Americans need us.

Nation and hometown. Colorful markings identify this aircraft as an Air National Guard bird (author's collection).

We have to believe in our Republic. We have to believe that whoever gets elected will be making those right decisions that put us in harm's way.

That's part of it and part of it's camaraderie. Around the good old 167th, how many people do we know, how many people do we have an opportunity to work with for any number of years? That's the beauty of the Guard, that you can be with people for a long period of time and develop those friendships. You don't want to let your buds down. If we're going to go to war, we're going to go together and we're going to come back together.

Another motivator for me is also making sure that I can help train those people to come back. That's why we did tactics training when we were over there. That's why we talked about a whole bunch of different things. We'd just sit around and have those little bull sessions and say, "Did you think of this; did you think of that?"

Master Sergeant Dave Twigg, loadmaster

After being in the military sixteen years and flying for fourteen of them, there's not really a whole lot of adventure left. I've been an incredible amount of places—all fifty states, many foreign countries, many continents.

But to keep doing it—I like the job. I like the military way of life. To a certain degree it carries over into my home life as well. My kids with homework, they know their personal responsibilities. Especially my daughter. She's eighteen and she's a very responsible person. My son is eleven, and we can tell day by day that he's accepting the responsibilities that come with normal life.

It satisfies me to do my part, however small it is, to keep the military heritage we have. The American dream for a lot of people would not get fulfilled if our military didn't do what we do. That gives me a good sense of personal pride to say I believe I've done my part and will continue to do my part until I reach retirement age. I want to stay as long as I can.

Master Sergeant Doug Ferrell, loadmaster

When I was a child, I grew up right across from the air base. I used to watch the planes fly. Every drill weekend, I would run out in my front yard when the planes would fly by. My father, who was a private pilot, took me up in a Cessna when I was five years old and I was hooked. I said, "This is what I'm going to do with the rest of my life."

Then when my brother joined the unit, I saw the places he got to go. He brought me in and I joined up and became a loadmaster like him. The travel is great. The people are great, and when we went to war, I don't think I could have thought of a better group of people to go with.

Colonel Roger Nye, pilot, air operations officer

I got into it because somebody said, "Why don't you come down and take a test and see if you can become a pilot?" That sounded like fun. That's why I started. Why do you stay twenty-five years? I guess my answer to that is—last Sunday I took my wife's brother and his family to D.C. Walked up the steps of the Lincoln Memorial and saw Abe sitting there. Then we walked down and saw all the names on the wall. We walked on over to the World War II Memorial and around to Korea and all the others. I guess it's the pride in being part of those things. The day before, we went to Gettysburg. Being a part of what so many have dedicated their lives to.

Freedom doesn't come free. How do you explain patriotism and where did it come from? I don't know. I wouldn't be doing anything else. I couldn't imagine doing anything else other than trying my best to lead this group of people to go out and do incredible things. I don't think they realize how incredible the things are that they're doing. OK, we're flying a C-130 from A to B. But that medical equipment you just dropped off saved how many people?

Colonel Eric Vollmecke, pilot, wing commander

I went to the Citadel. It's not a military academy with a mission solely to produce officers. The reason the Citadel was created was to form citizen-soldiers. Even though I spent seven years on active duty, I'm most proud of being a citizen-soldier. Especially today, our reservists and guardsmen can pack up in a matter of hours, go up to the fight, and be just as effective as their active-duty counterparts. I take a lot of pride in that.

My dad was a Korean War veteran. He raised us to serve our country. I see a lot of my colleagues in the civilian world who never served in the military, now in their late forties like me, asking the question, "What more can I do? Life hasn't given me everything I wanted." They're going through some of these mid-life crisis things, but I feel like I've been fortunate to experience so much through the military. I'm serving something greater than myself and I'm also doing something very exciting.

Brigadier General Wayne "Speedy" Lloyd (ret.), former commander of the West Virginia Air National Guard

I'd like people to know they've got great young Americans out there responding to the taskings of their government and doing an outstanding job in all corners of the world. And I would like for them to know that the United States military never goes anywhere and does anything for which we're not tasked by our civilian leadership.

So if people are for any reason unhappy with what they see going on in the world, they need to realize that when they go to the voting booth, they decide who leads our country. If they have a particular direction they want us to go, they need to exercise their right to vote and choose the people who will lead us in that direction. If their opinion is the dominant one, then their people will be elected.

The military responds to the direction of the civilian leadership, and I think these young Americans who are out there are doing an outstanding job putting their lives on the line to further the cause of the United States of America.

27

FINAL THOUGHTS

There are things I would not care to remember, but I wouldn't have given it up for the world.
—Master Sergeant Doug Ferrell, 167th AW

Lieutenant Colonel Bill Clark, pilot

What surprised me the most is probably the time and commitment that is now involved and the toll and the wear and tear it's taking on the families and the civilian employers. I expected this to be like Desert Storm: We go over for a few months and then we're done. We go home and from then on we do a couple deployments to the desert. Not this continuing activation, people being gone for two years. People coming home and they were self-employed and now the business is gone. People coming home to empty households, people coming home to divorces, people coming home to businesses that have eliminated their job. I didn't expect it to be like this. I expected it to be over and done in a year or so.

Captain Brandon Taksa, pilot

Something that people don't get when they watch this on TV—Iraq and Afghanistan—is how poor the people there are. How their focus and their way of doing business is not anything like what you or I do. The way they live their lives is completely different.

For most of them, day-to-day is just survival. They're not planning for their retirement. They're not thinking about what their kids are going to be when they grow up. They are literally just trying to get through today and maybe tomorrow if today's going all right. You know, we think over here in America, you're destitute if you're living month to month and you're having trouble paying your bills. Those folks are living in a mud hut.

Staff Sergeant Tony Dunnigan, intelligence specialist

I remember the mosque that was bombed in Samarra. [On February 22, 2006, insurgents blew up the Golden Mosque of Samarra, one of the most revered Shiite shrines in Iraq.] We were in theater at the time. We had been over the city before, and so we were able to get pictures of our own, not through the plane's equipment, but through our own digital cameras. We were able to take pictures of the city. Then we went back into the same area not long after the bombing, and the before-and-after was very disheartening, to see something we thought was really beautiful, and to come back and see it destroyed.

Part of our mission going back up to the area was to watch for indicators of more violence. We were there quite extensively. We were watching the crowds to make sure nothing else sprung up from this.

Before, with the dome, you could see the gold. At the time we were up there the sun was on it just right. It was picturesque, and we took advantage of that and took pictures. When we went back, it looked like any bombed or ruined area.

Major Mike Langley, pilot

I want to tell you something that happened to me two nights ago. My wife and I were lying in bed watching Fox News, and it was reporting on some of our Marines on the ground in Fallujah and the fighting that was going on. I'm sitting there and I'm watching it and my wife, Kirsten, is talking about it, how she feels like we should have kept more of our troops over there and taken a harder line to get things settled at the beginning.

We're having this discussion and I said if that had happened, I might have still been over there, and you never can tell whether more troops would have worked. But the next day I told her I feel guilty for being home, because there are still people over there. Even though I did my part and did what I was supposed to do, I feel guilty that we still have people over there and I'm not there.

Major Carla Riner, pilot

On my second deployment, I found myself being an enabler for many people. People both in my squadron and not in my squadron would come to me just head in hands, tearful, upset, homesick, just needing somebody to talk to.

On the first deployment, I could barely keep myself together, I was just, like, yecch, I hate this. The second time, somehow, I guess I was meant to play that role for people in some way because I always try to make people feel, you know, "Hi, how you doing?" Trying to spread a little sunshine or whatever, but I really got the opportunity to be somebody else's stronghold, somebody else's shoulder to lean on.

After I got back, I actually had a few traumas. I got upset and I cried about it because I had to be strong for those people there, but once I got home, I let it upset me. That was very surprising to me, that I handled as much as I did and kept it all very calm and cool for them, but then when I wasn't "on," so to speak, I actually had to release it for myself because I couldn't carry it around any more.

Captain Tony Henry, civil engineer

My wife didn't want to vote last time and I said, "I just got back from Iraq, fighting for you to have this right. You better vote."

She said, "Yes, dear."

Colonel Roger Nye, pilot, operations group commander

What I did over there was really nothing. Yeah, I contributed, but when you drive up to a checkpoint and you see the eighteen-year-old with an M-16, or handling a dog—if that dog alerts on a vehicle, now what's the next step? And these kids are going over there and doing the things they're doing. Most of them are doing what they want to be doing. They feel it's an honor. I don't think the American people realize young people are still joining the military because they want to be a part of something great. And what's happening over there is something great, no matter how the media shows it.

Lieutenant Colonel Steve Truax, operations officer

What was kind of uplifting to me was when I began to really understand how the war was being fought, how they do the different airways and the deconfliction and all that. Seeing it done for real. You can train all your life and never see what's going to work and what's not going to work. But by the end, I thought, "I see how they manage airplanes in a contingency." That was kind of an epiphany, also to see how well the American military adapts to large operations. People are just used to taking initiative and making things work, and it kind of becomes part of your psychology. I'd see people managing these huge amounts of cargo and these complex air movement tables, and they were doing it very naturally.

I thought, you know, ninety percent of the people in the world would be very intimidated with that kind of responsibility. I think that's something that sets American military personnel apart from nonmilitary people: they're just very comfortable with operating on a big scale.

Colonel Eric Vollmecke, pilot, wing commander

Part of the challenge we have as guardsmen and reservists is maintaining our relevance with the active duty. At the end of the day, it means being combat-ready. What was really amazing to me is not only was this unit better prepared than most of the other Air National Guard and Reserve wings, but also better than the active duty. So when we went to the fight, we were better trained, and we proved it in the way we flew.

For reservists, who live two lives, to be able to maintain that is a lot to be proud of. Everybody likes to hear the war stories and what we did there. But where the real credit needs to be placed is all the years, day in, day out, weekends, doing the training. Coming up here, flying at night, probably having only two weekends off a month, many times working all weekends. That part needs to be understood. So many people paid the price during all those years when we really weren't at war, and that deserves a lot of credit.

With American and West Virginia flags flying, a flight of four C-130s returns to Martinsburg on August 1, 2003, after one of several desert deployments. Props spinning and engines roaring, the planes taxi back to their home parking spots. Crews fondly refer to the Herk's propellers as the "Four Fans of Freedom" (courtesy the 167th Airlift Wing).

I was on a mountain-climbing expedition in Nepal in the fall of 1989. One lesson from that experience, like my war experience, is that you must start out strong and prepared. That's because as things start getting tough, with each step comes more doubt. You must fight these negative thoughts and stay focused on the reasons to keep climbing.

The same thing applies with coming to war. I paid the price to be a military aviator, years and years of hard training, balancing a family and a civilian career. But when the time came and the country called, I went and did my part.

It's hard now to go into a book store and see all these books on leadership, self-improvement, and self-fulfillment and give that stuff a second look. The secret is the same now as a thousand years ago. It all comes from hard work, a sense of purpose, and a hunger to constantly challenge yourself.

Brigadier General Wayne "Speedy" Lloyd (ret.) former commander of the West Virginia Air National Guard

It gave me a lot of pride in the Air National Guard in that we were certainly on a footing with our active-duty counterparts. When the time comes and we're called on to do things, we can function at a level that is commensurate with the active duty, and we can do a job that is equal to what they can do. We can make the hard decisions that are necessary to support a war effort. The guys are out there doing the job every day in the most professional way it can be done. Our experience is there; in most cases our crews and maintenance people are more experienced than our active-duty counterparts because we've been around the business a lot longer.

Master Sergeant Doug Ferrell, loadmaster

You would look at faces of troops you were carrying, and the next day you would hear of a car bomb exploding. It would go through your mind: "Did I just take that guy up there and get him killed?" That was one thing that was hard to live with. That was kind of sad. There are things I would not care to remember, but I wouldn't have given it up for the world. I'm glad I got to be able to take part in it and do my part for the country and the unit.

Lieutenant Colonel Sandie Duiker, flight nurse

I enjoy what I do, not the suffering and things like that, but I'm looking around here and I'm an old dog. What I see as my job—training. My question to the Air Force is when we get ready to send people out the door, are we teaching our younger and middle people the right things? Or are we getting hung up on some whiz bang that is irrelevant?

If I can look in the mirror and say OK, I made some errors, granted, but with what I knew I did the best I could do, then screw 'em. The biggest thing was doing it right. I think that's what drives our train.

Colonel Eric Vollmecke, pilot, wing commander

I guess my first reaction when I see wounded soldiers is: "Are they going to be made whole again?" I'll give you one example. I was not flying the mission, but I was commanding at the time. This crew from Charleston, West Virginia, came back and landed and a pilot said, "Sir, if I ever complain about having to fly in combat zones, kick me in the butt, because I just flew back this wounded soldier who lost his right leg to an IED. After we landed he asked to see me. I went back to see him and here he was all patched up, but very alert. He said to me, 'Thank you for taking me out of there.' He was actually thankful that he was the only person injured on that patrol because he was the sergeant in command." To hear about that kind of spirit is really something.

Captain Andrew Schmidt, executive officer to Col. Vollmecke in Kandahar

I did find it was really weird going back to my civilian job after getting back from Afghanistan. It wasn't post-traumatic stress disorder, but I had a problem with people's perspectives.

There's so much stuff over there involving decisions that are life and death. What is very bizarre becomes normal. You're just under intense pressure, and that becomes the norm. You don't sleep much; that becomes the norm. You don't get to blow off steam; that becomes the norm. "Bad things happen" means a bunch of people got killed today. You just adjust because that's part of your military training. You move on.

You come back and you find people here more upset over things that don't really matter. You know, "Somebody rear-ended me and I have to take a half day off work to get my fender redone, and the insurance company's messing this up and my life's terrible." Who cares?

You get angry because once you've had an experience like this, you find that people can't put things in perspective.

And I had this overwhelming thing with my wife when I came home. I wanted to throw everything away. I couldn't believe how cluttered everything

The simple life. Captain Andrew Schmidt's quarters in Afghanistan (courtesy the 167th Airlift Wing).

was. I had lived out of a bag for four months. I had three uniforms and three sets of PT [Physical Training] gear, an alarm clock, and a toiletries kit. That's what I had. Then you come home and you're staring at all your possessions and you're like, "Why do I need all this?"

Staff Sergeant Michael Seavolt, security policeman

We were there for Thanksgiving, Christmas, and New Year's. A lot of people got depressed, kind of got down. Yeah, I missed my family and I wanted to be home. But by the same token, I was with guys who volunteered to do what I'm doing. No one told us to go; we went on our own free will. It's kind of cool to always remember that you spent one Christmas or one Thanksgiving in a war zone. It's at the unfortunate expense of my family, but for me it was just being with the guys, being with your friends. There's a bond between us now that you just can't break. We did this together.

From the author's journal, undated

Back from the deployment, waiting for the next one. Strange dream last night. Flying a routine night training mission, low-level out of Martinsburg. We're on NVGs over the Shenandoah Valley, a peaceful place with the friend-ship of neighbors, the taste of crisp apples, the smell of new-mown hay. Home.

Then the tracers begin streaming up at us. Hard break to the right. Wide awake.

For now, at least, we have left the war. But the war has not left us

EPILOGUE

In February of 2006, the last C-130 flew away from the West Virginia Air National Guard base at Martinsburg, and the 167th Airlift Wing began a conversion to the C-5 Galaxy, the largest aircraft in the Air Force fleet. Some members of the unit retired. Some transferred to other C-130 wings. But most retrained to fly or maintain the C-5 and eventually returned to Baghdad and other hotspots where we had flown the C-130.

As of this writing, Operation Enduring Freedom continues in Afghanistan, and Operation Iraqi Freedom grinds on in Iraq. Meanwhile, natural disasters take place each year, and American airlifters always provide aid. Every two minutes or less, an American military transport plane takes to the skies. While you read this, somewhere in the world a crew from the 167th or another airlift wing is strapping into seats, running checklists, flipping switches, starting engines.

Please wish them Godspeed.

GLOSSARY

AAA: Antiaircraft artillery, often referred to as "triple-A."

ACARS: Aircraft Communication Addressing and Reporting System. On civilian airliners, a digital link to the company for receiving instructions, weather information, etc.

A-10: The A-10 Thunderbolt, more commonly called the Warthog because of its ugly lines. An Air Force ground attack jet.

AC-130: The attack version of the C-130 Hercules, also known as the Spectre gunship.

AGL: Above Ground Level. Altitude above the ground, as opposed to altitude measured from sea level.

AEW: Air Expeditionary Wing, a deployed Air Force unit.

AMC: Air Mobility Command, the Air Force command that handles the airlift mission.

APU: Auxiliary Power Unit, a small turbine engine on an aircraft, distinct from the engines that propel the aircraft, used to provide electricity and compressed air, usually for ground use.

ARA: Airborne Radar Approach, an instrument approach during which the navigator provides guidance to the runway based on his radar picture without use of any ground-based navigational aids.

ATOC: Air Terminal Operations Center. A facility for handling passengers and cargo.

AW: Airlift Wing. A wing consists of one or more squadrons of airplanes, their crews, and all the sections that support the crews, from maintenance to food service to finance.

AWACS: Airborne Warning and Control Station, a plane that monitors all air traffic in the battlespace and coordinates flight operations of military aircraft.

Bingo fuel: The fuel level at which you must turn back to land (or refuel in the air).

B-52: The B-52 Stratofortress, a heavy bomber that dates from the 1950s.

BUA: Battlefield Update Assessment, a daily briefing for a commanding general.

BX: Base Exchange, the department store on an Air Force base.

C-5: The C-5 Galaxy, a four-engine turbofan transport built by Lockheed, the largest aircraft in the USAF inventory.

C-130: The C-130 Hercules, a four-engine turboprop transport aircraft built by Lockheed.

C-141: The C-141 Starlifter, a four-engine turbojet transport built by Lockheed, recently retired by the Air Force.

CAOC: Combined Air Operations Center, a control center for all air operations in a given theater.

CASF: Contingency Aeromedical Staging Facility, essentially a passenger terminal for wounded soldiers being transported by air.

CATM: Combat Arms Training and Maintenance, part of an Air Force Security Police section that trains Air Force personnel in the use and care of small arms.

CCAT: Critical Care Air Transport Team, an aeromedical team consisting of a physician, a critical-care nurse, and a cardiopulmonary technician.

CENTAF: Air Force, Central Command, the Air Force command responsible for the Middle East.

CJTF: Combined Joint Task Force, an ad hoc grouping of forces from different services formed to accomplish a specific mission.

CLS: Combat Lifesaver, a nonmedical Army soldier trained in emergency medicine as a secondary mission.

Combat Controller: An elite Air Force air traffic controller who is also trained to parachute into hostile areas and set up lights and navigational aids so friendly aircraft can land.

CSH: Combat Support Hospital, an Army hospital located in or near the combat zone.

DCU: Desert Camouflage, Utility. Desert fatigues.

DIRMOBFOR: Director of Mobility Forces. A general officer in charge of airlift and tanker aircraft.

E-MEDS: Expeditionary Medical Squadron, an Air Force medical unit in a deployed location.

EMT: Emergency Medical Technician.

EOD: Explosive Ordnance Disposal, teams that defuse or destroy bombs.

ERO: Engine-running onload or offload. A procedure used by airlift crews to minimize ground time in a hostile area.

F-16: The F-16 Fighting Falcon. Its pilots prefer to call it the Viper. A single-engine fighter used by the Air Force.

F/A-18: The F/A-18 Hornet. A two-engine fighter used by the Navy and Marine Corps.

FARP: Forward Arming and Refueling Point, a remote, temporary spot where aircraft can quickly take on more fuel or weapons, then continue their mission.

Firebase: See FOB, Forward Operating Base.

FLIR: Forward-Looking Infrared, a surveillance system installed on certain aircraft.

Flight Engineer: An enlisted aircrew member on the C-130 who monitors and operates aircraft systems, calculates aircraft performance numbers, coordinates tactical and emergency procedures, and runs most checklists.

FOB: Forward Operating Base, an Army camp located in or near a combat zone. A secured position used to support military operations.

Frag: In Air Force parlance, "frag" does not mean killing an officer. It refers to a "fragmentary order," a fragment of a larger order. An aircrew's frag tells them where and when to fly. If they arrive ahead of schedule, they "beat the frag."

Giant Voice: An emergency public address system in a tent city.

GPWS: Ground Proximity Warning System, an aircraft system that warns aircrew members of impending ground impact.

HF: High frequency radio.

HR: Human Remains.

ID: Infantry Division, as in Third ID.

IED: Improvised Explosive Device, or makeshift bomb.

ILS: Instrument Landing System, a precision approach to guide an aircraft to landing.

IMU: Islamic Movement of Uzbekistan.

IOE: Initial Operating Experience. An airline acronym that refers to a pilot's on-the-job training, flying passengers while he's under the supervision of an instructor, IOE comes immediately after classroom and simulator training.

KC-130: An aerial refueling version of the C-130 Hercules, used by the Marine Corps.

KC-135: A four-engine turbojet aerial refueling aircraft built by Boeing, used by the Air Force.

KIA: Killed in Action.

Loadmaster: An enlisted aircrew member on the C-130 who supervises the loading and handling of cargo, calculates weight and balance numbers, rigs the airplane for airdrops, and monitors passengers.

LZ: Landing Zone.

M-4: A light, carbine variant of the M-16 rifle.

M-9: A nine-millimeter semiautomatic pistol made by Beretta. The U.S. military's standard-issue handgun.

M-249: The Squad Automatic Weapon, a light machine gun.

MAC: Minimum Altitude Capable. Flying as low as your nerves can stand. A tactical procedure to avoid hostile fire.

MANPAD: Man-portable air defense system, a shoulder-fired missile.

MARS: Military Affiliate Radio System, a program in which licensed amateur shortwave radio operators provide an adjunct to the normal channels of military communications. MARS operators often provide phone patches to allow service members to call family members by radio.

MASF: Mobile Aeromedical Staging Facility, a smaller and more mobile version of the CASF.

MRE: Meal, Ready to Eat. Nonperishable field rations.

MRT: Maintenance Recovery Team, mechanics sent to fix an aircraft broken down away from its home station.

MSL: Mean Sea Level. Altitude above sea level, as opposed to altitude measured from above ground level.

MWS: Missile Warning System, a system on an aircraft that detects when an antiaircraft missile has been launched at the aircraft.

NATO: North Atlantic Treaty Organization.

Navigator: An aircrew member on the C-130 who assists pilots in navigation, terrain clearance, approach procedures, and communication.

NCO: Noncommissioned Officer. Includes all ranks of sergeants, and in some services, corporals and warrant officers. In the Navy, all ranks of petty officers.

NVGs: Night Vision Goggles. Also sometimes referred to as NOGs, for Night Observation Goggles, or NODs, for Night Observation Devices.

OEF: Operation Enduring Freedom, the U.S. military response to the 9/11 attacks.

OIF: Operation Iraqi Freedom, the U.S.–led invasion of Iraq.

OSI: The Air Force's Office of Special Investigations.

PJ: Pararescue Jumper, an elite Air Force medic trained to recover aircrews and other personnel in hostile environments.

Raven: An Air Force security policeman trained to protect aircraft and aircrews in hostile areas.

RPG: Rocket-Propelled Grenade.

SAFIRE: Surface-to-air fire. A SAFIRE incident is when a plane takes hostile fire from the ground.

SCNS: Self-Contained Navigation System. An aircraft navigation system that uses internal gyroscopes and does not depend on satellites or ground-based navigation aids.

SKE: Station-Keeping Equipment. A system that allows planes to fly in formation in all weather.

Sailboat Fuel: Air. Nothing. When you're flying with an empty cargo compartment, you're "hauling sailboat fuel."

SAM: Surface-to-air missile.

SERE: Survival, Evasion, Resistance, Escape. An acronym for survival training given to aircrew members and others considered "at high risk of capture."

TACP: Tactical Air Control Party, Air Force forward air controllers who travel with Army units to direct air strikes.

TALCE: Tanker/Airlift Control Element. Coordinates aircraft parking, loading, unloading, and other support functions for airlifters and aerial tankers.

TCN: Third Country National. A foreigner brought into an overseas military camp as a civilian staff member, for example, a Bangladeshi working in a U.S. military dining hall in Kuwait.

TIC: Troops in Contact. An encounter with the enemy. A firefight.

TIT: Turbine Inlet Temperature, a measure of a jet engine's power setting.

VBIED: Vehicle-Borne Improvised Explosive Device, or car bomb.

VHF: Very high frequency radio.

WEZ: Weapons Engagement Zone. The effective range of a given weapon.

WMD: Weapons of Mass Destruction. Can mean nuclear, biological, or chemical weapons.

XO: Executive Officer, the officer who is second in command of a given unit.

Zulu Time: Greenwich Mean Time, also known as Coordinated Universal Time, originally Mean Solar Time at Britain's Royal Observatory. When military personnel conduct missions across time zones, references to local times could create confusion. Instead, they use Zulu time references.

SOURCES

Interviews and Letters

Abbot, Bobby. Technical Sergeant. Interview, 25 July 2006.
Alderton, John. Chief Master Sergeant. Interview, 5 August 2006.
Atkinson, Clayton. Staff Sergeant. Interview, 13 July 2006.
Barrow, Christopher. Technical Sergeant. Interview, 25 July 2006.
Barrow, Jay. Technical Sergeant. Interview, 25 July 2006.
Bayne, Michael. Senior Master Sergeant. Interview, 2 May 2004.
Brake, Roy. Master Sergeant. Interview, 8 May 2006.
Brown, Derek. Staff Sergeant. Interview, 9 June 2005.
Clark, William. Lieutenant Colonel. Interview, 28 July 2004.
Cordova, John. Master Sergeant. Interview, 9 October 2006.
Creighton, Corey. Staff Sergeant. Interview, 28 September 2004.
Deyerle, Lee. Technical Sergeant. Interview, 10 June 2005.
Duiker, Sandie. Lieutenant Colonel. Interview, 29 September 2004.
Dunnigan, Tony. Staff Sergeant. Interview, 13 April 2007.
Faller, Kerrie. Staff Sergeant. Interview, 5 June 2005.
Ferrell, Doug. Master Sergeant. Interview, 12 May 2006

Foley, Michael. Major. Interview, 9 June 2005.
Garrett, Curtis. Captain. Interview, 4 May 2004.
Gillenwater, Billy. Chief Master Sergeant. Interview, 31 July 2005.
Grimm, John. Technical Sergeant. Interview, 2 June 2005.
Gross, Peter. Major. Interview, 6 September 2007.
Henry, Tony. Captain. Interview, 13 October 2006.
Holcomb, Scott. Technical Sergeant. Interview, 5 June 2005.
Jackson, Don. Master Sergeant. Interview, 30 April 2005,
Jenness, Dave. Technical Sergeant. Interview, 8 May 2006.
Kendle, Gerry. Master Sergeant. Interview, 4 August 2006.
LaFollette, Kenny. Technical Sergeant. Interview, 14 June 2005.
Lane, Jeff. Major. Interview, 6 June 2004.
Langley, Michael. Major. Interview, 4 May 2004.
Lawrence, Fred. Technical Sergeant. Interview, 3 February 2007.
Lemon, Michael. Second Lieutenant. Interview, 9 December 2006.
Leverknight, Bob. Technical Sergeant. Interview, 27 June 2005.
Levy, Karl. Major. Interview, 2 July 2004.
Lloyd, Wayne. Brigadier General. Interview, 9 April 2004.

Martz, Harry. Chief Master Sergeant. Interview, 5 June 2005.

McDonald, Steve. Senior Master Sergeant. Interview, 3 February 2006.

McMillie, Michael. Lieutenant Colonel. Interview, 14 June 2005.

Miller, Michael. Master Sergeant. Interview, 15 April 2006.

Morris, Les. Master Sergeant. Interview, 13 July 2004.

Myers, Joe. Lieutenant Colonel. Interview, 8 April 2004.

Nicholson, Tim. Master Sergeant. Interview, 14 October 2007.

Nye, Roger. Colonel. Interview, 18 April 2006.

Perkowski, Shaun. Lieutenant Colonel. Interview, 7 July 2006.

Phillips, Bob. Master Sergeant. Interview, 17 May 2005.

Porter, David. Lieutenant Colonel. Interview, 16 February 2005.

Powell, James. Major. Interview, 13 May 2005.

Ratcliffe, John. Master Sergeant. Interview, 23 March 2005.

Riley, Travis. Staff Sergeant. Interview, 25 July 2006.

Riner, Carla. Major. Interview, 3 August 2004.

Robichaud, Rich. Lieutenant Colonel. Interview, 10 June 2005.

Rollyson, Eddie. Staff Sergeant. Interview, 9 December 2006.

Ruckh, Mark. Major. Letter, 16 November 2003

Runkles, Brad. Staff Sergeant. Interview, 29 September 2004.

Schmidt, Andrew. Captain. Interview, 9 October 2006.

Seavolt, Michael. Staff Sergeant. Interview, 12 May 2006.

Shafer, Randall. Senior Master Sergeant. Interview, 20 April 2005.

Shambaugh, Roland. Senior Master Sergeant. Interview, 4 May 2004.

Shambaugh, Vince. Technical Sergeant. Interview, 9 December 2006.

Shipway, Tim. Technical Sergeant. Interview, 27 April 2004.

Sigler, Christopher. Major. Interview, 12 July 2006.

Smith, Steve. Technical Sergeant. Interview, 6 January 2006.

Surratt, Curtis. Master Sergeant. Interview, 11 May 2005.

Taksa, Brandon. Captain. Interview, 15 June 2005.

Thomas, Jesse. Colonel. Interview, 21 March 2005.

Truax, Steve. Lieutenant Colonel. Interview, 7 April 2004.

Twigg, Dave. Master Sergeant. Interview, 16 October 2005.

Vollmecke, Eric. Colonel. Interview, 6 May 2006.

Walker, Chris. Major. Interview, 8 April 2004.

Wolkstein, Andrew. Lieutenant Colonel. Interview, 9 June 2004.

Books

The Aeronautical Information Manual.

The 9/11 Commission Report.

The Iraq Study Group Report.

Air Force Technical Order 1C-130-1, the C-130 Flight Manual.

Air Force Instruction 11-2C-130, Volume Three.

Air Force Manual 3-3.35B, Combat Aircraft Fundamentals.

INDEX